GENDER AND CANDIDATE COMMUNICATION

GENDER AND CANDIDATE COMMUNICATION

VideoStyle, WebStyle, NewsStyle

Dianne G. Bystrom
Mary Christine Banwart
Lynda Lee Kaid
Terry A. Robertson

A volume in the series *Gender Politics, Global Issues*, edited by Dorothy Stetson and Barbara Burrell.

Published in 2004 by
Routledge
711 Third Avenue
New York, NY 10017
www.routledge-ny.com

Published in Great Britain by
Routledge
2 Park Square
Milton Park, Abingdon
Oxon OX14 4RN U.K.
www.routledge.co.uk

Copyright © 2004 by Taylor & Francis Books, Inc.
Routledge is an imprint of the Taylor & Francis Group.

All rights reserved. No part of this book may be reprinted or reproduced or utilized in any form or by any electronic, mechanical, or other means, now known or hereafter invented, including photocopying and recording, or in any information storage or retrieval system, without permission in writing from the publishers.

Library of Congress Cataloging-in-Publication Data
   Bystrom, Dianne G.
     Gender and candidate communication : videostyle, webstyle, newsstyle / by Dianne Bystrom with Mary Christine Banwart ... [et al.].
     p. cm. — (Gender politics, global issues)
     Includes bibliographical references and index.
     ISBN 0-41594-682-4 (hdbk) — ISBN 0-41594-683-2 (pbk) 1.
Women political candidates—United States. 2. Women political candidates—Press coverage—United States. 3. Mass media and women—United States. 4. Communication in politics—United States. 5. Political campaigns—United States. I. Title. II. Series.

HQ1236.5.U6B97 2004
324.7'3'0820973—dc22
                                                           2004004977

Contents

PART I   Women, Communication, and Politics

1 Women, Communication, and Politics:
    An Introduction   3

2 VideoStyle, WebStyle, and NewsStyle:
    A Framework for Gendered Analysis   9

PART II   Campaign Advertising: Gendered Messages, Gendered Reactions

3 VideoStyle: Communication Messages through
    Campaign Advertising   29

4 The Interaction of Electoral Status, Political Party,
    and VideoStyle   47

5 VideoStyles in the 2002 Kansas Governor's Race:
    A Case Study   81

6 Voter Reactions to Candidate VideoStyle   93

PART III   Candidate Web Sites: Gendered Messages, Reactions

7 WebStyle: Communication Messages through
    Candidates' Web Sites   113

8 WebStyles in a North Carolina U.S. Senate Race and
    a Montana Gubernatorial Race: A Case Study   143

9 Voter Reactions to Candidate WebStyle   165

PART IV Media Coverage of Candidates: Gendered Messages, Gendered Reactions

        10 NewsStyle: Media Coverage of Candidate Presentation   173

        11 NewsStyles in the 2000 New York U.S. Senate Campaign: A Case Study   189

        12 Gendered Reactions to Media Coverage   203

PART V Gender and Political Communication in Future Campaigns

        13 Gendered Political Campaign Communication: Implications for the Future   213

Notes   221

References   227

Index   237

Part I
Women, Communication, and Politics

1
Women, Communication, and Politics:
An Introduction

In 1982, Virginia Sapiro suggested that a "central research question for those who study women's political roles is why, given the lack of legal or obvious structural barriers to recruitment of female elites, are women still so underrepresented among political officials" (1982: 61). More than twenty years later, those who study women as political candidates still seek to respond to that question. Although the number of women holding political office has steadily but slowly increased, uncovering the barriers that restrict female candidates from election to public office is important if we seek fair representation.

A poll conducted by Roper-Starch Worldwide and underwritten by Deloitte and Touche provides insight into the public's perception of female candidates and how these perceptions may serve as potential barriers. The poll, released January 13, 2000, focuses on the viability of female candidates being elected to the presidency. Although such findings should not be applied automatically to the viability of female candidates being elected to gubernatorial and congressional offices, the responses do offer further understanding of the cultural mind-set about female candidates.

In the poll results, one-third of the population surveyed indicated "there are general characteristics about women that make them less qualified to serve as president" (Deloitte and Touche 2000: 2), suggesting that women must still overcome traditional stereotypes. Additionally, a majority of those polled (51 percent) indicated that a man could do a better job than a woman leading the nation during a crisis and in making difficult decisions, the top two qualities believed "very important" in a presidential candidate (Deloitte and Touche 2000).

Due to such public perceptions about female candidates, combined with the added weight of media framing and stereotyping (e.g., Kahn 1993, 1996; Witt, Paget, and Matthews 1995), it remains important for female candidates to define strategically and successfully their own image and issue messages through traditional mass media, such as television, as well as through new forms of mass media, such as the Internet. In addition, as we explore the barriers that face women candidates and generate gender expectations, it is important to consider news coverage of mixed-gender political races to understand how the media shape our attitudes about the viability of female candidates. Finally, once we identify communication styles and strategies utilized by female and male candidates, analyzing how those strategies function to shape candidates' images and perceptions in voters' minds remains an area in need of research and analysis.

This book will analyze three aspects of gender and political campaigns: how female and male candidates present themselves to voters through their mass media messages (television spot ads and Web sites), how the media present these candidates through their news coverage, and how voters respond to the candidates' mass media strategies. The significance of this work stems from our comprehensive examination of the messages as we identify female and male communication styles used in mass media settings, coupled with our research on the news coverage of candidates in mixed-gender races and our study of how voters respond to the strategic messages designed by the candidates. Female and male candidates use similar self-presentation strategies as well as strategies that differ; however, voter perceptions dictate the ultimate success and appropriateness of those candidate images.

Women as Political Candidates

This comprehensive examination of the communication by and about women in federal and statewide political campaigns is possible because of the increased number of women running for Congress and governor beginning in the 1990s. Before the 1990 election, the largest number of women to hold office in the U.S. Congress was twenty-five (Dolan 1997). In the 108th Congress, elected in 2002, that number more than doubled, as seventy-three women served in Congress in 2004 (fourteen senators, fifty-nine representatives). The number of women serving as their state's governor has also doubled—from three in 1991 to an all-time high of eight in 2004.

The path to women's election as political office holders has been slow but mostly steady over the past thirteen years. For example, the number of women seeking seats in Congress increased from 77 in 1990 to 117 in 1992, 121 in 1994, 129 in 1996, and 131 in 1998. In 2000, the number of women seeking seats in Congress fell slightly, to 128. But in 2002, a record 135 women ran for Congress (Center for American Women and Politics

2002). In terms of their representation, the number of women serving in the U.S. Senate increased from four in 1991 to seven in 1993, nine in 1995, 1997, and 1999, thirteen in 2001, and fourteen in 2003. The number of women serving in the U.S. House of Representatives has increased from twenty-eight in 1991 to forty-seven in 1993, forty-eight in 1995, fifty-four in 1997, fifty-six in 1999, and fifty-nine in 2001 and 2003 (Center for American Women and Politics 2004).

More women also are seeking their state's top executive office, though the numbers running for governor have fluctuated over the past decade. In 1990, there were eight female candidates for governor. In subsequent election years, three women ran for governor in 1992, ten in 1994, six in 1996, ten in 1998, five in 2000, and ten in 2002. Similarly, the overall number of women serving as their state's governor has fluctuated over the past decade, with three women serving as governor in 1991, 1993, 1997, and 1999. In 1995, four women served as governor; in 2001, five women served as governor; in 2003, six women served as governor; and, in 2004, a record eight women served as governor (Center for American Women and Politics 2002).

The women who ran for the U.S. Senate and state governorships—as well as their male opponents—between 1990 and 2002 provide the basis for our analysis of their mass media messages and their media coverage. We chose U.S. Senate and gubernatorial campaigns because they are conducted statewide and thus lead to candidate communication and media coverage that are broader, more consistent, and more comparable across races than local or congressional district campaigns.

Gendered Reactions to Political Candidates

In addition to an examination of how female and male candidates present themselves to potential voters through their television commercials and Web sites, this book considers how the media cover these candidates and how voters react to political candidate messages in presidential and mixed-gender gubernatorial and senatorial campaigns.

Sex stereotyping, which is more fully explained in chapter 2, and the phenomenon known as the "gender gap" provide a rationale for the examination of media coverage and voter reactions to political campaigns. Sex stereotypes have been defined as a "structured set of beliefs about the personal attributes of men and women" (Ashmore, Del Boca, and Wohlers 1986: 89). The act of sex stereotyping, then, refers to a normal cognitive process through which people simplify their perceptions about women and men by drawing inferences based on their beliefs about what members of a particular group are like (Ashmore, Del Boca, and Wohlers 1986: 89).

The gender gap, on the other hand, "refers to differences between women and men in political attitudes and voting choices" (Center for American Women and Politics 1997) but provides no explanation about what causes the difference (Seltzer, Newman, and Leighton 1997). Thus, the gender gap is neutral and can be used to examine the voting behavior, party identification, evaluations of presidential performance, and policy preferences of both women and men. Since the early 1980s, in both presidential and congressional races, women have preferred the Democratic candidate more often than men, whereas men have preferred the Republican candidate more often than women. In terms of party identification, larger proportions of women are Democrats, and larger proportions of men are Republicans. But party affiliation does not always explain the gender gap, as sometimes women voters prefer the Republican female candidate over the Democrat male candidate.

Over the past twenty or so years, the gender gap has expanded or narrowed by race and election year, with the largest gaps recorded in the 1996 and 2000 presidential campaigns. In 2000, the gender gap in the presidential race was of similar magnitude to the record set in the 1996 campaign, with women preferring Democrat Al Gore by twelve points and men favoring Republican George W. Bush by ten points. Women voters provided the margin of victory for U.S. Senate candidates Hillary Rodham Clinton (D-NY) by favoring her twenty-one points over her male opponent and Debbie Stabenow (D-MI) and Maria Cantwell (D-WA) by eight points each. Women also provided the margin of victory for gubernatorial candidates Jeanne Shaheen (D-NH) by twelve points and Ruth Ann Minner (D-DE) by thirty-six points (Center for American Women and Politics 2004).

The largest gender gap previously recorded in a presidential campaign was in 1996, with women favoring Democrat Bill Clinton by eleven points and men favoring Republican Bob Dole. The gender gap was also a factor in thirty-eight of the forty-nine races where the Voter News Services (VNS) conducted exit polls in 1996. That year, there were gender gaps in six of eleven gubernatorial races and twenty-eight of thirty-four senatorial races. Races with the largest gender gaps in 1996 included Democrat John Brennan versus Republican Susan Collins for the U.S. Senate in Maine, with women favoring Brennan by nine points and men favoring Collins by thirteen points, and Mary Landrieu (D-LA), who won her U.S. Senate race with women supporting her by nine points over male voters (Center for American Women and Politics 1997).

In 1994, fifty-one of the sixty-three races with VNS exit poll data showed gender gaps of four or more points; in forty-nine of those races, female voters supported the Democratic candidate more than male voters did. This included the U.S. Senate race of Dianne Feinstein (D-CA), whom women voters preferred by eleven points. In one of two exceptions (the Ohio attorney general's race), women voters supported the Republican woman candidate more than men did (Center for American Women and Politics 1997).

In 1992, thirty-four of fifty-one races with VNS exit poll data showed gender gaps of four or more points. In thirty of thirty-four races, women voters supported Democratic candidates more than men did. This included the U.S. Senate races of Democrat Barbara Boxer (D-CA) and Democrat Dianne Feinstein (D-CA), where women preferred both by fourteen points, and Democrat Patty Murray (D-WA) and Carol Moseley-Braun (D-IL), both of whom were preferred by women by seven points. In one of the four exceptions, female voters supported a Republican woman candidate more than did male voters (Center for American Women and Politics 1997).

In 1990, forty-three of seventy races with VNS exit poll data showed gender gaps of four or more points. Again, in thirty-nine of those forty-three races, female voters supported Democrat candidates more so than did male voters. This included the gubernatorial races of Dianne Feinstein (D-CA), whom women preferred by sixteen points; Barbara Roberts (D-OR), preferred by women by sixteen points; and Ann Richards (D-TX), chosen by 15 percent more women than men. In three of the four exceptions, female voters supported the Republican woman candidate at a greater rate than male voters (Center for American Women and Politics 1997).

In this book, we include political party affiliation and incumbent/challenger status in our analysis of how these U.S. Senate and gubernatorial candidates present themselves to voters through their television commercials as well as how voters respond to political ads from mixed-gender gubernatorial and senatorial campaigns and presidential campaigns.

Theoretical Underpinnings

The theoretical underpinnings of this book are grounded in research in a variety of disciplines, including sociology, psychology, and communication.

To study how female and male political candidates present themselves through their mass media messaging (political ads and Web sites), we turned to Goffman's (1973) theory of self-presentation, Kaid and Davidson's (1986) VideoStyle concept, Bystrom's (1995) application of Campbell's (1989) feminine style rhetorical construct to VideoStyle, and Banwart's (2002) application of these concepts to Web sites, that is, WebStyle.

To study how the media and public perceive and react to female and male political candidates, we applied theories of sex role stereotyping from cognitive psychology (Ashmore, Del Boca, and Wohlers 1986) and gender schema theory (Bem 1993). We call the media's presentation of female and male candidates to their readers NewsStyle.

Based on these theoretical perspectives, which are explained in chapter 2, the book analyzes differences in female and male candidate advertising and Internet strategies, news coverage of female and male candidates, and female and male reactions to media messages.

Methods

Four research methods—content analysis, experimental, survey, and case study research—are used in this book. The primary method used in our research is a content analysis of media messages from mixed-gender U.S. Senate and gubernatorial races. In excess of thirteen hundred spot ads, forty-eight Web sites, and eighteen hundred newspaper articles are included in the analysis. We use the ads, Web sites, and news coverage of candidates from mixed-gender races (versus those from male/male and female/female races) to control for gender. Our analysis also includes experimental research on responses of male and female voters to political messages as well as survey research responses reporting media use by women and men in political campaigns.

Finally, we employ the constructs of VideoStyle, WebStyle, and NewsStyle to study the individual campaigns of female and male political candidates in mixed-gender gubernatorial and U.S. Senate races. For these sections of the volume, a case study methodology is used.

Thus, this book analyzes data collected over a number of years to offer a comprehensive study of how female and male candidates present themselves to voters, and how the media and public respond to communication strategies and campaigns. In Parts II, III, and IV, we apply a similar, comprehensive approach to analyze gendered messages and responses to candidate VideoStyle (Part II, chapters 3 through 6), WebStyle (Part III, chapters 7 through 9), and NewsStyle (Part IV, chapters 10 through 12). In each part, we provide an updated overview of female and male U.S. Senate and gubernatorial campaign VideoStyle, WebStyle, and NewsStyle. Next, these constructs are applied to individual campaigns of female and male candidates running for governor and U.S. Senate in 2000 and 2002. Finally, the responses of female and male voters to candidate campaign commercials, Web sites, and media coverage are reported. In Part V, chapter 13, we summarize the theoretical and practical implications of our work for those interested in women's political campaigns and election to office, including women candidates and students and scholars of communication, political science, sociology, and women's studies.

2
VideoStyle, WebStyle, and NewsStyle: A Framework for Gendered Analysis

Our comprehensive look at gender and political communication includes not only an analysis of how female and male candidates present themselves through the candidate-controlled mediums of television ads and Web sites, but also an examination of how the media and voters react to these presentations. The framework for our analysis—VideoStyle, WebStyle, and NewsStyle—is based on theories from communication, sociology, and psychology that have been specifically applied to gender studies. This chapter explains these theoretical frameworks, the results of previous research relevant to our lines of inquiry, and the methods used in our analyses.

Analyzing Gendered Candidate Messages

The theoretical basis for our research on gender and candidate messages is drawn primarily from the concept of VideoStyle, initially introduced by Kaid and Davidson (1986). VideoStyle builds on the concept of "self-presentation" as discussed by Goffman (1973), providing a systematic method of analyzing the verbal content, nonverbal content, and production techniques in television spot ads. Since Kaid and Davidson's inaugural work, VideoStyle has been advanced to study the self-presentation of female and male candidates in political spot ads adding Campbell's construct of feminine style (Bystrom 1995; Bystrom and Kaid 2002; Bystrom and Miller 1999; Miller 1996) and adapted to the interactive features of the Internet and labeled "WebStyle" (Banwart 2002).

Goffman's Theory of the Presentation of Self

In explaining his dramaturgical theory of the "presentation of self," Goffman (1973) uses the metaphor of the theater to describe interpersonal communication. He describes people as actors who structure their performances to make impressions on their audience:

> When an individual appears in the presence of others, there will usually be some reason for him to mobilize his activity so that it will convey an impression to others which it is in his interests to convey. (1973: 4)

> He may wish them to think highly of him, or to think that he thinks highly of them . . . he may wish to ensure sufficient harmony so that the interaction can be sustained, or to defraud, get rid of, confuse, mislead, antagonize, or insult them. (1973: 3)

Regardless of the actor's motives or objectives, his or her ultimate interest, Goffman argues, is to "control the conduct of others, especially their responsive treatment" of the actor (1973: 3). However, the "asymmetry of the communication process" is maintained when others sense that the individual actor is manipulating his or her behavior (1973: 8). Because the "arts of piercing an individual's effort at calculated unintentionality seem better developed than our capacity to manipulate our own behavior," Goffman believes that the audience holds the ultimate advantage over the actor in the interpersonal communication process (1973: 8–9).

Kaid and Davidson's Construct of VideoStyle

The first attempt to describe systematically the style of political commercials was Lynda Lee Kaid and Dorothy Davidson's 1986 content analysis of fifty-five commercials from three 1982 U.S. Senate races in which they advanced their concept of "VideoStyle." Later, Dorothy Davidson Nesbit (1988) attempted to supplement this concept through interviews with incumbent U.S. senators, their challengers, and producers of their political spots.

As defined by Kaid and Davidson (1986), VideoStyle combines the verbal content, nonverbal content, and film or video production techniques of televised political advertising. Thus, VideoStyle encompasses all the ways in which political candidates present themselves to voters through their television advertising. As Kaid and Davidson note:

> When candidates use television to project themselves to voters, they engage primarily in a form of pseudointerpersonal communication in which they use television's visual element and its capacity to induce intimacy to portray themselves as they believe voters wish

to see them. Their methods of self-portrayal make up their videostyles. (1986: 185)

In constructing their concept of VideoStyle from Goffman's theory of the presentation of self, Kaid and Davidson point out that Goffman "did not envision the capacity to edit so finely that a presentation can be perfected and polished, controlled and rehearsed, timed and staged" (1986: 189). In fact, they argue that television advertising may actually supply the candidates with a communication channel through which nonverbal behavior (which is often considered more believable) can be controlled. Political commercials can be rehearsed, reshot, and redone until the right video image and message are achieved. Thus, they believe, televised political commercials afford the actors an advantage over the audience in the communication process (Kaid and Davidson 1986; Nesbit 1988).

Of course, the audience of actors in the interpersonal communication process is different from the audience of mass-communicated television ads. Whereas interpersonal communication usually involves small, homogeneous audiences that the actor knows in advance, the audience watching mass-communicated advertising is large, heterogeneous, and usually unknown to the candidate (Kaid and Davidson 1986). However, through various research strategies, candidates and their consultants can predict and determine the audience's receptivity to certain types and styles of political ads.

Whereas the ability to think on one's feet is important to candidates speaking to audiences in interpersonal settings, the ability to anticipate audience reactions is critical to candidates communicating through televised political advertising (Nesbit 1988). Thus, the presentation of self over television requires different abilities and skills of the political candidate—and his or her consultants—than does the interpersonal presentation of self.

The presentation of self through television is further complicated, Nesbit notes, because many people—not just the communicator—are involved in deciding the content, timing, frequency, and sequence of airing political commercials. "The spot is the composite of candidates' self images, producers' theories about how to market these candidates, and actual political situations," she observes (1988: 5). "However, in the competition between producer and candidate, it is the candidate who ultimately determines what the ingredients of his [or her] videostyle will be" (1988: 28).

Similar to Goffman's (1973) view that control over the conduct and responses of others is the goal of the interpersonal presentation of self, the purpose of VideoStyle in political advertising is to control the candidate's issue and image presentation through a commercial's verbal, nonverbal, and production content and affect how viewers think, feel, and act. Thus, candidate VideoStyles are designed to have cognitive, affective, and/or behavioral consequences (Nesbit 1988).

Commercials may use cognitive strategies to communicate information about the candidate's image qualities or issue concerns to increase his or her recognition among viewers. Affective strategies are used throughout campaigns to evoke favorable feelings (such as empathy, trust, and excitement) toward the candidate or negative emotions (such as fear, anxiety, and uncertainty) about his or her opponent. Similarly, behavioral strategies may be designed to elicit support for the candidate sponsoring the ad or rejection of his or her opponent. "The use of a cognitive or affective strategy to evoke certain feelings hinges on the relative importance that candidates and their producers place on cognition and affect in their theories of how voters decide" (Nesbit 1988: 30).

Systematic studies of the VideoStyles of televised political advertising reveal the strategies that politicians and their consultants presumably believe showcase the candidate in a way that most favorably affects how voters think about, feel about, and act toward the candidate. Research on candidate commercials utilizing the VideoStyle construct provide information about the content of the television commercials of incumbents and challengers as well as male and female candidates.

For example, Kaid and Davidson's pioneering 1986 study on the VideoStyles of U.S. Senate candidates revealed significant differences in the verbal and nonverbal messages and production techniques of incumbents and challengers. They found that incumbents used more positively focused ads, more testimonials, more slides with print, more formal attire, announcers, longer spots, and more verbal and visual emphasis on competence. Challengers used more negatively focused ads, a cinema verité production style, a personal "head-on" appearance, more frequent eye contact, and more casual dress, and did more speaking for themselves.

Although Kaid and Davidson's 1986 study is cited in several other works investigating gender as a variable in televised political advertising (Kahn 1993; Kahn and Geer 1994; Procter, Schenck-Hamlin, and Haase 1988; Trent and Sabourin 1993), Bystrom was the first researcher to utilize this construct specifically in examining the content of the commercials of male and female candidates to determine whether men and women present themselves similarly or differently in their VideoStyles. In her dissertation research (1995), she incorporated Campbell's (1989) concept of "feminine style" as well as other variables based on gender and communication into the construct of VideoStyle to study the campaign commercials of female and male candidates running against each other in U.S. Senate campaigns in 1990, 1992, and a special election in 1993.

Campbell's Concept of Feminine Style

According to Campbell (1989), women—relegated for centuries to the private sphere—learned to craft their rhetorical style so that it (1) is more personal in tone, (2) relies on personal experiences, anecdotes, and other examples, (3) is structured inductively, (4) invites audience participation, (5) addresses the audiences as peers, and (6) identifies with the audience's experience.

In contrast with feminine style, masculine speech strategies include (1) deductive logic and reasoning (the most common political speech strategy), in which the speaker presents his or her conclusions before giving examples), (2) affirmations of one's own expertise, (3) use of expert authority ("impartial" statistics or examples provided by a third party, such as a newspaper), and (4) the use of impersonal or incomplete examples (historical or hypothetical examples that are not connected to the experiences of the speaker or the audience) (Curtis, Shuler, and Grieve 1994; Dow and Tonn 1993).

A woman's goal when utilizing a feminine rhetorical strategy, Campbell says, is empowerment; thus, the goal is to persuade "listeners that they can act effectively in the world, that they can be 'agents of change'" (1989: 13). Although Campbell named this rhetorical style "feminine," she maintains that these strategies are not exclusive to women.

Prior to Bystrom's 1995 study of political advertising, Campbell's construct of feminine style was applied in historical analyses of early feminist rhetoric (Campbell 1989; Campbell and Jerry 1988), case studies of women orators such as former Colorado congresswoman Patricia Schroeder (Szpiech 1992) and Texas governor Ann Richards (Dow and Tonn 1993), analysis of feminist social group movements (Zurakowski 1994), and content analysis of Congressional speeches (Curtis, Shuler, and Grieve 1994).

Case studies of women political speakers have concluded that they synthesize gender expectations in their political discourse by using both "masculine" rhetorical strategies, such as formal evidence, deductive structure, and linear modes of reasoning, with elements of feminine style, such as personal anecdotes (Dow and Tonn 1993; Szpiech 1992).

In their study of five women and five men in the U.S. Congress, Curtis and colleagues (1994) found that eight of the ten used both feminine and masculine rhetorical strategies in their public addresses. However, women used a personal tone—a feminine style—more often than men, who were more likely to use a masculine deductive style.

Feminine style continues to be employed in the content analysis of the speeches of female and male political leaders. In her analysis of speeches presented at the 1992 Democratic and Republican national conventions, DeRosa (1996) found that speakers blended feminine and masculine speech strategies while concentrating on characteristically masculine issues. A content analysis (DeRosa and Bystrom 1999) of the nomination, keynote, and featured speeches delivered during the 1996 Democratic and Republican national conventions found a similar blending of feminine and masculine speech styles by men and women. However, the structure of their appeals, application of familial roles, use of attacks, and emphasis on masculine versus feminine traits and issues revealed striking differences between women and men and Republicans and Democrats.

For example, women of both political parties were much more likely to structure their appeals inductively—a feminine rhetorical strategy—whereas men employed a deductive (masculine) style at the 1996 conventions (DeRosa and Bystrom 1999). And whereas men emphasized their own political expertise, women built their credibility through a personal application of familial roles—particularly as wives and mothers.

Another significant difference was seen in the use of attacks, with men much more likely to use negative rhetoric than women.

However, both female and male speakers at the 1996 conventions employed stereotypically masculine traits (such as leadership, action, and past performance) and issues (such as taxes, the economy, employment, and crime) in their political rhetoric (DeRosa and Bystrom 1999). Unlike 1992, when "women's issues" were systematically ignored, downplayed, or simply avoided (Daughton 1995), 1996 saw the Democrats paying considerable attention to such issues as education, health care, the environment, and child care.

Bystrom's Application of Feminine Style to Campaign Commercial VideoStyle

Bystrom (1995) combined Campbell's (1989) feminine style with Kaid and Davidson's (1986) VideoStyle in her content analysis of political television advertisements from mixed-gender U.S. Senate campaigns in 1990, 1992, and a special election in 1993. She found that these female candidates used about the same percentage of attacks and talked about mostly the same issues and images as male candidates. However, these female candidates also smiled more, made more eye contact, spoke more often for themselves, appeared head on more often, dressed more formally, and invited viewer participation and action more often than male candidates. From these results, Bystrom proposed female and male VideoStyles for future investigations.

However, subsequent studies of the 1994 (Bystrom and Kaid 1996) and 1996 (Bystrom and Miller 1999) mixed-gender races for governor and U.S. Senate pointed to other differences in the VideoStyles of female and male candidates. In 1994, which was dubbed the "Year of the Angry White Man" by the media, male candidates were more negative than female candidates, but both emphasized about the same issues and image traits (Bystrom and Kaid 1996). In 1996, female candidates were more likely than male candidates to stress male traits such as toughness. Women also ran more negative ads, as compared to the men, and were less likely than the men to stress warmth and compassion (Bystrom and Miller 1999).

A study of the VideoStyles of mixed-gender U.S. Senate campaigns from 1990 to 1998 (Bystrom and Kaid 2002) found that female candidates had increased their use of attacks, as compared to their male opponents, over the decade. Female candidates also continued to dress more formally and smile more than men. However, the issues that female and male candidates mentioned in their television commercials seemed to be more attributable to the context of the election year than the gendered VideoStyle of the candidate. For example, both women and men focused on education, the environment, and senior citizens' issues in 1990; the economy, health care, and taxes in 1992–93; taxes and crime in 1994; taxes, senior citizens' issues, and education in 1996; and taxes, the economy, and senior citizens' issues in 1998.

In addition, the study of commercials from 1990–1998 mixed-gender U.S. Senate campaigns (Bystrom and Kaid 2002) found that female and male candidates emphasized similar images in their television commercials. They both emphasized stereotypically masculine traits such as strength, aggressiveness, performance, and experience, balanced with such stereotypically feminine attributes as honesty, sensitivity, and understanding. That is, both men and women seem to be presenting themselves as tough but caring—at least when running against each other.

Banwart's Adaptation of Feminine Style and VideoStyle to Construct WebStyle

In recent years, the Internet has provided political candidates and office holders with an important means of communicating with voters and constituents—and researchers with another way to look at the political communication of female and male politicians. As of June 2001, nearly all members of the U.S. House of Representatives maintained Web sites, some of which receive as many as a thousand hits a month (Niven and Zilber 2001). As of November 2002, all candidates in mixed-gender gubernatorial races, 83 percent of candidates in mixed-gender U.S. Senate races, and 66 percent of candidates in mixed-gender U.S. House races hosted Web sites (Banwart 2002).

Similar to television advertising, Web sites represent a form of communication that is controlled by the politician, rather than interpreted by the media. Researchers (Banwart 2002; Niven and Zilber 2001) are beginning to examine Web sites to see if female and male politicians present themselves differently when they use this form of communication.

In her research, Banwart adapted the use of feminine style and VideoStyle to an analysis of female and male candidate Web sites in the 2000 election and constructed the concept of WebStyle. Although the VideoStyle categories of verbal, nonverbal, and production content were largely applicable, the construct further required the development of variables to capture one of the most important features of Web sites: interactive content. Overall,

Banwart found several similarities, and some differences, in the WebStyles of the female and male candidates she studied. For example, she found that both female and male candidates discussed so-called feminine issues much more frequently than so-called masculine issues on their Web sites. Both female and male candidates were equally as likely to discuss the feminine issue of education. On masculine issues, male candidates were only slightly more likely to discuss taxes, whereas female candidates were slightly more likely to discuss the economy (Banwart 2002).

Among the differences Banwart found in the WebStyle presentations of women and men running for governor and Congress in 2000 were that women candidates in 2000 were much less likely than men to be shown with their families on their Web sites. The use of interactive content by female and male candidates remained largely similar, although female candidates were more likely to include a form for contributing in their sections for getting involved, suggesting that female candidates were less up front about requesting contributions from viewers. Female candidates' WebStyle was likely to feature a "feminine personal-professional" style, and male candidates' WebStyle tended toward a "masculine up-front" style.

Although the theoretical framework for our study of the campaign messages of female and male political candidates is built primarily on VideoStyle and feminine style, some researchers (Kahn 1996) have used the construct of sex stereotypes to analyze not only the messages of female and male candidates in their political ads, but also media coverage and voter reactions to their campaigns. Sex stereotypes, though sometimes employed in research to study campaign advertising messages, are used in this book primarily as a means of analyzing media coverage and voter reactions and are described next.

Analyzing Gendered Media Coverage and Voter Reactions

The theoretical basis for our research on gendered reactions by the media and voters to female and male political candidates and their campaign messages is primarily derived from the field of psychology. Particularly, we relied on Ashmore, Del Boca, and Wohlers (1986) explanation of sex, or gender, stereotypes as well as Bem's (1993) gender schema theory.

According to Ashmore et al., sex stereotypes are a "structured set of beliefs about the personal attributes of men and women" (1986: 89). These attributes can include personality traits, physical characteristics, and expected behaviors associated with women or men as part of a gendered group. Such stereotypes are not necessarily bad—although they could be incorrect, overgeneralized, and rigid—because they are the result not of "aberrant or bizarre cognitive structures and processes," but rather of "normal" cognitive activity (1986: 89).

The act of sex stereotyping, then, refers to a normal cognitive process through which people simplify their perceptions about women and men by drawing inferences based on their beliefs about what members of a particular group are like. Scholars who study sex stereotypes are more concerned with perceived differences between women and men and look at sex stereotypes from both the cultural (group-level) and personal (individual-level) perspectives.

Sex stereotypes are used in this analysis as a means of explaining the differences in how the media as well as individual voters view and describe female and male political candidates. From our viewpoint, sex stereotypes have a circular relationship—sex stereotypes are found in our culture, which shapes how reporters see and report their worlds, which in turn reinforces the beliefs held by members of the society.

Closely related to the construct of sex stereotypes is Bem's gender schema theory, which is based on the assumption that "gender schematicity" is the acceptance of gender polarization learned from the culture (1993: 125). Bem argued that this polarization begins in childhood, at which time children learn to accept or reject what is appropriate or inappropriate for their sex based on definitions learned from their culture. Such polarization is problematic for both women and men, constraining roles for both.

Sex stereotyping has been used in previous research studying the content of the newspaper coverage of female and male candidates (Kahn 1991, 1992, 1994a, 1994b, 1996; Kahn and Goldenberg 1991) as well as their campaign appeals (Kahn 1993, 1996) and the effects of this coverage on voters (Kahn 1992, 1994b, 1996). Sex stereotypes also have been used to study the reactions of voters to candidates (Sapiro 1982; Huddy and Terkildsen 1993; Leeper 1991). Finally, sex stereotypes (Banwart and Carlin 2001; Bystrom 2003; Iyengar, Valentino, Ansolabehere, and Simon 1997; Kaid, Myers, Pipps, and Hunter 1984; Wadsworth, Patterson, Kaid, Cullers, Malcomb, and Lamirand 1987) and gender schema theory (Hitchon and Chang 1995; Hitchon, Chang, and Harris 1997) have been used to analyze voter reactions to male and female political ads.

Kahn's Application of Sex Stereotypes to Campaign Coverage and Effects

Extensive studies by Kim Fridkin Kahn (Kahn 1991, 1992, 1994a, 1994b; Kahn and Goldenberg 1991) examining the newspaper coverage of women candidates running for election in the 1980s found that this medium not only stereotypes female candidates by emphasizing "feminine traits" and "feminine issues," but also questions their viability as candidates. In an experimental design, fictitious female candidates gained viability when they received the same media coverage usually given to male incumbents (Kahn 1992, 1994b).

However, Kahn (1994b, 1996) also has noted that gender-stereotyped newspaper coverage, which reduces a woman candidate's perceived viability, can sometimes be used to a woman candidate's advantage—for example, by emphasizing warmth and honesty. Such positive stereotypes may actually create a favorable electoral environment for women candidates, Kahn (1994b) argues.

Kahn's 1996 book, *The Political Consequences of Being a Woman: How Stereotypes Influence the Conduct and Consequences of Political Campaigns*, provides the most comprehensive look to date on the impact of sex stereotypes on candidate advertising appeals, media campaign coverage, and voter reactions. By consciously considering the sex stereotypes held by female and male voters, Kahn argues that both women and men candidates can structure their campaign appeals to either capitalize on these beliefs or work to dispel them, depending on the context of the electoral environment.

Sex stereotypes can also influence the media coverage of the political campaigns of female and male candidates, in terms of both quantity and quality. Kahn found that newspapers responded to the gender of candidates by affording women less issue coverage and more image coverage than their male opponents—even though women were just as likely as men to emphasize issues in their campaign ads. And by emphasizing the horse race nature of the campaign, newspaper coverage often provided voters with negative information about the women candidates' viability.

Finally, Kahn found that sex stereotypes can impact the way male and female voters perceive women and men candidates. Often these stereotypes can lead to favorable evaluations of women candidates, who are considered more compassionate and honest, with expertise on such feminine issues as education, health care, and women's issues. However, if such issues are not salient to the campaign, women may need to emphasize masculine image characteristics, such as toughness and strength, and masculine issues, such as the economy or foreign policy, to counter sex stereotypes and establish their competence.

Kahn's research (1992, 1994b, 1996) on voters' stereotyping of male and female candidates confirms earlier studies. For example, research by Sapiro (1982), Huddy and Terkildsen (1993), and Leeper (1991), among others, found that women candidates are perceived as more compassionate and honest, with particular expertise on education, health care, and women's issues, whereas men candidates were considered more competent and knowledgeable, particularly on issues of the economy, the military, and foreign policy.

Beyond Kahn: The Construction of NewsStyle

Studies conducted since Kahn's work on the media coverage of women running for both governor and the U.S. Senate have confirmed many of her findings and given some hope that media coverage of women candidates might be improving in the 1990s and into the twenty-first century.

For example, a study examining the coverage of a gubernatorial campaign by two major newspapers (Serini, Powers, and Johnston 1998) confirmed many of Kahn's (1992, 1994a, 1994b, 1996) findings that women receive less issue coverage and more negative assessments of their viability as candidates. A study examining media coverage of the 1996 races for the Illinois House of Representatives (Miller 2001) also found some differences in the issue coverage of female and male candidates, but to a lesser degree.

Smith's (1997) study of newspaper coverage of female and male U.S. Senate and gubernatorial candidates in eleven races in 1994 provides "cautious inference" that reporters are treating women and men more equally. In this study, women and men received about the same quantity and quality of coverage. Women received less coverage in open races (races without an incumbent candidate), more coverage in gubernatorial races, and more neutral coverage overall. Although this study found that the "rule was one of rough parity in coverage," it concluded that "most exceptions to the rule were at the expense of female candidates" (Smith 1997: 79).

Similarly, a study of two gubernatorial campaigns found that while women and men were treated more equitably in media coverage, female candidates received more negative coverage than their male opponents (Rausch, Rozell, and Wilson 1999). And in his study of 1998 gubernatorial candidates, Devitt (1999) found that while male and female candidates for governor received about the same amount of coverage, women received less issue-related coverage than men did.

The 2000 campaign provided an opportunity to study not only the media coverage of women running for governor and the U.S. Senate (Bystrom, Robertson, and Banwart 2001; Banwart, Bystrom, and Robertson 2003; Robertson, Conley, Scymcznska, and Thompson 2002), but also the short-lived presidential candidacy of Elizabeth Dole (Aday and Devitt 2001; Bystrom, forthcoming; Heldman, Carroll, and Olson 2000). A study of newspaper coverage of women and men running for their party's nomination for U.S. Senate and governor in the 2000 primary races (Bystrom, Robertson, and Banwart 2001) found that these women received more coverage than men in terms of quantity, and that the quality of their coverage—slant of the story and discussion of their viability, appearance, and personality—was mostly equitable. Still, these women candidates were much more likely to be discussed in terms of their role as mothers and their marital status, which can affect their viability with voters.

Robertson and colleagues (2002) also studied the newspaper coverage of women candidates for governor and U.S. Senate in the 2000 general election. They found that women received more much coverage—as well as more favorable coverage—in their campaigns, as compared to previous research. However, significant differences were discovered in the quality of their coverage. For example, women were much more likely than men to be described in terms of their gender, marital status, and children. And, perhaps surprisingly, men were much more associated with the feminine issue of education in the general election than women, with 32 percent of male-candidate-focused articles and 11 percent of female-candidate-focused articles discussing the issue. Still, their study led the researchers to conclude that a gradual evolution is taking place within newspapers' coverage of women running for political office. Although some stereotyping does exist, the playing field for female candidates is flattening, they determined.

In their comparison of the media coverage of women and men in the 2000 primary and general elections, Banwart, Bystrom, and Robertson (2003) found that female candidates received more newspaper coverage than male candidates in U.S. Senate and gubernatorial races, with more than 95 percent of the articles mentioning female candidates, compared to about 75 percent of the articles mentioning male candidates. In terms of the quality of their media coverage, they found that the slant of male candidates' news coverage became more negative, while coverage of female candidates remained more neutral from the primary to general election. Yet these advantages did not translate to greater discussions of female candidates' viability in these races, as viability coverage remained equitable for female and male candidates during both the primaries and general election.

Further, the news coverage across both primary and general election races continued to define female candidates in terms of their gender, children, and marital status (Banwart, Bystrom, and Robertson 2003). Such news coverage can ultimately affect how voters view female candidates' ability to hold political office by reinforcing their "other" status in the male-dominated world of politics as well as images of them as mothers and wives, who have traditionally carried less authority and competence in the public arena (Witt, Paget, and Matthews 1995).

This potential disadvantage for female candidates may be further exacerbated when news coverage is more likely to link male candidates with issues and traits voters have more commonly associated with female candidates. For example, male candidates in 2000 were associated at significantly higher percentages in their general election coverage (32 percent) than in their primary coverage (9 percent) with education and schools—a traditionally "feminine" issue—while still being associated with the traditionally "masculine" issues of taxes and the economy in both the general (43 percent, 41 percent) and primary (22 percent, 11 percent) election (Banwart, Bystrom, and Robertson 2003). Women candidates, on the other hand, were twice as likely to be associated with the feminine issue of health care in the general election (17 percent) compared to the primary (8 percent), while their association with issues concerning the budget, unemployment/jobs, and immigration—traditionally masculine issues—decreased or became nonexistent in their general election coverage (Banwart, Bystrom, and Robertson 2003).

The portrayal of candidate image traits did not differ significantly between the primary coverage and the general election coverage for either female or male candidates, except on the image strategy of using an "above-the-trenches" posture, i.e., a technique whereby candidates try to create the image that they are somehow removed from politics (Banwart, Bystrom, and Robertson 2003). Thus, those traits on which female and male candidates significantly differed in their primary coverage again emerged with significant differences in their general election coverage. Such traits included associating male candidates more with the feminine trait of honesty, the challenger strategy of being a voice for the state, and the use of a personal tone—an element of feminine style—than female candidates (Bystrom, Robertson, and Banwart 2001).

In addition to examining the media coverage of women running against men for governor and the U.S. Senate, the 2000 campaign provided a rare opportunity for scholars to analyze the media's treatment of a woman campaigning for a major political party nomination for president. Three studies (Aday and Devitt 2001; Bystrom, forthcoming; and Heldman, Carroll, and Olson 2000) examining the newspaper coverage of Elizabeth Dole—the first woman to seek a major political party nomination for president since former U.S. representative Patricia Schroeder's short-lived consideration in 1988—during seven months in 1999 found that she received less equitable coverage in terms of quality and especially quantity as compared to her male opponents. Although polls consistently showed Dole as a distant runner-up to George W. Bush for the Republican nomination for president, she not only received significantly less coverage than Bush, but also less coverage than Steve Forbes and John McCain, who at the time were behind her in the polls.

In terms of the quality of coverage, all three studies found that Dole received less issue coverage than Bush, Forbes, or McCain. However, according to the two studies (Bystrom, forthcoming; Heldman, Carroll and Olson 2000) that considered the types of issues mentioned, Dole's issue coverage was balanced between such stereotypically masculine issues as taxes, foreign policy, and the economy and such stereotypically feminine issues as education, drugs, and gun control.

The findings regarding Dole's image coverage were mixed. Aday and Devitt (2001) found that Dole received significantly more personal coverage, including descriptions of her personality and appearance, than the male candidates studied. However, Heldman, Carroll, and Olson (2000) found that the media did not pay much attention to her appearance but did make reference to her personality in three-fifths of the articles studied. Bystrom's study (forthcoming), which was limited to media coverage in Iowa, found that Dole was less likely than Bush to be covered in terms of her image, including appearance and personality.

Although these studies show that media biases toward women candidates still exist, it does appear that coverage is becoming more equitable. Women running for governor and the U.S. Senate in 2000 received more coverage, in terms of quantity, than men in both the primary and general elections, and mostly equitable coverage in terms of quality during the primary campaign (Banwart, Bystrom, and Robertson 2003; Bystrom, Robertson, and Banwart 2001; Robertson et al. 2002).

For future women presidential candidates, it is somewhat promising to note that Elizabeth Dole's media coverage in 1999 was more balanced and less stereotypical than found in earlier studies, particularly in the range of issues mentioned and the lack of attention to her appearance and personality. Still, Dole received less coverage than male candidates, even those running behind her in the public opinion polls.

The media coverage studies of female and male candidates by Robertson, Banwart, and Bystrom provide the basis for our construct of NewsStyle. According to the most recent analyses, we see female and male political candidates receiving more equitable media coverage, especially in terms of quantity, with some improvements in quality. However, women political candidates still may be disadvantaged by media that portray them in stereotypical ways, especially in terms of their image traits and marital status and family. The media also affects voters' perceptions of candidates by stressing male candidates' attention to stereotypically feminine issues and image traits.

Gendered Reactions to Candidate Communication

Sex stereotypes (Banwart and Carlin 2001; Bystrom 2003; Iyengar et al. 1997; Kaid et al. 1984; Wadsworth et al. 1987) and gender schema theory (Hitchon and Chang 1995; Hitchon, Chang, and Harris 1997) also have been used to study the reactions of women and men to the political ads of female and male candidates.

Early studies of women's political advertising (Kaid et al. 1984; Wadsworth et al. 1987) found that masculine strategies work best for women candidates in their political ads. However, more recent studies (Banwart and Carlin 2001; Bystrom 2003) found that women were most effective when balancing stereotypically feminine and masculine traits. Hitchon and Chang (1995) and Hitchon, Chang, and Harris (1997) found that neutral—as opposed to emotional—appeals worked best for women candidates in terms of audience recall, especially for issue stances. As for issue emphasis, Iyengar and colleagues (1997) found women were more effective when communicating about stereotypical female issues.

In an experimental design, Kaid and colleagues (1984) found that female candidates can be just as successful as male candidates in their television advertisements, especially when they appear in settings traditionally associated with men. In fact, the woman candidate they studied received her highest overall rating while wearing a hard hat at a construction site, perhaps because the appearance of a female in that role was somewhat novel to the audience.

Similarly, in another experimental design, Wadsworth and colleagues (1987) found that audiences responded more favorably to hypothetical women candidates who used masculine (aggressive, career-oriented) rather than traditionally feminine (nonaggressive, family-oriented) strategies in their television ads. Femininity is not a valued trait, they assert; rather, viewers valued women candidates who were honest, smart, experienced, and rational. The researchers advised that a career-oriented approach is the best style and strategy for women candidates.

In their experiment on two 1992 U.S. Senate campaigns and the 1994 gubernatorial campaign in California—all of which pitted a woman against a man—Iyengar and colleagues (1997) concluded that women candidates were more effective in communicating with voters through commercials that focused on such stereotypically female issues as women's rights, education, and unemployment than such stereotypically male issues as crime and illegal immigration. Like Kahn (1996), these researchers advise women candidates to "consider their constituents' stereotypes when designing their advertising strategies" (Iyengar 1997: 96) but to "pick the characteristics which will resonate best with voters based on the issue environment during that particular campaign season" (1997: 98).

Using gender schema theory, Hitchon and Chang (1995) suggest that voters' stereotypical beliefs may interfere with their processing of political ads. In an experimental design, they found that subjects recalled more mentions of family and visuals of appearance when the candidate was a woman. They had better recall of male candidates' names and campaign activities. Neutral appeals by women produced high levels of total recall and issue recall.

Hitchon, Chang, and Harris (1997) also used gender schema theory in their experimental design to assess audience reactions to the emotional tone of the political advertisements of female and male candidates. Similar to Hitchon and Chang (1995), they found that women received better evaluations from audiences when they employed neutral tones. They suggest that "women can benefit by adopting a rational, unemotional approach in mass media messages" (Hitchon et al. 1997: 64).

Other researchers (Kaid 1994, 1998; Kaid and Johnston 1991, 2001; Kaid and Tedesco 1999) have examined the reactions of female and male respondents to male presidential ads. Their results mirror the characteristics of the gender gap, as explained in chapter 1, with women more likely to evaluate the Democratic candidate more positively than men, and men more likely to evaluate the Republican candidate more positively than women.

For example, in the 1996 presidential campaign—in which female voters preferred President Bill Clinton by eleven points over male voters at the polls—Kaid and Tedesco (1999) found identifiable differences in the reactions of women and men to Clinton's and Bob Dole's ads. Women were more negative toward Dole and more positive toward Clinton in the pretest.

After viewing their ads, women's evaluation of Clinton's image increased significantly, while their evaluation of Dole decreased significantly.

Overall, researchers have found that female voters tend to provide male presidential candidates with higher evaluations after seeing their video messages (Kaid and Holtz-Bacha 2000). There are often clear differences in how male and female voters react to the same candidates. These differences are less pronounced, however, when male and female voters react to Internet presentations or media portrayals of candidates.

Methods

This book utilizes three primary research methods: content analysis to examine more than thirteen hundred political ads, forty-eight Web sites, and more than eighteen hundred newspaper stories; experimental designs to test the reactions of respondents to political ads and Web sites; and survey research to examine gender differences in media use during political campaigns. A case study approach was used to examine the individual campaigns of women and men running for governor and the U.S. Senate.

One of the most frequently used methodologies in political, mass, and public communication (Frey, Botan, Friedman, and Kreps 1991; Kaid and Wadsworth 1989), content analysis has been recognized as a powerful and valuable research technique for (1) making "objective, systematic, and usually quantitative" (Kaid and Wadsworth 1989) descriptions of communication content and (2) "making replicable and valid inferences" from data analyzed within the context that the communication occurs (Krippendorf 1980). Thus, content analysis is a particularly useful research methodology to examine, describe, and assess how these male and female candidates present themselves to voters through their political television commercials and Web sites and how the media present these candidates to voters through newspaper coverage within the context of their campaigns and election years.

As with other research methodologies, content analysis begins with the formulation of hypotheses or research questions (Kaid and Wadsworth 1989). The other steps include (1) selecting the sample to be analyzed, (2) defining the categories to be applied, (3) outlining the coding process and training the coders who will implement it, (4) implementing the coding process, (5) determining reliability and validity, and (6) analyzing the results of the coding process (Kaid and Wadsworth 1989: 199). These procedures were used to content analyze the television commercials, Web sites, and newspaper articles for our studies in chapters 3, 4, 5, 7, 8, 10, and 11.

The experiments reported in chapters 6 and 9 used a basic pretest-posttest experimental design. That is, participants responded to a set of pretest questions, then were exposed to stimuli—either candidate campaign commercials or Web sites—and finally completed a set of posttest questions.

The pretest survey asked respondents for demographic and media use information and had them complete semantic differential scales regarding the images of specific political candidates. Also used in the posttest, this scale was developed over many years and has been used frequently to measure candidate image with high reliability (Kaid 1995). The posttest also included questions designed to determine other types of reactions to the spots or Web sites.

Information for chapter 12 came from portions of the questionnaires about media use that were contained in experimental sessions on advertising and Web site reactions and from surveys of voters after the general elections in 1996 and 2000.

Part II
Campaign Advertising: *Gendered Messages, Gendered Reactions*

3
VideoStyle: *Communication Messages through Campaign Advertising*

With significantly more women entering the political arena, researchers are becoming increasingly interested in exploring differences and similarities in the campaign communication styles and strategies of female and male candidates. Studies investigating the role of gender in campaign communication have become more feasible, from a methodological perspective, since the 1992 election, when record numbers of women sought and won political office.

Televised political ads provide an important resource for documenting the communication styles and strategies of political candidates, as they remain one of the few candidate-controlled (rather than media-mediated) communication tools of the modern political campaign. The importance of television advertising to today's political campaign is underscored by the significant financial resources devoted to such communication. For example, according to the Alliance for Better Campaigns (2001), the nation's broadcast industry took in between $770 million and $1 billion in political advertising spending in the 2000 campaign. Studies examining the influence of political advertising on voter perceptions of candidates and their issues and images show that this money may be well spent (see Geiger and Reeves 1991; Joslyn 1980; Kern 1989; Patterson and McClure 1976; West 2001). For example, a study of the 1992 U.S. Senate races in California found that commercials influenced perceptions of candidate recognition, favorability, electability, and voting preference (West 2001).

Several researchers (Bystrom 1995) have argued that television and the control it offers over campaign messages, especially in transmitting information on image and issues, is even more important for women candidates, who are often framed in stereotypical terms by the media (see the discussion of Kim Kahn's work in chapter 2). Media coverage of women candidates oftentimes emphasizes their traditional roles as wives and mothers and focuses on their appearance, personality, and personal lives (see Braden 1996; Witt, Paget, and Matthews 1995). For example, the hairstyles of former Texas governor Ann Richards and U.S. Senate candidate Lynn Yeakel, Yeakel's wardrobe, and U.S. Senator Barbara Mikulski's weight and physical appearance were subjected to media scrutiny during the 1992 and 1994 campaigns; former U.S. Senator Carol Moseley Braun's smile was noted in her media coverage during her 1992 and 1998 campaigns; and former First Lady Hillary Rodham Clinton's hairstyle and wardrobe were often commented on by the media during her 2000 race for the U.S. Senate (see Witt, Paget, and Matthews 1995; chapters 10 and 11 herein). Newspaper coverage further stereotypes women candidates by associating them with "feminine traits" and "feminine issues" and according them less coverage that often focuses on their viability as candidates (see chapter 2).

In light of such stereotypical treatment by the media, women candidates can use political advertising to counter such images and present themselves in their own ways and words. Through an examination of the verbal, nonverbal, and production content—collectively, the VideoStyle—of the televised political commercials of female and male candidates opposing each other in races for the U.S. Senate and governor in the 1990 through 2002 elections, this study seeks to determine the similarities and differences between female and male candidate VideoStyles and to define whether certain characteristics are unique to gender.

Candidate VideoStyles: U.S. Senate and Gubernatorial Races 1990–2002

This chapter reports the results of studies conducted on the television advertising used by women and men candidates when competing against each other for seats in the U.S. Senate and governor's office in 1990, 1992–93, 1994, 1996, 1998, 2000, and 2002. Mixed-gender U.S. Senate and gubernatorial races were selected because such campaigns usually rely heavily on television advertising to provide candidate information to statewide audiences. Each of these studies used a coding process involving a code sheet and detailed code book investigating the VideoStyle—the verbal, nonverbal, and production content—of these ads.[1] The coding process was based on a 1986 study by Kaid and Davidson (which delineated the elements of VideoStyle), with revisions to include gender-based expectations discussed in communication and political science literature.

These studies coded for demographic information on the candidates along with three types of commercial content: verbal, nonverbal, and production content. Verbal content included the presence or absence of negative attacks, the issues mentioned, the image qualities highlighted, and the structure of the appeals made. Nonverbal content included assessing the setting of the ad, identifying who is speaking and who is pictured in the ad, and examining the candidate's voice, facial expressions, body movement, gestures, and dress. Production content included the ad's format, camera shots and angles, and length.

Other categories interwoven throughout the coding were designed to measure for differences between women and men candidates on several variables that have been previously associated with gender. For example, communication studies have shown that women establish more eye contact than men, use more facial expressions, are more expressive, smile more, and wear normative clothing to win approval (Pearson, Turner, and Todd-Mancillas 1991). In addition, certain issues, image characteristics, and appeal strategies have been identified as "masculine" or "feminine" in political science and communication literature (Benze and Declercq 1985; Johnston and White 1994; Huddy and Terkildsen 1993; Kahn 1993; Trent and Sabourin 1993). For example, women have been associated with such issues as education, health care, and the environment and such image traits as compassion, cooperation, and honesty. Men have been associated with such issues as taxes, the economy, crime, and defense and such image traits as toughness, aggressiveness, and emphasis on their accomplishments.

Advertisements analyzed in these studies were obtained from the Political Communication Center at the University of Oklahoma. The sample of ads analyzed from the 1990 through 2002 campaigns totaled 1,389, including 195 ads from 1990, 233 from 1992, 7 from a special-election U.S. Senate race in 1993, 318 from 1994, 152 from 1996, 166 from 1998, 163 from 2000, and 155 from 2002. Of the total sample, 686 ads were from female candidates, and 703 ads were from male candidates. About 60 percent of the ads were from U.S. Senate campaigns, with the remaining 40 percent from gubernatorial races. About 49 percent of the ads were for female candidates, and 51 percent were for male candidates (see Table 3.1).

Through our statistical analyses, we found differences and similarities in the VideoStyles of these female and male candidates, which are summarized in Table 3.2 and described below. The differences in the sample size on certain variables are due to the year in which the ads were coded. For example, certain issues—such as youth violence—were included in most but not all of the election years studied. The variable that coded presence of demographics shown in the ads was not included in the coding for 1996. Of the advertisements coded for 1990 and 1992, only the U.S. Senate spots included coding for the sex of the dominant speaker, facial expression, and dominant dress; the 2002 ads did not include coding for these variables.

Verbal Content of Candidate VideoStyle

Although female and male candidates were similar in the focus, type, and structure of their verbal appeals to voters through their television commercials, some significant differences were found in the issues and image traits they emphasized as well as in their appeal strategies.

TABLE 3.1 Female and Male Candidate Advertising Analyzed 1990–2002

	Total	Female Ads	Male Ads
Year			
1990	195 (14%)	98 (50%)	97 (50%)
1992	233 (17%)	87 (37%)	146 (63%)
1993	7 (1%)	7 (100%)	0 (0%)
1994	318 (23%)	181 (57%)	137 (43%)
1996	152 (11%)	65 (43%)	87 (57%)
1998	166 (12%)	66 (40%)	100 (60%)
2000	163 (12%)	84 (52%)	79 (48%)
2002	155 (11%)	98 (63%)	57 (37%)
Level			
Governor	535 (39%)	282 (53%)	253 (47%)
Senate	854 (61%)	404 (47%)	450 (53%)
Status			
Incumbent	406 (29%)	97 (24%)	309 (76%)
Challenger	393 (28%)	281 (72%)	112 (29%)
Open Race	590 (43%)	308 (52%)	282 (48%)
Party			
Democrat	645 (46%)	439 (68%)	206 (32%)
Republican	744 (54%)	247 (33%)	497 (67%)
Outcome			
Won	700 (50%)	292 (42%)	409 (58%)
Lost	689 (50%)	394 (57%)	295 (43%)

Focus of Appeal. Although female and male candidates have differed in their use of negative and positive ads over the years, an analysis of the seven election cycles studied found them to be similar over time. For example, 59 percent of the female candidates' ads were coded as candidate-positive, compared to 62 percent of the male candidates' ads. Conversely, 32 percent of the female ads and 30 percent of the male ads were coded as opponent-negative. The remaining 9 percent of the female ads and 8 percent of the male ads were coded as comparative.

In addition to overall focus, we coded for the presence or absence of an attack. Although female candidates' ads were more likely to contain an attack (48 percent) compared to male candidates' ads (42 percent), the differences were not significant over time. These findings are particularly interesting when compared to Bystrom and Kaid's (2002) study of female and male candidates' ads from mixed-gender U.S. Senate campaigns in the 1990s. That study found women significantly more likely (49 percent) than men (38 percent) to include an attack in their television ads.

When we examined the purpose and dominant strategies used in the attack ads of female and male candidates from 1990 through 2002, some significant differences emerged (see Table 3.2). Although the negative ads

TABLE 3.2 Significant Differences in Advertising Content by Gender

	Female Ads	Male Ads
Verbal Content		
Purpose of Attack [a]	($n = 320$)	($n = 293$)*
Personal character	22%	13%
Issue stands	41%	45%
Group affiliation	3%	12%
Opponent's background	5%	3%
Opponent's performance	28%	27%
Dominant Strategy [b]	($n = 319$)	($n = 292$)*
Humor/ridicule	8%	6%
Negative association	72%	80%
Name-calling	17%	8%
Guilt by association	3%	7%
Issues	($n = 686$)	($n = 703$)
Economy in general	15%	9%*
Education/schools	31%	22%*
Crime/prisons	10%	14%*
Health care	20%	13%*
Senior citizens' issues	18%	13%*
Welfare	1%	5%*
Women's issues	9%	4%*
	($n = 470$)	($n = 411$)
Youth violence	4%	1%*
Appeal Strategies	($n = 686$)	($n = 703$)
Incumbency stands for legitimacy	6%	11%*
Use of statistics	17%	22%*
Own accomplishments	31%	37%*
Taking the offensive position	24%	18%*
Attack opponent's record	40%	32%*
	($n = 470$)	($n = 411$)
Make gender an issue	7%	2%*
Character Traits	($n = 686$)	($n = 703$)
Toughness/strength	36%	30%*
Experience in politics	21%	29%*
Sensitivity/understanding	16%	20%*
Nonverbal Content		
Demographics Pictured	($n = 621$)	($n = 616$)
Family of candidate	9%	20%*
Children (not candidate's)	33%	26%*
Sex of Dominant Speaker	($n = 554$)	($n = 603$)*
Male	60%	75%
Female	36%	21%
Cannot determine	5%	4%

TABLE 3.2 (continued) Significant Differences in Advertising Content by Gender

	Female Ads	Male Ads
Candidate as Speaker	(n = 554)	(n = 603)*
Yes	29%	24%
No	71%	77%
Facial Expression[c]	(n = 457)	(n = 485)*
Smiling	47%	31%
Attentive/serious	53%	69%
Dominant Dress[a]	(n = 439)	(n = 468)*
Formal	80%	52%
Casual	21%	48%

Note: "Not applicable" not included in all analyses in table.
[a] "Cannot determine" not included in analysis.
[b] "Other" not included in analysis.
[c] "Frowning/glaring" and "other" not included in analysis.
* Significant at $p \leq .05$.

of both women (41 percent) and men (45 percent) were most likely to attack the issue positions of their opponents, the negative ads of female candidates (22 percent) were more likely to attack their opponent's personal characteristics than the negative ads of male candidates (13 percent) were. The negative ads of male candidates were more likely to attack their opponent's group affiliations (12 percent compared to 3 percent).

The negative ads of female and male candidates also showed significant differences in the dominant strategy used (see Table 3.2). The dominant strategy used in the negative ads of both female and male candidates was negative association, although men used this in 80 percent of their negative ads compared to 72 percent of the female ads. The negative ads of female candidates were more likely to use name-calling (17 percent compared to 8 percent).

Type and Structure of Appeal. The type of the appeal (logical, emotional, or ethical) as well as the structure of the reasoning used (inductive or deductive) also measures the verbal content of political candidate Video-Style. Logical appeals are in favor of some position (either to support the candidate or attack an opponent). Emotional appeals are designed to invoke particular feelings or emotions in viewers, such as happiness, goodwill, pride, patriotism, or anger. Ethical appeals focus on the qualifications of the candidate or attack the qualifications of the candidate's opponent by telling what the candidate has done or is capable of doing, or how reliable the candidate is.

In terms of types of appeals, there were no significant differences in male and female candidates in the seven election cycles studied. Both female and male candidates were most likely to use logical appeals (45 percent,

44 percent), followed by ethical appeals (33 percent, 31 percent) and emotional appeals (22 percent, 25 percent).

Furthermore, there was no difference in the structure of reasoning—inductive versus deductive—used by male and female candidates. Interestingly, the ads of both female (64 percent) and male (63 percent) candidates relied predominantly on the feminine style of inductive reasoning, which is characterized by proceeding from a series of examples or specifics to draw a general conclusion. Deductive reasoning, of course, is the opposite (proceeding from the general to the specific) and is considered more typical of masculine reasoning. In the years studied, deductive reasoning was used in 27 percent of the ads of female candidates and 30 percent of the ads of male candidates.

Appeal Strategies. We also looked at appeal strategies used, including feminine and masculine style strategies as outlined by Campbell (1989) and other researchers (Curtis, Shuler, and Grieve 1994; Dow and Tonn 1993), and incumbent and challenger strategies, as noted by Trent and Friedenberg (2000). Few significant differences were found in the appeal strategies of female and male candidates (see Table 3.2).

In terms of feminine versus masculine appeal strategies, the ads of male candidates were significantly more likely to use the "masculine" strategy of statistical evidence (22 percent) as compared to female candidates' spots (17 percent). Otherwise, their ads made similar use of the feminine style strategies of personal tone (female 32 percent, male 29 percent), addressing viewers as peers (female 30 percent, male 29 percent), relying on personal experiences (female 21 percent, male 21 percent), identifying with the experiences of others (female 12 percent, male 12 percent), and inviting participation and action (female 10 percent, male 8 percent); they were also similar in use of the masculine strategy of employing expert authorities (female 20 percent, male 19 percent).

In terms of incumbent and challenger appeal strategies, the ads of male candidates were significantly more likely to include the incumbent strategies of emphasizing one's own accomplishments (37 percent compared to 31 percent of female ads) and "incumbency stands for legitimacy" (11 percent compared to 6 percent of the female ads). The ads of female candidates were significantly more likely to include the challenger strategies of attacking the opponent's record (40 percent compared to 32 percent of the male ads) and taking the offensive position (24 percent compared to 18 percent).

However, the ads of female candidates and male candidates were similar in the use of such incumbent strategies as taking an "above-the-trenches" approach (13 percent, 14 percent) and using endorsements (7 percent, 7 percent) as well as the challenger strategies of calling for changes (31 percent, 27 percent), acting as a voice for the state (22 percent, 23 percent), emphasizing optimism and hope for the future (19 percent, 19 percent), yearning for traditional values (11 percent, 9 percent), and identifying with the philosophical center of the party (5 percent, 4 percent).

In some of the years analyzed, we also coded for the use of gender as an issue (see Table 3.2). Although female and male candidates rarely used this strategy, women were significantly more likely to make gender an issue in their ads (7 percent) than male candidates (2 percent).

Issue Emphasis. When we examined the overall content of the ads, we found that 62 percent of the ads of women candidates and 64 percent of the ads of men candidates focused on campaign issues rather than candidate images. Of the 21 issues studied, female and male candidates showed significant differences in their emphasis of eight issues (see Table 3.2). The ads of female candidates were significantly more likely than the ads of male candidates to discuss the economy, a masculine issue (15 percent to 9 percent), as well as the feminine issues of education (31 percent to 22 percent), health care (20 percent to 13 percent), senior citizens' issues (18 percent to 13 percent), women's issues (9 percent to 4 percent), and youth violence (4 percent to 1 percent). The ads of male candidates were significantly more likely to discuss crime and prisons (14 percent to 10 percent) and welfare (5 percent to 1 percent). Crime is usually considered a masculine issue, and although welfare is generally considered a feminine issue, some of the male candidates discussing this issue talked about efforts to limit the numbers of families receiving welfare benefits.

Also of note, female and male candidates did not differ significantly in their discussion of taxes (29 percent, 28 percent), unemployment and jobs (18 percent, 20 percent), dissatisfaction with government (10 percent, 10 percent), the federal budget (8 percent, 9 percent), the environment and pollution (7 percent, 7 percent), cost of living and inflation (4 percent, 3 percent), ethics and moral decline (4 percent, 3 percent), defense (4 percent, 3 percent), drugs and drug abuse (2 percent, 3 percent), international issues (2 percent, 3 percent), recession and depression (2 percent, 1 percent), immigration (2 percent, 1 percent), and poverty (1 percent, 1 percent).

Image Emphasis. Overall, 38 percent of the ads of female candidates and 36 percent of the ads of male candidates focused on candidate images rather than campaign issues. Few differences were found in the particular images emphasized in the ads of female candidates versus male candidates running in mixed-gender campaigns for U.S. Senate and governor (see Table 3.2). Of the fourteen traits studied, female and male candidates' ads showed significant differences on only three—toughness and strength, experience in politics, and sensitivity and understanding. Interestingly, female candidates were significantly more likely to emphasize the masculine trait of toughness and strength (in 36 percent of their ads compared to 30 percent of male candidates' ads), and male candidates were significantly more likely to discuss the feminine trait of sensitivity and understanding (in 20 percent of their ads compared to 16 percent of female candidates' ads). Male candidates also were significantly more likely to discuss their experience in politics—a masculine trait—more often than female candidates (29 percent compared to 21 percent).

Of note, there were no significant differences found between female and male candidates in their emphasis on the feminine traits of honesty and integrity (30 percent, 28 percent), trustworthiness (21 percent, 22 percent), cooperation (12 percent, 13 percent), or Washington outsider status (7 percent, 8 percent), nor on the masculine traits of past performance (35 percent, 39 percent), aggressiveness and being a fighter (37 percent, 33 percent), qualifications (25 percent, 22 percent), being action-oriented (33 percent, 32 percent), leadership (32 percent, 37 percent), competency (19 percent, 20 percent), or knowledge and intelligence (14 percent, 13 percent).

Nonverbal Content of Candidate VideoStyle

The second aspect of VideoStyle involves the nonverbal components of a candidate's self-presentation. Significant differences were found in the people pictured in candidates' ads, speakers used, and candidate facial expression and dress (see Table 3.2).

Interestingly, the ads of male candidates were significantly more likely to feature their families (20 percent compared to 9 percent of female ads), whereas the ads of female candidates were significantly more likely to include children who were not the candidate's (33 percent compared to 26 percent of the male ads).

The ads of both women (60 percent) and men (75 percent) candidates were most likely to feature a male dominant speaker. However, the fact that male candidates used a male dominant speaker more frequently than female candidates, as well as the fact that female candidates were more likely than male candidates (36 percent compared to 21 percent) to use a female dominant speaker, accounted for a significant difference in this measure of nonverbal content (see Table 3.2). Female candidates also were significantly more likely (29 percent) than male candidates (24 percent) to speak themselves in their ads.

Women candidates exhibited several forms of nonverbal behaviors in their political ads—normative clothing and smiling facial expressions—that are associated with women in their everyday life as a means to win approval (Pearson, Turner, and Todd-Mancillas 1991). For example, although formal attire (business or professional dresses, men's suits and women's pantsuits) was preferred by both female (80 percent) and male (52 percent) candidates over casual dress (sweaters or casual shirts, slacks or jeans, and athletic wear), the difference in this preference was statistically significant.

Women also were more likely to exhibit another stereotypically feminine nonverbal behavior in their ads—they smiled more often than men (in 47 percent of their ads compared to 31 percent of male candidates' ads). Male candidates (69 percent) were more likely to have an attentive or serious expression in their ads compared to female candidates (53 percent).

Except for these differences, female and male candidates were similar in the nonverbal content of their televised political ads. For example, the ads of both female (40 percent) and male (37 percent) candidates were most likely to use an inside setting in their ads (22 percent female, 27 percent male), no setting (26 percent female, 26 percent male), or combination/other (female 12 percent, male 10 percent) instead of an outside setting. The ads of both women (58 percent) and men (55 percent) were most likely to picture the candidates and other people in their ads, followed by candidate and opponent (female 12 percent, male 15 percent), candidate only (female 12 percent, male 11 percent), people other than candidate (female 8 percent, male 9 percent), candidate's opponent (female 7 percent, male 6 percent), and no one (female 3 percent, male 4 percent).

Female and male candidates were also similarly likely to picture senior citizens (female 33 percent, male 28 percent) and ethnic and racial minorities (female 31 percent, male 33 percent) in their ads. And they exhibited about the same amount of eye contact, a feminine trait: always (female 5 percent, male 9 percent), almost always (female 10 percent, male 7 percent), sometimes (female 29 percent, male 27 percent), and never (female 56 percent, male 57 percent).

Production Content of Candidate VideoStyle

The final element of VideoStyle relates to the production content of spots. Production techniques are an important element of candidate VideoStyle, as they can help determine the impression an audience gets. For example, a close-up camera angle is more intimate and makes a candidate seem warmer and friendlier. Fast motion and quick editing styles can make a candidate seem more dynamic and active.

In terms of production content, there were no significant differences between female and male candidates in the 1,389 ads included in this analysis. Both female and male candidates preferred twenty- to thirty-second spots (93 percent, 92 percent); ads sponsored by the committee for election or reelection of the candidate (95 percent, 90 percent), with men having more national political party and issue-based group sponsors than women; and an opposition-focused format (30 percent, 30 percent) followed by testimonials (female 16 percent, male 22 percent), documentaries (female 15 percent, 14 percent male), introspection (female 13 percent, male 12 percent), issue dramatization (female 10 percent, male 9 percent), issue statement (female 10 percent, male 9 percent), and bandwagon excitement (female 3 percent, male 4 percent).

We also coded for camera angles and dominant shot and again found no significant differences between the ads of female and male candidates.

The ads of both female (90 percent) and male (88 percent) candidates were most likely to feature straight-on dominant camera angles and medium (female 51 percent, male 50 percent) or tight (female 35 percent, male 35 percent) shots.

Conclusion

This analysis of some 1,400 ads from female and male candidates running against each other in U.S. Senate and gubernatorial races from 1990 through 2002 showed many similarities in their VideoStyles. However, significant differences also emerged.

For example, contrary to the findings of Bystrom and Kaid's 2002 study of female and male VideoStyles in mixed-gender U.S. Senate races in the 1990s, this analysis found no significant differences between women and men in their use of negative advertising. Women candidates did use negative attacks more often than men candidates and ran more opponent-negative focused ads during the seven election cycles studied, but the differences were small and not statistically significant. The fact that the difference in the use of negative advertising between female and male candidates was significant in Bystrom and Kaid's 2002 study and not in this analysis may be explained by several factors.

First, the Bystrom and Kaid study looked only at mixed-gender U.S. Senate races; perhaps the inclusion of mixed-gender gubernatorial races in this analysis narrowed the gap between female and male candidates in their use of negative ads. That is, perhaps female gubernatorial candidates are less negative then female U.S. Senate candidates. When we analyzed our data set by level of race, that is indeed what emerged. For example, in the 1996 campaign—the year that Bystrom and Kaid found women significantly more negative than men—there was a sharp contrast in the number of attacks issued by female gubernatorial candidates (in 22 percent of their ads) and U.S. Senate candidates (in 64 percent of their ads). Also, when we isolated the U.S. Senate races in 1994 and 1996 within our data set, we found that women candidates ran significantly more negative-slanted ads, compared to positive-slanted ads, than men candidates. In 1994 mixed-gender U.S. Senate races, 39 percent of female ads and 26 percent of male ads were negative. In 1996, 62 percent of female ads were negative and 29 percent of male ads were negative in such races.

We also considered that the difference in findings between Bystrom and Kaid's 2002 study and this analysis may be the inclusion of the 2000 and 2002 campaigns; perhaps they were less negative than campaigns in the 1990s. We did find that female U.S. Senate candidates were much less negative in 2002; only 28 percent of their ads that year issued an attack. However, in 2000, 58 percent of the ads of female U.S. Senate candidates included an attack. Of interest, female gubernatorial candidates were comparatively more negative than female U.S. Senate candidates in those years, with 62 percent of their ads issuing a negative attack in 2002 and 65 percent of their ads attacking their opponent in 2000.

In any case, the use of negative attacks by women—and in slightly greater percentages than their male opponents—defies conventional wisdom, which holds that women should not use such aggressive, unfeminine strategies and would, in fact, raise the level of civil discourse. Their use of negative attacks could be related to their status as challengers (41 percent of the 686 female ads in this analysis were by challengers, compared to 16 percent of the 703 male ads) or perhaps to the obstacles they face as women candidates, including stereotyping by the media and voters that not only limits the expectations of their appropriate role in society but also questions their viability as candidates. Women candidates may be willing to use more negative ads to show they are tough enough for politics and as a way to defy stereotypical norms. The interaction of candidate status—as incumbents, challengers, and open-race contenders—and VideoStyle is explored in chapter 4; chapter 10 looks at stereotypes in their media coverage.

Although female and male candidates were similar in their use of negative attacks, they differed in the purpose of the attacks and strategies used. Though attacking one's opponent on the issues was the preferred attack purpose in the ads of both women and men, the spots of women candidates were significantly more likely to criticize their opponent's personal character. And although negative association was the preferred attack strategy in the ads of both women and men, the spots of women were significantly more likely to use name-calling in their negative attacks.

Attacking the opponent's character, rather than his or her stance on the issues, and name-calling are seen as much more personal. Here, female candidates may be taking advantage of voter stereotypes, which find women to be more caring and compassionate. That is, women candidates may be given more latitude than men candidates to make personal attacks, as they enter the race with the stereotypical advantage of being considered kinder. Of course, defying stereotypical norms also may backfire for women candidates. Male candidates, on the other hand, may feel more constrained by stereotypical norms when it comes to attacking the personal characteristics of their female opponents. So they lash out significantly more often at their opponents' group affiliations, which is another way to question their character. The fact that male candidates were significantly more likely than female candidates to use "guilt by association" in their negative ads underscores this strategy. Voter reactions to candidate VideoStyles are explored further in chapter 6.

Confirming Bystrom and Kaid's 2002 study, female and male candidates are increasingly similar in the issues they discuss in their ads and especially in the image traits they emphasize and appeal strategies they use. The similarities and differences that did emerge are interesting from a gendered perspective.

For example, the top issue in the ads by female candidates—and one that was discussed significantly more often than in the ads for male candidates—was the stereotypically feminine concern of education and schools, followed by taxes, health care, unemployment and jobs, and senior citizens. The ads of female candidates in this analysis also discussed the feminine issues of health care, senior citizens' issues, and women's issues significantly more often than the ads of their male opponents. Here, women candidates may be conforming to stereotypical expectations that consider them to be experts on such concerns.

The top issue in ads for male candidates, on the other hand, was taxes, followed by education and schools, unemployment and jobs, health care, and senior citizens' issues. The only issues discussed significantly more often in the ads of male candidates, compared to female candidates, were crime and prisons, a masculine issue, and welfare, a feminine issue. However, these findings are further illuminated by the results of recent surveys (see, for example, League of Women Voters/*Ladies Home Journal* 1996) that show that male and female issue preferences are more complicated.

For example, most public opinion surveys taken in recent election years have found that female and male respondents are most concerned about the economy. But when you ask what concerns them most about the economy, male respondents said taxes were too high, whereas female respondents were concerned about "increasing jobs, wages and benefits" (League of Women Voters/*Ladies Home Journal* 1996). The fact that male candidates discussed taxes most often whereas female candidates were significantly more likely to discuss the economy in general underscores the gendered differences found among voters in their issue concerns.

The fact that male candidates talked significantly more about crime and prisons whereas female candidates discussed youth violence significantly more also plays to these gendered preferences among voters. For example, a League of Women Voters/*Ladies Home Journal* poll (1996) found that both male and female respondents were concerned about crime in about equal proportions. However, when they were asked what concerned them about crime, male respondents were more likely to talk about the need to "arrest and put away criminals," whereas female respondents were concerned with "the underlying social problems, such as jobs and schools, that are associated with crime."

As we approach the 2004 elections in the midst of international conflicts, threats of terrorism, and homeland security concerns, two issues stand out for their lack of discussion. International issues were discussed in only 4 percent of male candidates' ads and 3 percent of female candidates' ads. Defense was discussed in only 3 percent of male candidates' ads and 4 percent of female candidates' ads. Whereas recent public opinion polls show that citizens are worried about such international issues, they are more concerned about the economy and jobs and almost equally concerned with health care in 2004. For example, a survey conducted on January 12 through 15, 2004, showed that voters were most interested in hearing from the presidential candidates on the economy and jobs (26 percent of those surveyed), almost twice as many as those wanting to hear from them about the war in Iraq and foreign policy (14 percent). And 11 percent of those surveyed said they were most interested in hearing from the candidates about health care and Medicare (CBS News 2004). There were fewer differences between female and male candidates in the images they emphasized and appeal strategies they used. However, the traits they chose to emphasize both defied and underscored stereotypical expectations about the roles and behaviors of women and men in today's society. The top traits emphasized in the ads by women candidates were aggressiveness and being a fighter, toughness and strength, past performance, leadership, and being action-oriented—masculine attributes—and honesty and integrity, a feminine quality. The top traits emphasized in the ads by men candidates were past performance, leadership, aggressiveness and being a fighter, being action-oriented, toughness and strength, and experience in politics—all masculine attributes. Of these traits, women candidates were significantly more likely to emphasize toughness and strength than men candidates, and men candidates were significantly more likely to discuss their experience in politics than women.

The differences in the image attributes emphasized by men and women candidates may be related to their background, political experience, status, and gender-related traits. Men's ads were more likely to boast about their performance, leadership, and especially their experience in politics—perhaps because 44 percent of the 703 male ads in this analysis were by incumbents. The fact that women candidates countered by portraying themselves as aggressive and tough may underscore their status as challengers fighting gender stereotypes. Perhaps more interesting than women's use of masculine images to portray themselves is men's increasing use of feminine attributes. Although the top traits they discussed were all stereotypically masculine, male candidates did emphasize the stereotypically feminine quality of sensitivity and understanding significantly more often than female candidates and discussed the feminine traits of honesty and integrity, trustworthiness, and cooperation in almost equal proportions as female candidates. As Bystrom and Kaid (2002) have noted, the inclusion of women in these races may have prompted the men to reveal their feminine as well as masculine sides in seeking votes.

The appeal strategies used in female and male candidates' ads were closely related to the traits they emphasized and thus also are interesting from a gendered perspective. Both female and male candidates were equally as likely to use all of the elements of Campbell's (1989) construct of feminine style—inductive structure, personal tone, addressing the audience as peers, relying on personal experiences, identifying with the experiences of others, and inviting audience participation. Male candidates did rely on statistics (a masculine strategy) significantly more often than female candidates, and female candidates were significantly more likely to make gender an issue in their ads—an indication that at least some women are campaigning as women candidates and not as political candidates who happen to be women. The fact that both women and men candidates used elements of feminine style in similar proportions may suggest, as other researchers (Bystrom and Kaid 2002) have observed, that this style works best for thirty-second spots in the more intimate medium of television.

Perhaps again related to men's predominant status as incumbents and women's predominant status as challengers in this sample of ads, male candidates were significantly more likely to use the incumbent strategies of "incumbency stands for legitimacy" and emphasizing one's accomplishments, whereas female candidates were significantly more likely to use the challenger strategies of taking the offensive position and attacking the opponent's record. Otherwise, the ads of female and male candidates were similar in their use of both incumbent and challenger strategies. Further analysis of the interaction of candidate status on their advertising VideoStyle is provided in chapter 4.

In the nonverbal content of their appeals, it is interesting to note that women have continued to dress significantly more formally than men do in their television commercials as well as to smile significantly more often than men do. Both of these nonverbal characteristics reflect gender-based norms and stereotypical expectations. For example, the choice of attire reflects the gender-based norms that society imposes on women as they face the challenge of portraying themselves as serious and legitimate candidates. And smiling is regarded as a nonverbal strategy that women use to gain acceptance in everyday life. Perhaps women candidates are more likely than men candidates to smile in their ads for the same reasons—to gain acceptance from viewers in the traditionally male political environment.

Because societal gender stereotypes more often associate women with families and children, it is interesting to note who is pictured in female and male candidates' ads. Whereas women candidates may be distancing themselves from their roles as wives and/or mothers by picturing their families in only 9 percent of their ads, men candidates showed their families in 20 percent of their ads over the twelve years studied. At the beginning of the decade, men pictured themselves with their families in 12 percent of their ads, whereas women were pictured with their families in 9 percent of their ads (Bystrom and Kaid 2002). In 2002, men were pictured with their families in 19 percent of their ads, whereas women were shown with their families in 11 percent of their spots. In picturing their families or not, both male and female candidates are confronting societal stereotypes. Women candidates may want to show voters that they are more than wives and mothers and to dismiss any concerns voters may have over their abilities to serve in political office due to family obligations. Men candidates, on the other hand, may want to round out their images beyond business and politics with voters by portraying themselves as loving husbands and fathers.

Interestingly, the ads of female candidates were significantly more likely than the ads of male candidates to picture other people's children—not their own—in their ads. Perhaps this is the way that female candidates show their concern for family issues without picturing their own families.

Confirming earlier VideoStyle research (Bystrom 1995) female candidates were significantly more likely than male candidates to speak for themselves in their ads and, thus not surprisingly, significantly more likely than male candidates to use a woman as the dominant speaker in their ads. This finding also may be related to the production content of the ads analyzed, with male candidates more likely to use a testimonial format—featuring the endorsements of others—than female candidates.

The fact that no significant differences emerged in the production content of female and male political ads most likely indicates a standardization in the business of producing television commercials and even, perhaps, a leveling of the field in the quality of the political consultants and production companies that women and men can afford to hire to run their campaigns.

Female and Male VideoStyle

Does recent research show distinct female and male VideoStyles? Our research analyzing the content of female and male candidate television commercials in mixed-gender races for the U.S. Senate and governor over twelve years leads us to conclude with a (qualified) yes.

In her 1995 study analyzing ads in mixed-gender U.S. Senate campaigns in 1990, 1992, and 1993, Bystrom proposed distinct female and male VideoStyles. From her findings, she concluded that women candidates generally used verbal strategies identifying with their states, invoking change, inviting action, and attacking their opponents on their records; pictured themselves with their opponents; used more intensifiers in their language; made more eye contact; smiled more; dressed formally more; spoke more often for themselves in their ads; used live audio from the candidate; and used more slides with print and superimpositions. Men candidates generally emphasized their trustworthiness; pictured themselves and others; looked more serious and attentive; dressed casually more; used someone else head-on; used other-person live sound; used more testimonials; and used a variety of spot lengths.

Seven years and three campaign cycles later, Bystrom and Kaid (2002) found that most of these distinctions had disappeared when looking at female and male VideoStyle over the course of one decade through the ads of female and male candidates in mixed-gender U.S. Senate campaigns. Still, throughout the 1990s, women U.S. Senate candidates were more likely to use negative attacks, dress formally, and smile more often in their ads, and men candidates used fewer negative attacks and dressed casually more often.

This analysis adds two more election cycles—2000 and 2002—as well as the ads of female and male candidates in mixed-gender gubernatorial races from 1990 to 2002 to the mix. Based on our analysis of male and female candidates' ads in mixed-gender U.S. Senate and gubernatorial races from 1990 through 2002, we propose that female VideoStyle is characterized by an attention to feminine issues, balance of masculine and feminine image traits, blend of feminine style and challenger appeals, a smiling facial expression, and formal dress. Male VideoStyle is characterized by a balance of masculine and feminine issues and images, blend of feminine style and incumbent appeals, inclusion of family, serious facial expression, and casual dress.

This analysis further concludes that the presence of female and male candidates in a statewide, mixed-gender race impacts the discourse of the campaign. That is, both female and male candidates are likely to blend a mix of feminine and masculine issues, images, and appeals when running against each other for political office.

4
The Interaction of Electoral Status, Political Party, and VideoStyle

As illustrated in chapter 3, certain differences—and similarities—do exist in female and male candidate VideoStyles. However, due to the number of women running for the statewide offices (U.S. Senate and gubernatorial) typically examined in such studies, researchers (e.g., Banwart 2002; Bystrom 1995; Bystrom and Kaid 2002; Robertson 2000) have not examined the VideoStyles of female and male candidates by status (incumbent, challenger, open race), political party, and outcome of their race. Therefore, using the same data set described in chapter 3 from mixed-gender U.S. Senate and gubernatorial races waged between 1990 and 2002, this chapter responds to the question of whether female and male VideoStyles differ by these variables.

Incumbent, Challenger, and Open Race VideoStyles

Differences in how candidates campaign based on whether they are incumbents at the time of the election, challenging the incumbent, or running in an open race (in which neither candidate is an incumbent) has been well outlined by Trent and Friedenberg (2000). Incumbent strategies include creation of pseudoevents, making appointments to jobs and/or positions in the party, creation of task forces to look into issues of public concern, appropriation of funds and/or grants, consultation with international leaders, manipulation of economic or domestic issues, receipt of party and political leader endorsements, focus on accomplishments, use of an "above-the-trenches" posture, use of campaign surrogates, and using a foreign-policy issue to create a crisis, but these also have been successfully co-opted by nonincumbent candidates. Similarly, challenger strategies can be used by incumbents and include the following: attacking the opponent's record, using an offensive stance in issue discussion, calling for change, being optimistic about the future, emphasizing traditional values, representing the party's centrist approach, and having surrogates deliver the attacks.

In their initial study of candidate VideoStyle (which focused on male versus male candidates running for the U.S. Senate), Kaid and Davidson (1986) determined that incumbent candidates did, in fact, use more testimonials, run more ads with a positive focus, dress more formally, use announcers or voices other than their own in their ads, and stress their competence more than challenger candidates. Challenger candidates were more likely to use ads with a negative focus, incorporate tight head-on shots, have more eye contact with the viewer, dress more casually, and speak for themselves in their ads.

Based on their extensive research of presidential advertising, Kaid and Johnston found that differences emerged in the VideoStyles of incumbent and challenger candidates running for president from 1952 to 1996. For example, incumbents were more likely to emphasize their character traits and concerns of the group; use ethical or source credibility appeals; use anonymous announcers, music, testimonial and documentary formats, and cinema verité; and emphasize their accomplishments and the trappings of being the incumbent. Challenger candidates were more likely to emphasize economic concerns and aggressiveness, speak for themselves, feature themselves head-on and with tight camera shots, use question-and-answer formats and special effects, attack the record of the opponent, and take an offensive stance on the issues (Kaid and Johnston 2001: 94).

Our examination of the VideoStyles of female and male candidates running in mixed-gender races from 1990 to 2002 indicates that differences do exist based on the status of the candidate (see Table 4.1). Further, most of the differences exist between female and male incumbents and female and male challengers, suggesting that fewer differences emerge between candidates running in open races, that is, races in which their status is equal.

Incumbents

Verbal Content: Focus, Attacks, and Message Design. Although there were no significant differences in the focus (candidate positive, opponent negative, or comparative) of the ads run by incumbent candidates (see Table 4.1), differences did emerge in the presence of an attack in the ad. Even when female and male candidates both possessed incumbent status in their races, female incumbents were still more likely to issue attacks in their ads (44 percent) as compared to male incumbents (30 percent) and more likely to attack their opponent's background (33 percent) than male incumbents (1 percent). Granted, both female (40 percent) and male (46 percent) incumbents were most likely to attack their opponent's issue

TABLE 4.1 Significant Differences in Female and Male VideoStyle by Candidate Status

	Incumbent		Challenger		Open Race	
	Female	Male	Female	Male	Female	Male
			Verbal Content			
Focus	(n = 97)	(n = 309)	(n = 281)	(n = 112)	(n = 308)	(n = 282)
Candidate-positive	—	—	58%	38%*	—	—
Opponent-negative	—	—	31%	38%	—	—
Comparative/ cannot determine	—	—	11%	24%		
Negative Attack Present	44%	30%*	45%	67%*	—	—
Purpose of Attack	(n = 40)	(n = 92)			(n = 154)	(n = 126)
Personal characteristics	18%	11%*	—	—	21%	14%*
Issue stands	40%	46%	—	—	46%	50%
Group affiliation	0%	11%	—	—	3%	8%
Opponent's background	33%	1%	—	—	1%	6%
Opponent's performance	10%	32%	—	—	29%	23%
*Dominant Content**			(n = 274)	(n = 110)		
Logical appeals	—	—	45%	28%	—	—
Emotional appeals	—	—	23%	37%	—	—
Ethical appeals	—	—	32%	35%	—	—
	(n = 97)	(n = 295)	(n = 279)	(n = 112)	(n = 245)	(n = 209)
*Fear Appeals Present**	17%	7%	6%	15%	19%	12%
*Structure**	(n = 97)	(n = 309)				
Inductive	54%	61%	—	—	—	—
Deductive	34%	36%	—	—	—	—
Cannot determine	12%	3%	—	—	—	—
*Emphasis**	(n = 97)	(n = 309)	(n = 281)	(n = 112)		
Campaign issues	54%	71%	60%	45%	—	—
Candidate image	46%	29%	40%	55%	—	—
Issues	(n = 97)	(n = 309)	(n = 281)	(n = 112)	(n = 308)	(n = 282)
Unemployment/ jobs	6%	22%	17%	6%	—	—
Cost of living/ inflation	—	—	—	—	6%	3%
Economy in general	—	—	17%	3%	—	—
Education/schools	31%	17%	31%	20%	—	—
Crime/prisons	19%	11%	6%	14%	11%	18%
Health care	—	—	21%	7%	21%	9%

50 • Gender and Candidate Communication

TABLE 4.1 (continued) Significant Differences in Female and Male VideoStyle by Candidate Status

	Incumbent		Challenger		Open Race	
	Female	Male	Female	Male	Female	Male
Senior citizens' issues	—	—	19%	7%	—	—
Environment	0%	10%	7%	2%	9%	5%
Dissatisfaction with the government	—	—	11%	21%	—	—
Women's issues	13%	3%	—	—	10%	4%
					(n = 245)	(n = 209)
Recession/depression	—	—	—	—	4%	1%
Strategic Appeals	(n = 97)	(n = 309)	(n = 281)	(n = 112)	(n = 308)	(n = 282)
Personal tone	—	—	—	—	32%	25%
Call for change	—	—	—	—	26%	36%
Traditional values/yearn for the past	—	—	11%	20%	—	—
Use of endorsements	10%	4%	3%	9%	—	—
Use of statistics	—	—	14%	25%	—	—
Use of expert authorities	—	—	23%	13%	—	—
Attack record of opponent	37%	24%	—	—	—	—
	(n = 97)	(n = 295)			(n = 245)	(n = 209)
Above the trenches	25%	16%	—	—	8%	14%
			(n = 174)	(n = 112)		
Make gender an issue	—	—	10%	1%	—	—
Character Traits	(n = 97)	(n = 309)	(n = 281)	(n = 112)	(n = 308)	(n = 282)
Honesty/integrity	37%	26%	27%	42%	—	—
Toughness/strength	—	—	—	—	39%	21%
Past performance	—	—	27%	16%	—	—
Aggressive/fighter	—	—	36%	23%	37%	29%
Leadership	—	—	30%	20%	—	—
Experience in politics	18%	41%	17%	6%	—	—
Action oriented	25%	36%	29%	17%	—	—

Nonverbal Content/Production Content

Setting	(n = 90)	(n = 299)				
No setting	18%	22%*	—	—	—	—
Inside	37%	32%	—	—	—	—
Outside	26%	40%	—	—	—	—
Combination/other	20%	7%	—	—	—	—

The Interaction of Electoral Status, Political Party, and VideoStyle • 51

TABLE 4.1 (continued) Significant Differences in Female and Male VideoStyle by Candidate Status

	Incumbent		Challenger		Open Race	
	Female	Male	Female	Male	Female	Male
Who Is Pictured	(n = 97)	(n = 309)				
No one	2%	2%*	—	—	—	—
Candidate only	7%	11%	—	—	—	—
Opponent	12%	5%	—	—	—	—
Candidate and opponent	2%	11%	—	—	—	—
Candidate and others	64%	64%	—	—	—	—
People other than candidate	12%	7%	—	—	—	—
Demographic Groups Represented	(n = 97)	(n = 295)	(n = 279)	(n = 112)	(n = 245)	(n = 209)
Men	—	—	62%	41%	—	—*
Women	—	—	58%	39%	—	—*
Candidate family	5%	13%*	11%	26%	8%	25%*
Children (not family)	—	—	35%	18%	—	—*
Ethnic/racial minorities	27%	39%*	—	—	—	—*
Dominant Speaker*			(n = 223)	(n = 96)		
Candidate	—	—	34%	34%	—	—
Government official/office holder	—	—	31%	4%	—	—
Anonymous announcer	—	—	29%	53%	—	—
Citizen/constituent	—	—	4%	1%	—	—
Combination	—	—	3%	6%	—	—
Sex of Dominant Speaker*	(n = 90)	(n = 297)	(n = 228)	(n-98)	(n = 236)	(n = 208)
Male	62%	75%	58%	76%	61%	76%
Female	34%	21%	37%	25%	35%	20%
Combination	3%	4%	5%	0%	5%	5%
Eye Contact *			(n = 173)	(n = 78)		
Never	—	—	49%	42%	—	—
Sometimes	—	—	35%	9%	—	—
Almost always	—	—	11%	14%	—	—
Always	—	—	6%	35%	—	—
Facial Expression*	(n = 65)	(n = 252)				
Smiling	48%	26%	—	—	—	—
Attentive/serious	52%	74%	—	—	—	—

TABLE 4.1 (continued) Significant Differences in Female and Male VideoStyle by Candidate Status

	Incumbent		Challenger		Open Race	
	Female	Male	Female	Male	Female	Male
Dress *	(n = 63)	(n = 241)	(n = 187)	(n = 74)	(n = 189)	(n = 154)
Formal	83%	54%	78%	49%	80%	52%
Casual	18%	47%	22%	51%	20%	48%

Note: Percentages indicate frequencies within gender.
* Significant at $p \leq .05$.

stands when they did attack. However, female incumbents were more likely to attack their opponent's performance (25 percent) and their personal characteristics (24 percent) than male incumbents (16 percent and 11 percent). Male incumbents were more likely to attack their opponent's group affiliation (17 percent) than female incumbents (4 percent).

Although the use of an inductive structure when presenting a message is considered an element of "feminine style" (Campbell 1989), the overall use of an inductive design was most common with incumbent candidates in mixed-gender races. Male incumbents were, however, more likely to structure their messages inductively (61 percent) than female incumbents (54 percent), and both female and male candidates used a deductive structure about equally. Based on the finding that 12 percent of female incumbents were likely to use a design that was not dominantly deductive or inductive, we propose that perhaps female incumbents have presented a more complex argument structure in their advertising. With regard to the type of arguments presented, female and male incumbents were just as likely to use logical, emotional, and ethical appeals, although female incumbents were more likely to include fear appeals in their ads (17 percent) than male incumbents (7 percent). Although this may, on the surface, appear to be a unique strategy employed by female incumbents as compared to male incumbents, further analysis indicates that the use of fear appeals is grounded in the type of race in which the candidates are running. When incumbent females and challenger males were compared, no significant differences arose between the candidates' use of fear appeals; likewise, when incumbent males and challenger females were compared, there were no significant differences.

Verbal Content: Issues Versus Image. When we examined whether the advertising of incumbents focused on campaign issues or candidate image, interesting results emerged. First, although both female and male incumbents were more likely to focus on campaign issues in their advertising, the differential between focusing on campaign issues and candidate image was far more distinct for male incumbents. Specifically, 71 percent of male incumbents' ads focused on issues, whereas 29 percent focused on image;

female incumbents were more likely to balance the issue/image differential, with 54 percent of their ads focusing on issues and 46 percent focusing on image.

One explanation for this apparent difference in focus could be related to gender; that is, female incumbents may focus more diligently on continuing to develop a viable image, even though they are seeking reelection to their office. However, we find a more grounded explanation when the challengers' focus on issues or image is examined (see Table 4.1). Notably, when the percentages were paired, 54 percent of female incumbents' ads and 45 percent of male challengers' ads focused on campaign issues, and 46 percent of female incumbents' ads and 55 percent of male challengers' ads focused on image, resulting in no significant differences. When the male incumbents' ads were paired with female challengers' ads, the emphasis on issues and image, which on the surface appears similar, instead resulted in significant differences. Thus, in races with a male incumbent and female challenger, 71 percent of the male incumbents' ads were focused on issues, as were 60 percent of the female challengers' ads; 29 percent of the male incumbents' ads were focused on image, as were 40 percent of the female challengers' ads. With these findings, it is important to revisit the potential for a gendered explanation.

Based on these findings, both male incumbents and female challengers are more likely to focus on issues rather than candidate images. Yet while the male incumbent can afford to be more focused on the issues than his female challenger, a traditional incumbent strategy (Trent and Friedenberg 2000), the female challenger perhaps needs to dedicate more time than her male incumbent opponent to introducing herself, establishing name identity, explaining her background, emphasizing the strengths that she brings to the office, and developing appeals that illustrate her viability and legitimacy to successfully hold office. The question that our explanation leaves unanswered is why the same pattern would not emerge when the female is an incumbent and the male a challenger if the difference is solely based on status. Clearly this must indicate some type of dynamic emerging between gender and status. With the prevalence of attacks in male challengers' ads (67 percent), their equal use of opponent-negative focused ads and candidate-positive ads (38 percent), and their frequent use of comparative ads (24 percent), one explanation suggests that the types of messages presented specifically by male challengers requires female incumbents to focus less on issues and more on image development, or perhaps even responses to negative advertising. On the other hand, as female challengers focus on advertising messages that present their stands on issues *and* establish their viability, male incumbents are able to run a more traditionally incumbent race wherein they focus on the issues, use endorsements, appear "above the trenches," and are more positive (Kaid and Davidson 1986; Kaid and Johnston 2001; Kahn 1993). It remains unanswered which strategy is in response to the other, but it is clear that female and male incumbents—as do female and male challengers—find differing dynamics at play based on their status and gender that require appropriately developed responses.

Verbal Content: Issue Discussion. When the issues incumbent candidates discussed in their advertising were analyzed, some differences did emerge. Of all the issues examined, female incumbents have addressed education and schools (31 percent; male incumbents, 17 percent) most frequently, followed by crime and prisons (19 percent; male incumbents, 11 percent) and taxes (18 percent). Female incumbents also have been significantly more likely to discuss women's issues (13 percent; male incumbents, 3 percent). Male incumbents have addressed unemployment and jobs most frequently (22 percent; female incumbents, 6 percent), followed by health care (19 percent) and taxes (18 percent). Male incumbents also have been significantly more likely to discuss environmental issues (10 percent; female incumbents, 0 percent).

Verbal Content: Emphasis on Appeals and Character Traits. The use of strategic appeals by female and male incumbents differed little across the variables analyzed. Although female incumbents used endorsements from important party leaders in only 10 percent of their ads, they were still significantly more likely to use them than male incumbents (4 percent), and female incumbents were more likely to attack the record of their opponent (37 percent; male incumbents, 24 percent) and use an "above-the-trenches" posture in their ads (37 percent; male incumbents, 37 percent), a traditional incumbent strategy (Trent and Friedenberg 2000). Since arguments for source credibility also can be presented by others, benefits may be derived from the endorsements of others whose power can reassure voters that the female candidate is competent and has the credentials be a public leader (Witt et al. 1995). Typically the endorsements that reinforce the female candidate's credentials, legitimacy, and character have been from men (Banwart 2002; Witt et al. 1995) or institutional sources. Until more women political leaders are viewed with the same credibility as men political leaders, this will no doubt continue to be the only option for female candidates seeking source credibility arguments from other political figures.

The emphasis on specific character traits also differed little between female and male incumbent candidates. When examining emphasis across all character traits, past performance was the trait most frequently emphasized by female (52 percent) and male (54 percent) incumbents. Female incumbents also frequently emphasized their toughness and strength (42 percent), followed by their leadership abilities (38 percent). Male incumbents frequently emphasized their leadership abilities (48 percent) and their experience in politics (41 percent). The fact that female incumbents frequently emphasized their toughness and strength is not surprising, as female candidates must counter what are perceived as weaknesses—such as a lack of toughness—in order to overcome stereotypes (Kahn 1993). Further, when candidates are perceived as possessing such masculine traits as toughness, they are viewed as more capable of handling issues rated of higher importance (Huddy and Terkildsen 1993). Female incumbents were more likely to emphasize their honesty and integrity (37 percent; male incumbents, 26 percent), whereas male incumbents were more likely to emphasize their experience in politics (41 percent; female incumbents, 18 percent) and being action-oriented (36 percent; female incumbents, 25 percent).

Nonverbal and Production Content. In an examination of the nonverbal and production content in the female and male incumbents' ads (see Table 4.1), male incumbents were more likely to use an outside setting in their advertisements (40 percent), whereas female incumbents were more likely to use an inside setting (37 percent). Both female and male incumbents were equally likely to picture the candidate and other people in their ads (64 percent), yet female incumbents were more likely to feature their opponent (12 percent) and people other than the candidate (12 percent), whereas male incumbents were more likely to feature the candidate *and* opponent in their ads (12 percent) and just the candidate (11 percent). Consistent with our findings of male VideoStyle overall, male incumbents were significantly more likely to feature their family in their advertisements (13 percent) than female incumbents (5 percent), but male incumbents also were more likely to feature racial and ethnic minorities in their advertising (39 percent).

Although male speakers tended to dominate the voices in political candidate advertising overall, female incumbents' ads were significantly less likely to feature a male voice in their ads (62 percent) as compared to male incumbents (75 percent) and more likely to feature a female voice (34 percent; male incumbents, 21 percent). Both female and male incumbents were most likely to be attentive and serious in their advertising. However, when candidates smiled, female incumbents were more likely to do so (48 percent) than male incumbents (26 percent). Similarly, both female and male incumbents were most likely to be formally attired in their advertising, although female incumbents were significantly more likely to wear formal attire (83 percent) than male incumbents (54 percent).

Challengers

Verbal Content: Focus, Attacks, and Message Design. We have already discussed the differences in the focus of female and male challengers' ads, use of attacks, and the emphasis of advertising. It is important to note that, as Table 4.1 indicates, female challengers did use logical appeals more frequently (45 percent) than male challengers (28 percent), and male challengers used emotional appeals more frequently (37 percent) than female challengers (23 percent). Both female and male challengers used ethical appeals in slightly more than one-third of their advertising.

Verbal Content: Issue Discussion. In their issue discussion (see Table 4.1), female challengers most frequently discussed education and school issues (31 percent), followed by taxes (28 percent) and health care (21 percent). Male challengers most frequently discussed taxes (34 percent), followed by dissatisfaction with the government (21 percent), and education and school issues (20 percent). There is some consistency in the most frequently discussed issues when the incumbent is paired with the challenger, in that female incumbents and male challengers both frequently discussed education and school issues (although female incumbents did so more frequently than male challengers) and taxes (although male challengers did so more frequently than female incumbents). Similarly, male incumbents and female challengers both frequently discussed health care and taxes; however, female challengers discussed both of these issues in a higher percentage of their advertising.

The differences that emerged between female challengers and male challengers in issue discussion primarily resulted from female challengers simply discussing the issues more frequently than male challengers. For instance, female challengers discussed education and schools, health care, senior citizens' issues, the economy, unemployment and jobs, and environmental issues more frequently. Male challengers did discuss crime and prison issues and dissatisfaction with the government more frequently. The relevance of the overall emphasis (dominantly positive or dominantly negative) of the advertising again should be included in this discussion, as 60 percent of female challengers' ads were predominantly focused on the issues compared to 45 percent of male challengers' ads. Therefore, as we concluded earlier, the gender-status dynamic does influence the content of the advertising in dominant emphasis, focus, attacks, and—logically—the frequency of issue discussion.

Verbal Content: Emphasis on Appeals and Character Traits. When examining appeal strategies, male challenger candidates have employed a mix of incumbent, challenger, and masculine strategies more frequently than female challengers (see Table 4.1). For instance, male challengers were more likely to use the incumbent strategy of incorporating endorsements from political leaders in their advertising (9 percent) than female challengers (3 percent), although not with much frequency. In 25 percent of their ads, they employed the masculine strategy of using statistics, and in 20 percent of their ads, they used the challenger strategy of emphasizing traditional values and yearning for the past; female challengers used these appeals less frequently. Female challengers used expert authorities to support their candidacy or positions more frequently (23 percent) than male challengers (13 percent), and female challengers made gender an issue in 10 percent of their advertising. Of these differences, we highlight two in particular—the use of endorsements and the use of expert authorities.

An interesting point is that while female incumbents used endorsements from political leaders at greater frequencies than male incumbents, and females and males in open races used endorsements at approximately the same frequency, male challengers used this strategy more frequently than female challengers. A closer examination indicates that female incumbents and male challengers included endorsements in approximately the same number of ads (10 percent and 9 percent, respectively), whereas male incumbents and female challengers also used endorsements at approximately the same frequency (4 percent and 3 percent, respectively). Therefore, we again argue that although it appears there is a gendered difference, the difference between female and male challengers stems more from the dynamics of their respective races. In the use of expert authorities, however, the issue of gender does perhaps play a greater role. Witt and colleagues have argued that "[w]omen are born lacking one attribute men appear to acquire by accident of gender: authority" (1995: 81). As such, female candidates may turn to others to provide that authority on issues as well as to establish the legitimacy of their candidacy. Notably, female incumbents and females in open races did not use this strategy differently than their male counterparts. Thus as female challengers seek to establish their viability and present themselves as legitimate candidates, they may turn to the use of expert authorities—generally influential voices perceived to be objective—to strengthen their candidacies and reinforce their positions.

Across all three status categories—incumbents, challengers, and open-race candidates—female and male challengers differed most on the characteristics they emphasized in their advertising. Overall, female challengers most frequently emphasized being aggressive and a fighter (36 percent), followed by their toughness and strength (31 percent) and their leadership (30 percent). Male challengers most frequently emphasized their honesty and integrity (42 percent), followed by their toughness and strength (36 percent) and the characteristics of aggressiveness and being a fighter (23 percent). However, when the use of the traits by female and male challengers is directly compared, more significant differences emerge.

The fact that the female challengers emphasized many of the character traits more frequently than male challengers is of interest because male challengers more frequently emphasized candidate image in their advertising. A closer examination of the eight masculine traits included in our analysis found that female challengers emphasized five of those traits more frequently than male challengers, who did not emphasize any of the masculine traits at greater frequencies; of the five feminine traits included in our analysis, male challengers emphasized one only trait—honesty and integrity—more frequently (42 percent) than female challengers (27 percent), who also did not emphasize any of the feminine traits more frequently than male challengers. Further analysis of the candidates' use of honesty and integrity and being action-oriented indicates that the differences among challenger candidates has more to do with the race than with gender. Our analysis finds there are no significant differences between female incumbent/male challenger and male incumbent/female challenger emphasis of either honesty and integrity or being action-oriented.

However, the same cannot be said for the remaining significant differences between challenger candidates. Research has indicated that masculine traits are more highly valued in political candidates than "feminine" traits (Huddy and Terkildsen 1993; Riggle, Miller, Shields, and Johnson 1997; Rosenwasser and Dean 1989). Further, in experimental scenarios, female candidates who are perceived in their advertising to emphasize both feminine and masculine traits are viewed more favorably and are more likely to win the subjects' votes (Banwart and Carlin 2001). Therefore, female candidates—particularly female challenger candidates—see the value in frequently emphasizing these traits in their advertising.

Nonverbal and Production Content. In terms of the nonverbal and production content of the ads studied, the differences between female and male challengers primarily emerged in the demographics of those in the ads, dominant speakers, and in candidate presentation. Specifically, female challengers were more likely to include men (62 percent), women (58 percent), and children who are not family (35 percent) in their advertising; male challengers were more likely to include their family (26 percent) in their advertising.

Differences also existed in the dominant speaker used in the challengers' advertising. Whereas female challengers were most likely to feature the candidate as the dominant speaker (34 percent), male challengers were most likely to use an anonymous announcer (53 percent) in their advertising. Although both female and male challengers' advertising more commonly featured a male speaker (58 percent to 76 percent, respectively), male challengers were more likely than female challengers to feature a male voice, and female challengers were more likely (37 percent) than male challengers (25 percent) to feature a female voice as the dominant speaker. Although female candidates did use a female speaker as the dominant voice delivering the message in their advertising, they did not necessarily rely on a female announcer, citizen or constituent, or other office holder; in fact, female challengers were the female voice in 88 percent of the ads in which a female speaker was dominant.

In terms of the candidate's nonverbal presentation, both female and male challengers were reluctant to establish eye contact with the viewer; if female challengers did establish eye contact, they were most likely to do so sometimes (35 percent), whereas male challengers were more likely to do so always (35 percent). Consistent with overall findings, female challengers were more likely to dress formally in their ads (78 percent) as compared to male challengers (49 percent), and male challengers were more likely to dress casually (51 percent) as compared to female challengers (22 percent).

Open-Race Candidates

Verbal Content: Focus, Attacks, and Message Design. From the comparative analysis of female candidates and male candidates in open races, it appears that although some differences exist in the presentation of their VideoStyles, much of their style has been similar (see Table 4.1). For instance, candidates in open races were equally positive, negative, and comparative; equally included attacks in their advertising; and used logical, emotional, and ethical appeals at similar frequencies. Open-race candidates focused similarly on issues and images in their advertising and more frequently emphasized campaign issues (female candidates, 66 percent; male candidates, 64 percent) than candidate image (female candidates, 34 percent; male candidates, 36 percent). Candidates in open races did differ on the purpose of their attacks, however. Table 4.1 indicates that female and male candidates attacked their opponent's issue stands most frequently; however, female candidates in open races were more likely to attack personal characteristics (21 percent; male candidates, 14 percent) and their opponent's performance in past offices or positions (29 percent; male candidates, 23 percent). Male candidates were more likely to attack their opponent's group affiliation (8 percent; female candidates, 3 percent) and their opponent's background (6 percent; female candidates, 1 percent). Female open-race candidates were more likely to use fear appeals in their advertising (19 percent; male candidates, 12 percent), a distinct difference from the comparison between female and male challengers, but consistent with the comparison between female and male incumbents.

Verbal Content: Issue Discussion. Few differences emerged in our comparative analysis of issue discussion between female and male candidates in open races, with the issue agendas of open-race candidates the most similar across all status categories. The most frequent issue discussed by both female (33 percent) and male candidates (36 percent) was taxes, followed by education and school issues (female candidates, 31 percent; male candidates, 27 percent) and unemployment and jobs (female candidates, 23 percent; male candidates, 22 percent). When examining the differences between individual issue discussion (see Table 4.1), female candidates were more likely to discuss health care (21 percent), women's issues (10 percent), environmental issues (9 percent), the cost of living (6 percent), and the recession (4 percent) than male candidates, although male candidates more frequently discussed crime and prison issues (18 percent) in open races. The difference in issue discussion does not directly point to gender, however, with the issues more frequently discussed by female candidates crossing traditionally feminine and masculine categorizations, although male candidates in open races were more likely to discuss the masculine issue of crime and prison. Regardless, the issue agendas of candidates in open races did not appear to fall along traditional gendered stereotypes. Rather, the balanced frequency in discussing feminine and masculine issues may well illustrate the ability of open-race female candidates to more successfully balance the double bind in issue discussion.

Verbal Content: Emphasis on Appeals and Character Traits. The strategic appeals used by open-race candidates in their advertising were largely similar, although female candidates were more likely to use a personal tone in their ads (32 percent)—considered an element of the "feminine" style (Campbell 1989)—compared to male candidates (25 percent). Male candidates were more likely to call for change (36 percent) and present an above-the-trenches posture (14 percent), challenger and incumbent strategies, respectively. Although female candidates may have used a personal tone, characterized by the use of the word *I*, they also emphasized their toughness and strength as well as their ability to be aggressive and a fighter. We mention these in combination, as in 50 percent of the open-race female candidate ads in which a personal tone was used, the candidates emphasized their toughness and strength. In 46 percent of those ads using a personal tone, the female candidates emphasized their aggressiveness. Upon further analysis, although the female and male candidates did not differ in their use of the candidate as the dominant speaker (28 percent and 24 percent, respectively), in 84 percent of those ads in which the female candidate was the dominant speaker and 69 percent of those ads in which a male candidate was the dominant speaker, a personal tone was used. Therefore, the use of a personal tone may be an element of the VideoStyle of a female candidate in an open race, as the female candidate personally emphasizes her character traits.

Nonverbal and Production Content. In examining the nonverbal and production content of the open-race advertising, the similarities outweigh the differences (see Table 4.1). Certainly the appearance of the candidate's family in the advertisement is an element indicative of male candidate VideoStyle, as open-race male candidates were significantly more likely to feature their family (25 percent) than female candidates (8 percent) and at an even greater percentage difference than either incumbent or challenger candidates. Additionally, similar to the significant differences among female and male incumbents and challengers, female and male candidates in open races were most likely overall to use a male voice as the dominant speaker in their advertising. However, if a female voice was used, female candidate ads were significantly more likely to feature a female voice

(35 percent) than male candidates (20 percent). Finally, again a staple of female candidate VideoStyle overall, female candidates were significantly more likely to wear formal attire (80 percent) in their advertising; male candidates were most likely to wear formal attire (52 percent) but significantly more likely to wear casual attire (48 percent) than female candidates (20 percent).

Summary

Overall, our analysis of the VideoStyles of female and male candidates when compared by status indicates that certain differences exist when women and men run as incumbents and when women and men run as challengers. However, women and men running in open races are not bound by status implications—either the benefits or the constraints—and thus present far more similar VideoStyles. Characteristics of an incumbent VideoStyle in mixed-gender races includes a use of inductive reasoning, a focus on campaign issue ads as opposed to image ads, emphasis on past performance and leadership qualities, and the inclusion of candidates with other people in their advertising. In particular, female incumbents do tend to present a more complex argument in their advertisements, whereas male incumbents focus more on issues.

In mixed-gender races female and male candidate challengers differ more across character traits than either incumbent candidates or open-race candidates, with female challengers placing greater emphasis on masculine traits than male challengers. Female challenger characteristics include use of logical arguments, more frequent discussion of issues, and the use of expert authorities. Male challengers use more emotional arguments and are balanced in their use of positive and negative advertising but are significantly more likely to feature an attack, place greater emphasis on image advertising, and focus on their honesty and integrity. Female and male open-race candidates are similar across issue agendas, although we argue that the use of a personal tone is a characteristic most closely associated with female candidates in open races, and when emphasizing their aggressiveness and toughness, female candidates are more likely to make those assertions themselves.

Perhaps the most important findings from this analysis suggest that in many instances, the differences are not uniquely attributable to gender or status, but instead are a result of the combination of both variables. The dynamic between gender and status seems to have the greatest influence in the focus (positive, negative, comparative) of the ad, emphasis (issues or images), use of attacks, frequency of issue discussion, and use of endorsements. Therefore, as research moves forward in examining the use of VideoStyles by status in mixed-gender races, we must continue to explore the rich complexities in how these roles influence campaign strategies.

VideoStyles of Democrats and Republicans

The candidates' political party affiliation has been one of the least studied variables in examinations of the content of television advertisements run by females and males in mixed-gender races. One particular study (Kaid and Johnston 2001) that analyzed the VideoStyles of presidential candidates based on their party affiliation found numerous differences between Democrats and Republicans. For instance, they found Democratic presidential candidates have been more likely to use negative advertising, use fear and emotional appeals, attack their opponent's personal character, and emphasize partisanship. Further, Democrats have been more likely to use special effects, anonymous announcers, appeals to a group, and a cinema verité production style. Republican candidates were more likely to use positive spots, employ logical appeals, focus on foreign policy as an issue, show the candidate head-on, rely on government officials and surrogates as speakers in the ads, use testimonials and documentary formats, and include endorsements from foreign leaders. Such distinct differences at the presidential level suggest the need to examine whether such differences exist in statewide races, particularly when gender is introduced as a variable.

Verbal Content: Focus, Attacks, and Message Design

In examining the differences between female and male Democrat VideoStyle and female and male Republican VideoStyle, we first looked at the verbal content of the advertising (see Table 4.2). Whereas female Republicans (74 percent) and male Democrats (60 percent) were more likely than their counterparts to run candidate-positive advertising, the use of candidate-positive advertising was most common across both parties. Yet our findings indicate that female Republicans and male Democrats run more positive races than female Democrats and male Republicans. Specifically, female Democrats (39 percent) and male Republicans (32 percent) were more likely to run opponent-negative ads, and thus—not surprisingly—also were more likely to have attacks present in their advertising (female Democrats, 57 percent; male Republicans, 45 percent).

A closer look at the dynamics involved in the use of negative advertising indicates that female Republicans and male Democrats not only run fewer negative ads, but also run approximately the same amount of negative ads. As such, the difference in focus between female Republicans and male Democrats was not significantly different. Male Republicans, however, were more likely (59 percent) to run candidate-positive ads than female Democrats (50 percent); female Democrats were more likely (39 percent) to run opponent-negative ads than male Republicans (32 percent); and female Democrats also were more likely to run comparative ads (11 percent; male Republicans, 9 percent). Therefore, female Democrats are significantly more likely to use negative advertising than all other candidates.

TABLE 4.2 Significant Differences in Female and Male VideoStyle by Candidate Party

	Democrat		Republican	
	Female	Male	Female	Male
Verbal Content				
Focus	(n = 439)	(n = 206)	(n = 247)	(n = 497)
Candidate-positive	50%	69%*	74%	59%*
Opponent-negative	39%	23%*	20%	32%*
Comparative/cannot determine	11%	8%*	6%	9%*
Negative Attack Present	57%	37%*	31%	45%*
Purpose of Attack*	(n = 245)	(n = 75)		
Personal characteristics	24%	11%	—	—
Issue stands	41%	56%	—	—
Group affiliation	4%	17%	—	—
Opponent's background	7%	0%	—	—
Opponent's performance	25%	16%	—	—
Emphasis*	(n = 439)	(n = 206)		
Campaign issues	59%	68%	—	—
Candidate image	42%	33%	—	—
Issues	(n = 439)	(n = 206)	(n = 247)	(n = 497)
Taxes	27%	19%*	—	—
Cost of living/inflation	4%	8%*	4%	1%*
Economy in general	—	—	16%	8%*
Education/schools	39%	25%*	—	—
Crime/prisons	—	—	7%	14%*
Health care	25%	18%*	—	—
Welfare	—	—	1%	5%*
Dissatisfaction with government	8%	15%*	13%	8%*
Women's issues	—	—	6%	2%*
Defense	—	—	5%	2%*
International issues	1%	6%*	—	—
Strategic Appeals	(n = 439)	(n = 206)	(n = 247)	(n = 497)
Incumbency stands for legitimacy	5%	14%*	—	—
Voice for the state	—	—	31%	24%*
Personal tone	—	—	43%	32%*
Call for change	—	—	36%	28%*
Personal experience	19%	28%*	25%	18%*
Use of statistics	—	—	9%	23%*
Use of expert authorities	24%	17%*	12%	19%*
Emphasize own accomplishments	30%	46%*	—	—
Attack opponent's record	47%	30%*	—	—
Make gender an issue	—	—	6%	2%*
Character Traits	(n = 439)	(n = 206)	(n = 247)	(n = 497)
Toughness/strength	—	—	40%	31%*
Past performance	34%	49%*	—	—
Aggressive/fighter	40%	30%*	—	—

64 • Gender and Candidate Communication

TABLE 4.2 (continued) Significant Differences in Female and Male VideoStyle by Candidate Party

	Democrat		Republican	
	Female	Male	Female	Male
Leadership	26%	45%*	43%	34%*
Experience in politics	17%	38%*	—	—
Washington outsider	6%	13%*	—	—
Knowledgeable/intelligent	11%	18%*	18%	11%*
Qualified	—	—	26%	20%*
Trustworthy	—	—	15%	22%*

Nonverbal and Production Content

*Setting**	(n = 335)	(n = 172)		
No setting	31%	23%	—	—
Inside setting	39%	34%	—	—
Outside setting	17%	30%	—	—
Combination/other	13%	13%	—	—
*Dominant Shot**	(n = 258)	(n = 106)		
Tight	35%	18%	—	—
Medium	59%	61%	—	—
Long	1%	11%	—	—
Combination	6%	11%	—	—
*Who Is Pictured**			(n = 245)	(n = 496)
No one	—	—	4%	4%
Candidate only	—	—	17%	12%
Candidate's opponent	—	—	3%	7%
Candidate and opponent	—	—	9%	14%
Candidate and other people	—	—	62%	55%
People other than candidate	—	—	6%	9%
Demographic Groups Pictured	(n = 397)	(n = 172)	(n = 224)	(n = 444)
Family of candidate	10%	16%*	8%	21%*
Senior citizens	—	—	36%	27%*
*Dominant Speaker**			(n = 217)	(n = 433)
Candidate	—	—	41%	26%
Government official/office holder	—	—	23%	37%
Anonymous announcer	—	—	22%	30%
Spouse/family member	—	—	0%	1%
Citizen/constituent	—	—	12%	4%
Combination	—	—	3%	3%
*Sex of Dominant Speaker**	(n = 335)	(n = 171)	(n = 219)	(n = 432)
Male	68%	80%	47%	73%
Female	27%	17%	49%	23%
Cannot determine	5%	3%	4%	4%
*Eye Contact**			(n = 190)	(n = 320)
Never	—	—	47%	53%
Sometimes	—	—	34%	28%

TABLE 4.2 (continued) Significant Differences in Female and Male VideoStyle by Candidate Party

	Democrat		Republican	
	Female	Male	Female	Male
Almost always	—	—	13%	8%
Always	—	—	6%	11%
*Facial Expression**	(n = 259)	(n = 137)	(n = 198)	(n = 348)
Smiling	48%	25%	47%	34%
Attentive/serious	53%	75%	53%	66%
*Dress**	(n = 247)	(n = 133)	(n = 192)	(n = 336)
Formal	83%	58%	75%	50%
Casual	17%	42%	26%	50%

Note: Percentages indicate frequencies within gender.
* Significant at $p \leq .05$.

The purpose or object of the attack also differed significantly between female and male Democrats. Although both female (41 percent) and male (56 percent) Democrats most frequently focused on the issue stands of their opponents in the attacks, female Democrats were more likely to also attack the personal characteristics (24 percent) and their opponent's performance in past offices or positions (25 percent) in their advertising. Male Democrats were more likely to attack their opponent's group affiliations (17 percent) than female candidates (4 percent). When the purpose of the attacks was further analyzed, we found that, in fact, female Democrats also were more likely (24 percent) than male Republicans (14 percent) to attack their opponent's personal qualities, equally as likely to attack on issue stands (41 percent), and more likely to attack their opponent's background (7 percent; male Republicans, 4 percent). Male Republicans were more likely to attack their opponent's performance in past offices and positions (31 percent) than female Democrats (25 percent). Female Republicans, on the other hand, were more likely to attack their opponent's performance in past office and positions (40 percent) than male Democrats (16 percent) and were slightly more likely to attack their opponent's personal characteristics (15 percent; male Democrats, 11 percent). Male Democrats were more likely to attack their opponent's issue stands (56 percent) than female Republicans (43 percent) and their opponent's group affiliations (17 percent; female Republicans, 1 percent).

When examining the emphasis on campaign issues or candidate images, significant differences emerged only between female and male Democrats. Although both females (59 percent) and males (68 percent) were most likely to focus on campaign issues in their advertising, male Democrats were more likely to do so than female Democrats; female Democrats were more likely to focus on candidate image (42 percent; male Democrats, 33 percent). Further analysis comparing female Democrats versus male Republicans, and female Republicans versus male Democrats, indicates that the difference for Democrats is more closely related to the type of race in which the candidates are running and, thus, their opponents. The comparison of female Democrats' and male Republicans' ads resulted in no significant difference in emphasis on campaign issues or candidate image, and the comparison of female Republicans' and male Democrats' ads also did not yield any significant difference in emphasis of the ad.

Verbal Content: Issue Discussion

The emphasis on specific issue agendas found differences on both sides of the aisle. The most frequently discussed issue for female Republicans *and* male Republicans was taxes (female Republicans, 32 percent; male Republicans, 31 percent). The next most frequently discussed issues for female Republicans included unemployment and jobs (19 percent) and education and school issues (17 percent); the next most frequently discussed issues for male Republicans included education and school issues (20 percent) and unemployment and jobs (18 percent). Both female and male Democrats also most frequently discussed education and school issues in 39 percent and 25 percent of their ads, respectively. Female Democrats also discussed taxes (27 percent) and health care (25 percent) frequently in their ads, and male Democrats discussed unemployment and jobs (23 percent) and taxes (19 percent) in their advertising.

When we examined the differences between candidates in specific issue discussions, female Democrats were more likely to discuss taxes (27 percent), education and school issues (39 percent), and health care (25 percent) than their male counterparts (19 percent, 25 percent, and 18 percent); male Democrats were more likely to discuss the economy (8 percent), dissatisfaction with the government (15 percent), and international issues (6 percent) than their female counterparts (4 percent, 8 percent, and 1 percent). When differences arose between female and male Republicans, we found the female Republicans more likely to be engaging in issue discussion. For instance, female Republicans were more likely to discuss the economy (16 percent), dissatisfaction with the government (13 percent), women's issues (6 percent), defense (5 percent), and the cost of living (4 percent). Male Republicans were only more likely to discuss crime and prisons (14 percent) and welfare (5 percent). When we break issue discussion down by race—female Democrat versus male Republican, female Republican versus male Democrat—we find that the dynamic between gender and party does not seem to offer a thorough explanation regarding the frequency of issue discussion, but it does offer some insights.

First, although female Republicans and male Democrats may have discussed dissatisfaction with the government more than their counterparts, overall there are no significant differences when the candidates are compared to their opponents; thus, we argue that dissatisfaction with the government is truly a neutral issue. Although female Republicans discussed women's issues more than male Republicans, male Democrats discussed such issues as frequently as female Republicans; women's issues really *are* women's issues when female Democrats run against male Republicans, however. Welfare traditionally has been considered a feminine issue, yet male Republicans and male Democrats discussed the issue more frequently than their female opponents. And our results suggest that discussing the cost of living may be a Democratic issue more than a masculine issue, as female Democrats and male Democrats were more likely to discuss this issue than their Republican opponents. Although taxes, crime and prison issues, defense, and international issues also are traditionally considered "masculine" issues, female Democrats and male Republicans discussed these issues at similar levels of frequency. Overall, however, male Democrats seem to have the greatest emphasis on international issues, and female Republicans have been more focused on discussing defense than any of the other candidates. Health care and education and school issues, traditionally considered feminine issues, were discussed at similar frequencies by female Republicans, male Republicans, and male Democrats. But overall, female Democrats focused most frequently on both health care topics and education and school issues. Finally, of all the candidates, female Republicans less frequently discussed crime and prison issues, male Republicans less frequently discussed the economy, and male Democrats were least likely to discuss taxes.

Verbal Content: Emphasis on Appeals and Character Traits

The results of our analysis of strategic appeals used by the candidates do suggest possible patterns across feminine style, masculine style, incumbent style, and challenger style. Male Democrats were more likely to emphasize their own accomplishments (47 percent), use personal experience in their ad messages (28 percent), and use the "incumbency stands for legitimacy" strategy (14 percent). Female Democrats were more likely to use expert authorities (24 percent) and attack the opponent's record (47 percent) than their male counterparts (17 percent and 30 percent), the latter strategy being consistent with their greater likelihood to run negatively focused advertising than male Democrats. Thus, when female Democrats are compared to male Democrats, female Democrats appear to use more masculine and challenger strategies, whereas male Democrats use more feminine and incumbent strategies. Female Republicans more frequently—as compared to male Republicans—employed the strategies of using a personal tone (43 percent), calling for change (36 percent), being a voice for the state (31 percent), and using personal experience in their messages (25 percent), all of which have been considered either feminine or challenger strategies. Male Republicans were, however, more likely to use statistics (23 percent) and expert authorities (19 percent) than female Republicans (9 percent and 12 percent), both of which are considered traditionally masculine strategies.

In the analysis of character traits emphasized by the candidates in their advertising, the most frequently discussed character traits were far more similar between female and male Republicans than between female and male Democrats. Whereas female Republicans most frequently emphasized leadership (43 percent), toughness and strength (40 percent), and past performance (38 percent), male Republicans emphasized past performance (35 percent), being aggressive and a fighter (35 percent), and leadership (34 percent). Notably, the female and male Republicans shared the same seven most frequently emphasized character traits, the remainder of which were being action-oriented, possessing honesty and integrity, and emphasizing their experience in politics. Female and male Democrats, however, were more likely to most frequently emphasize different character traits. Whereas female Democrats most frequently emphasized their ability to be aggressive and a fighter (40 percent), their toughness and strength (34 percent), and their past performance (34 percent), male Democrats most frequently emphasized their past performance (49 percent), leadership (45 percent), and experience in politics (38 percent). Notably, the traits most frequently emphasized by all candidates were masculine traits.

Although the Republican candidates seemed to share a focus on emphasizing particular traits most frequently, they did differ in the amount of emphasis. For instance, female Republicans were more likely to emphasize their leadership (43 percent), their toughness and strength (40 percent), their qualifications (26 percent), and knowledge and intelligence (18 percent). Male Republicans more frequently emphasized their trustworthiness (22 percent), a traditionally feminine trait. Female Democrats emphasized only one trait more frequently than their male counterparts, that of being aggressive and a fighter (40 percent). Male Democrats, however, more frequently emphasized their past performance (49 percent), leadership (45 percent), experience in politics (38 percent), knowledge and intelligence (18 percent), and Washington outsider status (13 percent).

The emphasis by male Republicans on being trustworthy and the female Democrats on being aggressive and a fighter may occur because those are not traits traditionally associated with their gender; as scholars have argued, candidates have a tendency to emphasize the traits on which they are perceived as weak in order to overcome such perceptions (Kahn 1993). Further, when female Democrats and male Republicans were compared on both of these traits, no significant differences arose. Thus, perhaps the dynamic between their party and gender does have an influence in the types of traits emphasized. In other words, as a male Republican is emphasizing his trustworthiness, a female Democrat responds in kind to meet the image put forth by her opponent; likewise, as a female Democrat emphasizes her aggressiveness and ability to fight for programs, issues, and so on, the male Republican responds in kind. Notably, however, the dynamic was not at play with either of these traits when a female Republican and a male Democrat ran against each other.

One of the traits on which female Republicans placed greater emphasis than their male counterparts was an issue that female Republicans also placed greater emphasis on than male Democrats: toughness and strength. However, female Republicans and male Democrats were just as likely to emphasize leadership, being a Washington outsider, being knowledgeable and intelligent, and their qualifications. Male Democrats did place more emphasis on having experience in politics, an incumbent strategy, but 50 percent of the male Democrats' advertising was from incumbents in our sample and only 13 percent of the female Republicans' ads were from incumbents. Yet female Republicans apparently sought to compensate for their opponents' emphasis on having experience by emphasizing past performance—or previous accomplishments and achievements—that could provide similar benefits, although they did not have the same incumbent advantage.

Nonverbal and Production Content

An analysis of the nonverbal and production content also found differences between female and male Democrats and female and male Republicans (see Table 4.2). Specifically, both female and male Democrats used an inside setting most frequently, but female Democrats were more likely to use that setting (39 percent) as compared to male Democrats (34 percent), and male Democrats were more likely to use an outside setting (30 percent) than female Democrats (17 percent). Further, although both female and male Democrats most frequently used medium shots in their ads, female Democrats were more likely to use a tight shot (35 percent) than male Democrats (18 percent), and male Democrats were more likely to use a long shot (11 percent) than female Democrats (1 percent).

Of the people pictured in the ads, female and male Republicans were most likely to feature the candidate and other people, although female candidates were more likely to feature the candidate only (17 percent) and male Republicans were more likely to feature the candidate and other people (14 percent). Consistent with our findings throughout this chapter, both male Republicans and male Democrats were more likely to feature their families in their advertising than the female Republicans and Democrats. Whereas female Republicans more frequently featured senior citizens in their advertising (36 percent) than male Republicans (27 percent), overall the candidates seemed equally as likely to feature this demographic segment; in other words, there were no significant differences between the frequency of senior citizens appearing in the ads of female Democrats and male Republicans, and in female Republicans' and male Democrats' ads.

Female and male Democrats did not differ in the dominant speaker delivering their messages. Although both were most likely to feature male speakers, female Democrats were more likely to feature a female speaker (27 percent) as compared to male Democrats (17 percent). Female Republicans were most likely to feature the candidate as the dominant speaker in their advertising (41 percent), and male Republicans were most likely to feature a government official or office holder (37 percent). In a departure from prior findings in this chapter, female Republicans were more likely overall to feature a female voice as the dominant speaker in their ads (49 percent); male Republicans continued the male candidate trend of most frequently featuring a male voice in their advertising (73 percent).

When examining the nonverbal content of the advertising, female and male Republicans differed in their eye contact, facial expressions, and dress, whereas female and male Democrats differed in their facial expressions and dress. Not surprisingly, and consistent with previous findings in this chapter, female Democrats and female Republicans were both more likely to wear formal attire in their advertising than their male counterparts; male Democrats and Republicans were more likely to wear casual attire than their female counterparts. Similarly, female Republicans and female Democrats were more likely to smile in their advertising than male Republicans and Democrats, who were more likely to be seen as attentive and serious in their advertising than their female counterparts. However, it is important to note that overall, all candidates were most likely to be seen as attentive and serious in their advertising, and female Republicans, female Democrats, and male Democrats were most likely to be seen in formal attire; male Republicans wore either formal or casual attire equally as often.

Eye contact by the candidates is more complex, however. Although female and male Republicans were most likely overall to never have eye contact with the viewer, male Republicans were more likely to never have eye contact (53 percent) than female Republicans (47 percent), and female Republicans were more likely to sometimes have eye contact (34 percent; male Republicans, 28 percent). Yet when the candidates were compared with their opponents, it became apparent that female (64 percent) and male (68 percent) Democrats were significantly more likely to never have eye contact than male (53 percent) and female (47 percent) Republicans; female (6 percent) and male (11 percent) Republicans were significantly more likely to always have eye contact than male (2 percent) and female (4 percent) Democrats.

Summary

Although fewer defining patterns emerge when the VideoStyles of candidates in mixed-gender races are compared by party, certain characteristics are notable. For instance, races consisting of female Democrats and male

Republicans tend to be more negative than races consisting of female Republicans and male Democrats. Female Democrats are more likely to use negative advertising, attack their opponent's personal qualities and background, and discuss women's issues, education and school issues, and health care. Male Democrats are more likely to attack their opponent's issues stands and group affiliation and emphasize their experience in politics and past performance. Female and male Democrats are more likely to never have eye contact with the camera in their advertising.

Female and male Republicans present similar VideoStyles overall, although a particular characteristic of female Republicans is their emphasis on toughness and strength. Female and male Republicans both are more likely to attack their opponent's past performance in office or positions and are more likely to always have eye contact.

VideoStyles by Outcome

An important question has remained unanswered in the prior research focusing on female and male VideoStyles: do female and male VideoStyles differ when the candidates win or lose? With our extensive sample, we analyzed the verbal, nonverbal, and production content of winning and losing female and male candidates.

Verbal Content: Focus, Attacks, and Message Design

At a first glance, it appears that more differences do exist in the VideoStyles of female and male candidates who win, whereas fewer differences exist in the presentation of losing candidacies. Winning candidates overall most frequently ran candidate-positive ads, but winning male candidates were more likely to run such ads (70 percent) than winning female candidates (57 percent), and winning female candidates were more likely to run opponent-negative ads (34 percent) than winning male candidates (24 percent). Not surprisingly, then, winning female candidates also were more likely to issue attacks in their ads (49 percent) as compared to winning male candidates (33 percent). Of interest, however, is that we found no significant differences in the use of attacks in winning female candidates' advertising as compared to losing male candidates, yet losing female candidates were more likely to issue attacks and run opponent-negative ads as compared to winning male candidates. When attacks were issued, all candidates typically attacked their opponents' issue stands, although whether they won or lost, female candidates were more likely to attack their opponent's personal character. Losing male candidates were more likely to attack based on their opponent's group affiliation. A closer look at Table 4.3 indicates that when winning female and losing male candidates are paired, and losing female and winning male candidates are paired, any differences cease to exist when attacking the opponent's performance in

72 • Gender and Candidate Communication

TABLE 4.3 Significant Differences in Female and Male VideoStyle by Outcome of Race

	Won		Lost	
	Female	Male	Female	Male
Verbal Content				
Focus*	(n = 292)	(n = 408)	(n = 394)	(n = 295)
Candidate-positive	57%	70%	—	—
Opponent-negative	34%	24%	—	—
Comparative/cannot determine	9%	7%	—	—
Negative Attack Present*	49%	33%	47%	55%
Purpose of Attack*	(n = 139)	(n = 135)	(n = 181)	(n = 158)
Personal character	27%	14%	17%	13%
Issue stands	41%	47%	41%	43%
Group affiliation	4%	10%	3%	13%
Opponent's background	3%	1%	7%	5%
Opponent's performance	25%	28%	31%	27%
Dominant Content*	(n = 289)	(n = 402)		
Logical appeals	42%	46%	—	—
Emotional appeals	20%	27%	—	—
Ethical appeals	39%	27%	—	—
	(n = 257)	(n = 353)		
Fear Appeals Present*	16%	10%	—	—
Structure*	(n = 292)	(n = 408)		
Inductive	70%	61%	—	—
Deductive	21%	33%	—	—
Cannot determine	9%	6%	—	—
Issues	(n = 292)	(n = 408)	(n = 394)	(n = 295)
Taxes	32%	25%*	—	—
Economy in general	—	—	19%	7%*
Education/schools	31%	23%*	32%	20%*
Crime/prisons	9%	16%*	—	—
Health care	24%	14%*	—	—
Senior citizens' issues	20%	11%*	—	—
Welfare	0%	7%*	—	—
Environment	—	—	8%	4%*
Ethics/moral decline	—	—	4%	1%*
Women's issues	12%	3%*	—	—
Appeal Strategies	(n = 292)	(n = 408)	(n = 394)	(n = 295)
Incumbency stands for legitimacy	7%	15%*	—	—
Personal tone	—	—	36%	26%*
Address viewers as peers	24%	32%*	34%	26%*
Use of endorsements	12%	6%*	4%	8%*
Use of statistics	19%	25%*	—	—
Own accomplishments	37%	45%*	—	—
Taking the offensive position	24%	17%*	—	—

TABLE 4.3 (continued) Significant Differences in Female and Male VideoStyle by Outcome of Race

	Won		Lost	
	Female	Male	Female	Male
Attack opponent's record	42%	26%*	—	—
Make gender an issue	—	—	8%	2%*
Character Traits	(n = 292)	(n = 408)	(n = 394)	(n = 295)
Toughness/strength	—	—	37%	28%*
Aggressive/fighter	40%	32%*	—	—
Leadership	32%	48%*	32%	22%*
Experience in politics	26%	38%*	—	—
Knowledgeable/intelligent	—	—	16%	10%*

Nonverbal and Production Content

*Setting**	(n = 244)	(n = 353)		
No setting	28%	21%	—	—
Inside setting	39%	36%	—	—
Outside setting	19%	32%	—	—
Combination/other	14%	11%	—	—
Who Is Pictured*	(n = 292)	(n = 408)	(n = 394)	(n = 295)
No one	3%	5%	4%	3%
Candidate only	8%	8%	15%	15%
Candidate's opponent	9%	6%	5%	8%
Candidate and opponent	13%	15%	11%	15%
Candidate and others	56%	61%	60%	46%
People other than candidate	12%	6%	5%	12%
Demographics Pictured	(n = 257)	(n = 353)	(n = 364)	(n = 263)
Men	—	—	61%	49%*
Family of candidate	6%	18%*	11%	21%*
Children (not candidate's)	—	—	32%	24%*
Senior citizens	—	—	30%	21%*
Dominant Speaker*			(n = 308)	(n = 253)
Candidate	—	—	35%	25%
Government official/office holder	—	—	24%	31%
Anonymous announcer	—	—	31%	34%
Spouse/family member	—	—	0%	1%
Citizen/constituent	—	—	7%	5%
Combination	—	—	3%	4%
Sex of Dominant Speaker*	(n = 244)	(n = 350)	(n = 310)	(n = 253)
Male	66%	77%	55%	73%
Female	28%	19%	41%	25%
Cannot determine	5%	4%	4%	3%
Eye Contact*			(n = 251)	(n = 171)
Never	—	—	51%	50%
Sometimes	—	—	31%	30%

TABLE 4.3 (continued) Significant Differences in Female and Male VideoStyle by Outcome of Race

	Won		Lost	
	Female	**Male**	**Female**	**Male**
Almost always	—	—	13%	7%
Always	—	—	5%	14%
Facial Expression*	(n = 186)	(n = 298)		
Smiling	54%	28%	—	—
Attentive/serious	46%	73%	—	—
Dominant Dress*	(n = 177)	(n = 289)	(n = 262)	(n = 180)
Formal	80%	59%	79%	42%
Casual	20%	41%	21%	58%

Note: Percentages indicate frequencies within gender.
* Significant at $p \leq .05$.

past offices and positions, even though losing female candidates were slightly more likely to do so.

Both female and male winning candidates were most likely to use an inductive structure in the messages presented in their advertising, although winning female candidates were more likely to use this element of feminine style (70 percent) than winning male candidates (61 percent), and winning male candidates were more likely to use a deductive structure (33 percent; winning female candidates, 21 percent). Winning female candidates also were more likely to include fear appeals, doing so in 16 percent of their ads compared to 10 percent of winning male candidate ads. However, when the candidates were compared by race—winning females versus losing males, losing females versus winning males—no differences emerged in the use of fear appeals between winning males and losing females, although winning females did use the strategy significantly more than losing males.

Although winning males more often used logical appeals (46 percent) and emotional appeals (27 percent) than winning female candidates (42 percent and 20 percent), winning females placed more emphasis on ethical appeals (39 percent) than winning male candidates (27 percent). As the successful female candidates' ads were more likely to be from open races (see Table 4.3) and the successful male candidates' ads were more likely to be from races in which they were incumbents, it is logical that more of the female candidates' ads would seek to establish their credibility—and viability—to hold public office, since the ads would be from candidates who did not have the favor of incumbency. It is notable, however, that no differences in the types of appeals used emerged when winning female candidates and losing male candidates were paired, as well as when winning male candidates and losing female candidates were paired.

Verbal Content: Issue Discussion

Analysis of the issues discussed finds that more differences existed between winning female and male candidates than between losing female and male candidates. While both winning female and male candidates most frequently discussed taxes (winning females, 31 percent; winning males, 25 percent), followed by education and school issues (winning females, 31 percent; winning males, 22 percent), winning females were next most likely to discuss health care (24 percent), whereas winning males were next most likely to discuss unemployment and jobs (22 percent). When directly compared by each issue, winning female candidates generally discussed most issues more frequently than winning males. Although both most frequently discussed taxes, winning female candidates did so significantly more often (32 percent) than winning male candidates (25 percent) and were more likely to discuss education and school issues (31 percent), health care (24 percent), senior citizens' issues (20 percent), and women's issues (12 percent). Aside from the issue of taxes, all of the remaining issues—education and schools, health care, senior citizens' issues, women's issues—have been considered feminine issues, and clearly issues that female candidates should not be afraid to address, as they can still focus on feminine issues and win.

Crime and prison issues as well as welfare were discussed more frequently by winning males (16 percent) than winning females (9 percent). This appears to be a characteristic issue that winning males have focused on, as further comparisons—winning females versus losing males, losing females versus winning males—indicate that no differences exist in the discussion of crime and prison issues between winning females and losing males, although winning males did discuss the issue more than losing females. However, losing females discussed education and schools (32 percent) and the economy (19 percent) more than losing male candidates (20 percent and 7 percent), as well as the environment (8 percent) and ethics and moral decline (4 percent). When comparing the candidates with their opponents, it is clear that losing females discussed the economy more than all other candidates, and winning females discussed health care and women's issues more than all other candidates.

Verbal Content: Emphasis on Appeals and Character Traits

An examination of the appeal strategies used by candidates again found a greater number of significant differences between winning female and male candidates. As more winning males were incumbent candidates, it is not surprising that winning male candidates were more likely to employ the strategy of "incumbency stands for legitimacy" (15 percent; winning females, 7 percent). However, winning male candidates also used statistics (25 percent) and emphasized their own accomplishments (45 percent), both considered masculine strategies, and addressed viewers as peers (32 percent), considered a feminine strategy, more than winning female candidates. When winning female candidates employed strategies more frequently than winning males, they did so with masculine and challenger strategies. For example, winning female candidates more frequently attacked the opponent's record (42 percent), took the offensive position on issues (24 percent), addressed viewers as peers (24 percent), and used endorsements (12 percent).

However, it is worth noting that when the candidates are compared to their opponents—winning females versus losing males, losing females versus winning males—the strategies of using a personal tone, addressing viewers as peers, and the use of endorsements, long associated with gendered styles, perhaps should now be considered elements of a neutral style. In each comparison, there were no significant differences between the candidates' uses of these strategies. This comparison did find, however, that when male candidates won, they not only used more statistics than their female opponents, but also emphasized their own accomplishments more frequently, both considered masculine styles. Although winning female candidates were more likely to use the challenger strategies of taking the offensive position on issues and attacking their opponent's record, they did not do so significantly differently than the male candidates who lost the race. However, when female candidates lost, they took the offensive position on the issues, attacked the record of the opponent, and made gender an issue more frequently than their winning male opponents. Such findings suggest that although female candidates can use these strategies and still win, using them at significantly greater levels than their male opponents is not a successful campaign tactic.

As has become a trend with regard to outcome, winning female candidates and winning male candidates certainly differed in the character traits most frequently emphasized. Winning female candidates most frequently emphasized their past performance (41 percent), that they were aggressive and a fighter (40 percent), and their toughness and strength (35 percent). Winning male candidates, however, most frequently discussed their past performance (49 percent), their leadership (46 percent), and their experience in politics (38 percent). A review of differences on individual trait emphasis finds that although winning female candidates were more likely to emphasize their aggressiveness and willingness to fight for programs, issues, and so on (40 percent) than winning males (32 percent), winning male candidates were more likely to emphasize their leadership (48 percent) and experience in politics (38 percent), both masculine traits.

Losing female candidates most frequently emphasized toughness and strength (37 percent) and being aggressive and a fighter (35 percent) and action-oriented (32 percent). Losing male candidates were most likely to emphasize their honesty and integrity (35 percent) and being aggressive and a fighter (34 percent) and action-oriented (34 percent). When losing candidates differed, the losing female candidate was more likely to emphasize her toughness and strength (37 percent), leadership (32 percent), and knowledge and intelligence (16 percent) than losing male candidates.

When the candidates were compared with their opponents—winning females and losing males, losing females and winning males—distinct patterns regarding character trait emphasis emerged. Across all of the traits, toughness and strength, being aggressive and a fighter, cooperation with others, competency, knowledge and intelligence, being action-oriented, and trustworthiness did not show any significant differences between the candidates; in other words, winning females and losing males, and winning males and losing females, all emphasized these traits with the same frequency in their respective races. When both female and male candidates won, they emphasized past performance, leadership, and experience in politics; in addition, female candidates emphasized being qualified, and male candidates emphasized being sensitive and understanding. When female and male candidates lost, they were more likely to emphasize their honesty and integrity and being a Washington outsider.

Nonverbal and Production Content

The analysis of nonverbal and production content again yielded significant differences. With regard to setting, both winning female and male candidates most frequently used an inside setting, but female winning candidates were more likely to have no setting at all (28 percent) than winning males (21 percent), and winning male candidates were more likely to use an outside setting (32 percent; winning females, 19 percent). Both winning and losing candidates were most frequently pictured with others in their advertising, although winning males and losing females were more likely to use such images than their counterparts. However, winning females and losing males were more likely to feature people other than the candidate in their advertising. Reinforcing the trend of male candidates including their family in their advertising, no matter their categorization, both winning males and losing males were more likely to include these individuals than their winning and losing female counterparts. Additionally, losing females were more likely to include men (61 percent), children who were not family (32 percent), and senior citizens (30 percent) than losing males (49 percent, 24 percent, and 21 percent). When losing females and winning males were compared, however, no significant differences emerged, thus suggesting that the candidates are seeking to appeal to similar demographic segments within the context of their respective races.

When female candidates were unsuccessful in their electoral bids, they were more likely to be the dominant speaker in the ad (35 percent) when compared with losing males, and losing males were more likely to feature either an anonymous announcer (34 percent) or a government official or office holder (34 percent) as compared to losing female candidates. A comparison of losing female candidates and winning male candidates indicates that losing female candidates also were most likely to be the dominant speaker in their ads, whereas winning male candidates were most likely to feature a government official or office holder as the dominant speaker in their advertising. All candidates were most likely to feature a male voice as the dominant speaker in their ads, although winning and losing female candidates were more likely to feature a female voice as the dominant speaker when compared to their male counterparts.

The nonverbal presentation of the candidates did differ slightly depending on outcome. Losing female and male candidates were both most likely to never have eye contact with the camera, but losing male candidates (14 percent) were more likely to always have eye contact, and losing female candidates (13 percent) were most likely to almost always have eye contact. Winning female and male candidates did differ significantly in the facial expressions they used, with winning female candidates most likely to smile (54 percent) and also to do so more than winning male candidates (28 percent), whereas winning male candidates were most likely to be attentive and serious (73 percent) and to do so more than winning female candidates. With regard to attire, both winning females (80 percent) and males (59 percent) were more likely to dress formally. But when candidates lost, the females were most likely to dress formally (79 percent) and the males were most likely to dress casually (58 percent). Overall, however, females—whether winning or losing—dressed more formally than male candidates, and the male candidates dressed more casually than the female candidates.

Summary

Based on these findings, it is apparent that when women win election to political office—at least at the statewide level—they most certainly present VideoStyles different from those developed by male candidates who win election to political office. Specifically, winning female candidates' VideoStyle can be characterized as using more fear appeals, discussing issues more frequently—health care and women's issues specifically—and emphasizing qualifications more frequently. Winning male candidates' VideoStyle can be characterized by greater use of statistical appeals and emphasis on their own accomplishments, more frequent discussion of crime and prison issues, and an emphasis on being sensitive and understanding. Both winning female and male candidates use inductive reasoning and emphasize their past performance, leadership, and experience in politics.

The VideoStyle of losing female candidates is characterized by a more frequent use of attacks and likelihood of running opponent-negative advertising, discussion of the economy, being the dominant speaker in the ad, taking the offensive position on the issues, attacking the record of the opponent, and making gender an issue. Both losing female and male candidates emphasize their honesty and integrity and being a Washington outsider. Losing males also are more likely to attack their opponents' group affiliations.

Overall, it is apparent that differences do exist between the VideoStyles of winning females and males. In other words, there is not one specific prescription that will aid a candidate in winning his or her race. However, it is notable that when female candidates win, they are emphasizing masculine traits and both feminine and masculine issues most frequently, although more traditionally feminine than masculine issues. There is substantial issue discussion in the advertising of both winning female and male candidates, and particularly so in the ads of winning female candidates. Winning male candidates, however, also are incorporating a mix of feminine and masculine strategies to ensure their success.

Conclusion

Although our research indicates that gender does ground many of the choices made by female and male candidates in presenting their television advertising VideoStyles, status and party provide influential dynamics. For both female and male candidates, seeking a successful balance that takes each of these defining roles into careful consideration to develop the VideoStyle of a viable and successful candidate is of utmost importance. For researchers, illuminating the most influential of the dynamics is the greatest challenge.

5
VideoStyles in the 2002 Kansas Governor's Race: *A Case Study*

In the fall of 2002, Kansas voters found themselves in the middle of an electoral battle for their state's executive post. The battle was being waged by the state's insurance commissioner, a Democrat, and the state's treasurer, a Republican. Early in the general election cycle, the race appeared to be a sure win for Kathleen Sebelius (D) based on statewide polling data, but in the final days her opponent, Tim Shallenburger (R), narrowed the margin considerably. Although the media later would say that Sebelius' campaign followed a "winning formula" (Hanna 2002), the candidates' televised advertising—and the self-presentation strategies contained therein—reveal important reasons for the success of one candidate and the failure of the other.

By conducting an in-depth analysis of the advertising in one particular mixed-gender race, we are able to provide a more detailed understanding of how a female candidate successfully designed and established an appealing image that secured votes in a state known to advantage the opposing party. This case study further allows us to examine how the female candidate successfully established an incumbent status in an open race, challenged stereotypical gender roles, and strategically built an image that withstood attacks from her opponent and backlash when she responded in kind.

Kansas: The Sunflower State

The public opinion support for Sebelius, a Democrat, throughout the general election was a surprise for most election watchers from outside the state, as Kansas is typically considered a Republican stronghold. For instance, of the forty-four governors of the state, twelve have been Democrats and thirty-two have been Republicans. In 1996, a majority of Kansans (54 percent) preferred their native son Bob Dole for president, and in the 2000 presidential election, a majority (58 percent) favored George W. Bush (Kansas Secretary of State 1996; Kansas Secretary of State 2000). At the time of the 2002 midterm election, Republicans held the majority of seats in the State Senate and the State House and all but one statewide elected position, insurance commissioner.

2002 Kansas Governor's Race Background

The 2002 Kansas gubernatorial election occurred, as did many others, with the state facing large budget deficits. Many of the questions the candidates faced during the election were focused on their ideas for funding of state programs and solving the state's deficit. In addition to the budget problems, the citizens of Kansas were frustrated following a long and unproductive legislative session that left them with more questions than answers. As a result, the gubernatorial candidates campaigned with the knowledge that grim circumstances faced their state.

Sebelius began the campaign early. She spent $4 million (Hanna 2002), which set a record for the amount spent on a Kansas gubernatorial campaign (McLean and Grenz 2002). Not only did Sebelius have a larger campaign fund than her opponent—he raised $2.06 million (Hanna 2002)—but she also ran unchallenged in the primary and, therefore, did not have to spend much of her funds in a tough primary race. As a result, during late July and on the night of the primary election Sebelius launched ads focused toward the general election (McLean and Grenz 2002). She continued to run ads consistently throughout the fall and ultimately spent "the bulk of [her funds] on broadcast advertising, pounding home her message in a solid three months of television advertising" (Hanna 2002: 2). Her opponent, however, had to remain conservative with his money and was unable to launch his general election ads until September 24. Overall, Shallenburger created about half the number of general election ads as Sebelius and was able to air his ads approximately half of the amount of time during the general election. By running early ads and by spending more money than her opponent, Sebelius was able to ensure that voters heard her name—and her message—more than her opponent's throughout the fall. Sebelius' eventual win in the election was by a margin of 7 percent (Kansas Secretary of State 2002a), although Shallenburger made substantial gains in the polls, particularly during the final two weeks of the election.

Identifying the Campaign VideoStyles

In order to more thoroughly understand the VideoStyles developed by these two gubernatorial candidates, this case study analyzes not only the influence of gender, but also the influences of party affiliation, state history, current state issues, and the candidates themselves on the strategies used in televised ads and the ultimate success or failure of those strategies.

Both candidates' campaigns provided the compilation of the advertisements run during the general election cycle. A total of seventeen spot ads were analyzed in this study, eleven (65 percent) for Sebelius and six (35 percent) for Shallenburger.[1] The VideoStyle framework as initially developed by Kaid and Davidson (1986) and advanced by Bystrom (1995) was employed in this content analysis (see chapter 2).

Overall, the VideoStyles constructed by the candidates indicate that Sebelius created the predominant image of an incumbent in a technically open race, strategically balancing both "feminine" and "masculine" issue discussion, character trait emphasis, strategic appeals, and nonverbal cues. Shallenburger predominantly employed the image of a challenger, utilizing both feminine and masculine issue discussion, trait emphasis, and appeals, but was not able to effectively demonstrate a balance; he appeared either too soft or too harsh and thus did not merge both images successfully. Although prior research suggests that many of the differences between female and male candidate VideoStyle emerge more directly from the election cycle than from the gender of the candidates (Bystrom 1995; Bystrom and Kaid 2002), this case study suggests that the context of the race and the candidate's constraints and strategies must also be examined in order to develop a more fully representative scenario. Each candidate's VideoStyle is examined more fully to illuminate these findings.

Sebelius' VideoStyle

Sebelius' predominant development of an incumbent style (as defined by Trent and Friedenberg 2000) in her televised advertising was apparent not only throughout her issue discussions, image trait discussions, and verbal appeals, but also in her nonverbal strategies. It is notable how closely Sebelius tied part of her dominant issue discussion to the incumbent strategy of emphasizing successful past performance (Trent and Friedenberg 2000), her most frequently discussed character trait (see Table 5.2). She discussed three particular issues most frequently, one of which was health care (see Table 5.1). Sebelius' frequent discussion of health care stemmed largely from her emphasis on her past performance as the state's insurance commissioner. One ad in particular offers such an example:

> As Insurance Commissioner she cracked down on HMOs that deny hospital stays to new mothers, helped senior citizens save more than $7 million on prescription drugs, and blocked an out-of-state takeover of Kansas Blue Cross/Blue Shield. Because she knows affordable health care is really about something bigger than just your health. Endorsed by doctors, nurses, patients, and families. Kathleen Sebelius. Governor.

TABLE 5.1 Most Frequently Discussed Issues in Candidate Spot Ads by Candidate

Sebelius Ads (n = 11)	Shallenburger Ads (n = 6)
1. Health care (36%)	1. Crime (50%)
Education (36%)	2. Taxes (33%)
Dissatisfaction with government (36%)	Education (33%)
2. Senior issues (18%)	Dissatisfaction with government (33%)
Crime (18%)	Other (33%)
Other (18%)	3. Economy (17%)
3. Taxes (9%)	Job growth (17%)
Drugs (9%)	Environment (17%)

Note: Percentages total more than 100% within each category due to multiple issues discussed per artifact.

TABLE 5.2 Most Frequently Discussed Character Traits in Candidate Spot Ads by Candidate

Sebelius Ads (n = 11)	Shallenburger Ads (n = 6)
1. Past performance (64%)	1. Action-oriented proponent (50%)
2. Toughness/strength (55%)	2. Past performance (33%)
Action-oriented proponent (55%)	Sensitivity/understanding (33%)
3. Aggressive/fighter (36%)	Being of the people/commonality (33%)
4. Being of the people/commonality (27%)	3. Honesty/integrity (17%)
5. Honesty/integrity (9%)	Toughness/strength (17%)
Cooperation with others (9%)	Cooperation with others (17%)
Leadership (9%)	Leadership (17%)
Sensitivity/understanding (9%)	
Trustworthy (9%)	

Note: Percentages total more than 100% within each category due to multiple traits discussed per artifact.

Sebelius also frequently discussed education, and despite her experience as the insurance commissioner and prior experience with health care issues, education became Sebelius' signature issue throughout the campaign. As one media article noted, Sebelius was able to pull many of her votes from moderate Republicans based on her education platform (Hanna 2002), and she reiterated the issue throughout many of her ads. In the conclusion of one ad, titled "Dedicated," Sebelius personally delivered the message, stating, "As governor, I'll always put our children and schools first." An important strategy that she used throughout this ad was to offer her proposals in the form of statements that, to the uninformed voter, could suggest she had already been successful in accomplishing these outcomes. A male voiceover announced:

TABLE 5.3 Appeals Most Frequently Used in Candidate Spot Ads by Candidate

Sebelius Ads (n = 11)	Shallenburger Ads (n = 6)
1. Emphasize own accomplishments (64%) Above the trenches (64%)	1. Address viewers as peers (50%) Attack record of the opponent (50%)
2. Use expert authorities, nonpolitical (36%)	2. Emphasize own accomplishments (33%) Take offensive position on the issues (33%)
3. Use personal tone (27%) Address viewers as peers (27%) Call for changes (27%) Use statistics (27%)	3. Call for change (17%) Reinforce/promote traditional values (17%) Use personal experience, anecdotes (17%)
4. Attack record of the opponent (18%) Attack opponent on personal qualities (18%)	Use expert authorities, nonpolitical (17%) Attack opponent on personal qualities (17%)
5. Be voice for the state (9%) Invite viewer participation, action (9%) Reinforce/promote traditional values (9%) Use personal experience, anecdotes (9%)	

Note: Percentages total more than 100% within each category due to multiple appeals per artifact.

Kathleen Sebelius. As governor, dedicated to our schools, lift teacher pay from fortieth in the nation, cut government waste to get more dollars into the classroom, and promote local control so parents and educators decide what's best for their schools.

In creating her incumbent VideoStyle, Sebelius also was effective at emphasizing her own accomplishments (see Table 5.3), doing so in 64 percent of her ads. Simultaneously, she was active in establishing an above-the-trenches posture (64 percent of ads), both of which are considered incumbent strategies (Trent and Friedenberg 2000). The fact that Sebelius had sailed through the primaries without an opponent and had been an effective fund-raiser allowed her to enter the general election with the funds to immediately begin her ad campaign. Her opponent, on the other hand, suffered a tough, negative primary that required much time on the air. Shallenburger's budget was almost depleted at the conclusion of the primary (Hanna 2002), and he did not reappear on the air until late September. Sebelius, therefore, had approximately two months to run an ad campaign that could focus on her candidacy alone. In those ads, Sebelius used appeals that placed her above the political fray while reinforcing her accomplishments, plans, and qualifications, as did the following ad, which began airing on September 10, 2002:

Announcer: Over the years she's earned our trust. Saying no to special interests, putting the people of Kansas first, respecting our tax dollars.

Sebelius: As insurance commissioner, department spending has been reduced 19 percent. As governor, I'll cut the waste with a top-to-bottom audit of state government.

Announcer: Kathleen Sebelius. Tough performance audits to streamline government and control spending. Discipline, commitment, trust. Kathleen Sebelius. Governor.

The nonverbal (see Table 5.5) and production images (see Table 5.6) presented in these ads aided in reinforcing Sebelius' developing incumbent image. Sebelius' dominant attire in her ads was formal (82 percent of her ads), and the setting of many of her ads was a work environment. The production technique of cinema verité underscored the scenes in 64 percent of these ads, encouraging the perception that the ads were providing a live shot of the candidate. Sebelius was often seen working alone at a desk with the capital dome just outside the window and an American flag at the edge of the frame, at a desk with people dressed in formal suits discussing paperwork with her, or at a conference table during a meeting; in each of these shots she was portrayed as doing the business of government. One ad that focused on crime developed this image through the combination of verbal and visual content. The announcer began, "Our safety, our security. Every day it's a governor's concern." As the announcer said "every day," the ad cut to a shot of Sebelius working at a desk in an office, implying that she was already doing the work of a governor and that these were already her concerns. Similar images used throughout her advertisements reinforced that she was above the political fray of a campaign—the ads did not show images of the campaign—and that she was focused on working for the people.

Though Sebelius predominantly created the image of an incumbent, she also incorporated some challenger strategies through the combination of issue discussion and trait emphasis. For instance, Sebelius was not hesitant to call for change. In one ad she proclaimed that "Kansas needs a fresh start, a new leader with a proven record of real change," and in yet another an announcer proclaimed, "Exactly the change Kansas needs. Kathleen Sebelius. Governor." Timing is important here, however, as both of these examples are from ads aired after Shallenburger began running ads in the general election. The other instance in which Sebelius used that particular challenger strategy was in the ad she ran on the evening of the primary election, in which an announcer referenced the Republican primary's negative advertising and stated, "We can do better."

TABLE 5.4 Attack, General, and Group Appeals Most Frequently Used in Candidate Spot Ads by Candidate

Sebelius Ads	Shallenburger Ads
Attack Appeals	
(n = 11)	(n = 6)
Negative attack present (46%)	Negative attack present (50%)
(n = 5)	(n = 3)
Dominant purpose:	
1. Attack past performance (40%)	1. Attack issue stands (67%)
Attack personal characteristics (40%)	2. Attack personal characteristics (33%)
2. Attack issue stands	
General Appeals	
(n = 11)	(n = 6)
Type of appeal	
1. Logical (91%)	1. Logical (100%)
2. Emotional (46%)	2. Emotional (67%)
3. Credibility (27%)	3. Credibility (33%)
Structure of appeal	
1. Inductive (73%)	1. Inductive (100%)
2. Deductive (27%)	
Dominant emphasis	
1. Issues (91%)	1. Issues (67%)
2. Image (9%)	2. Image (33%)

Note: Percentages total more than 100% within each category due to multiple mentions per artifact.

Throughout her advertising, Sebelius also emphasized that she was able and willing to make tough decisions with regard to the state's financial situation and that she would be action-oriented in addressing a number of issues. Ultimately, she frequently reminded voters that the state could do better, and suggested not just that she could do the right things for the state, but also that she actually was already doing so—and all without offering, or being required to offer, specific solutions.

In addition to the challenger strategy of calling for change, in 46 percent of her ads Sebelius issued an attack (see Table 5.4). More specifically, she was most likely to attack her opponent's past performance and characteristics (40 percent). Sebelius' most negative ad was delivered by a female elementary school teacher, who claimed that "[a]s Speaker of the House Tim Shallenburger failed to adequately fund education. . . . Tim Shallenburger has the wrong priorities to be governor." However, the other attacks in her advertisements—on either her opponent's record or his personal qualities—were combined with positive messages about Sebelius. Therefore, even when using a challenger strategy of attacking the opponent, she incorporated the incumbent strategy of emphasizing her own accomplishments.

Sebelius effectively balanced feminine and masculine strategies throughout her advertising campaign, a strategy research has found to be most successful if not imperative for female candidates (Banwart and Carlin 2001). Although she frequently discussed what have been considered feminine issues—health care, education, and senior citizens' issues—she did so within a framework of masculine traits and appeals. For example, when discussing health care, she would emphasize her past accomplishments as insurance commissioner and also her toughness and strength, such as when she "crack[ed] down" on HMOs and "block[ed] an out of state takeover of Blue Cross Blue Shield." In addition to portraying her tough or strong business image, Sebelius was able to incorporate images of being sensitive in similar discussions of her past accomplishments—patting a senior citizen's arm as he sat in a chair and she bent down to talk with him. When discussing education, she did so within the framework of taking strong, decisive stands, yet coupled the verbal message with a visual of a classroom and children at work, while Sebelius turns to the camera, smiles, and crosses her arms.

With regard to other appeals (see Table 5.4), Sebelius was consistent in combining both masculine and feminine appeals. For instance, she was most likely to use a masculine logical argument in her appeals (91 percent of ads) but structured her arguments inductively (73 percent), considered a feminine style strategy. She established eye contact (see Table 5.5) with her viewer, considered a feminine strategy, at least sometimes in most (55 percent) of her ads. She also used a compact or closed posture (82 percent), considered a feminine strategy.

Overall, Sebelius' advertisements were issue-oriented (91 percent), were announced by a male voice-over (82 percent), and consistently used the production effects of computer graphics (100 percent) and music (100 percent).

Shallenburger's VideoStyle

Shallenburger predominantly used the challenger style of campaigning in this race, although he was not effective in consistently developing a strategically balanced image. His use of a challenger style is apparent not only throughout his issue discussions, image trait discussions, and verbal appeals, but also throughout his nonverbal strategies.

The verbal content of Shallenburger's ads most consistently employed the challenger strategy of attacking the opponent's record (Trent and Friedenberg 2000), which occurred in 50 percent of his advertisements (see Table 5.3). The use of this strategy also was closely related to his frequent discussion of the issue of crime (50 percent). The discussion of this

TABLE 5.5 Nonverbal Strategies Most Frequently Used in Candidate Spot Ads by Candidate

	Sebelius Ads (n = 11)		Shallenburger Ads (n = 6)	
Dominant Speaker				
Candidate	1	(9%)	2	(33%)
Anonymous announcer	9	(82%)	3	(50%)
Spouse or family member	—	—	1	(17%)
Citizen(s)/constituent(s)	1	(9%)	—	—
Sex of Dominant Speaker				
Male	9	(82%)	2	(33%)
Female	2	(18%)	4	(67%)
Candidate Dress (Dominant)				
Formal	9	(82%)	—	—
Casual	—	—	4	(67%)
Not applicable/candidate not present	2	(18%)	2	(33%)
Eye Contact				
Never	2	(18%)	2	(33%)
Sometimes	6	(55%)	2	(33%)
Always	1	(9%)	—	—
Not applicable/candidate not present	2	(18%)	2	(33%)
Facial Expression				
Smiling	1	(9%)	3	(50%)
Attentive/serious	8	(73%)	1	(17%)
Not applicable	2	(18%)	2	(33%)
Candidate Posture				
Compact/closed	9	(82%)	4	(67%)
Not applicable/candidate not present	2	(18%)	2	(33%)

Note: Percentages total more than 100% within each category due to multiple mentions per artifact.

issue was not framed as a platform issue, however, but rather as an attack on his opponent's past voting record as a member of the Kansas House of Representatives. For example, one ad stated: "She voted for all kinds of taxes and against the tough crime laws that protect our kids." It is of interest that most of these attacks were focused on reducing child-related crime, such as establishing drug-free school zones, making the sexual predator list

TABLE 5.6 Production Strategies Most Frequently Used in Candidate Spot Ads by Candidate

	Sebelius Ads (n = 11)		Shallenburger Ads (n = 6)	
Ad Format				
Documentary	—	—	1	(17%)
Issue statement	7	(64%)	2	(33%)
Opposition-focused	3	(27%)	3	(50%)
Other	1	(9%)	—	—
Production Technique				
Cinema verité	7	(64%)	4	(67%)
Slides	—	—	1	(17%)
Candidate head-on	1	(9%)	—	—
Other head-on	1	(9%)	1	(17%)
Combination	2	(18%)	—	—
Use of Special Effects				
Computer graphics/titles	11	(100%)	6	(100%)
Slow motion	3	(27%)	5	(83%)
Superimpositions	2	(18%)	—	—
Use of stills	2	(18%)	1	(17%)
Music	11	(100%)	6	(100%)
Focus	—	—	1	(17%)
Lighting	—	—	1	(17%)
Other	1	(9%)	—	—

Note: Percentages total more than 100% within each category due to multiple mentions per artifact.

public, and registering first-time child molesters—all of which were designed to increase the salience of the attack through emotional appeals.

As further evidence of his use of a challenger style, Shallenburger used the character trait of being action-oriented (Trent and Friedenberg 2000) in his focus on taxes, which ultimately became his signature issue in the campaign. He also addressed the viewers as peers when discussing this issue, a feminine style strategy. With regard to taxes, he presented the problem but offered only vague solutions that addressed the viewers as peers ("we"), thus incorporating a personal tone. For example, in one ad Shallenburger offered, "We will fund schools, we can grow the economy and create new jobs. It just takes the courage to say you're not going to raise taxes and find a better way."

Although education was discussed as frequently as taxes (33 percent; see Table 5.1), this particular issue was also discussed within the context of taxes. For instance, Shallenburger created one entire ad focused on education. However, the ad began with Shallenburger stating, "If we can find a better way to spend education tax dollars . . ."; an announcer later stated, "Tim Shallenburger will find better ways to fund schools. He'll cut waste and get tax dollars into the classroom."

When examining Shallenburger's use of feminine and masculine strategies, it becomes evident that he, too, combined the use of both types throughout his verbal and nonverbal content, although his ads incorporated more of a feminine style. Although he frequently used the incumbent traits of being action-oriented (50 percent) and emphasizing past performance (33 percent), many of his other frequently emphasized traits were traditionally feminine (see Table 5.2)—sensitivity and understanding (33 percent), being of the people and commonality (33 percent), honesty and integrity (17 percent), and cooperation with others (17 percent). The two additional traits frequently discussed were traditionally masculine traits, toughness and strength (17 percent) and leadership (17 percent), although these were present in only one ad. Further, his most frequently employed appeal, addressing viewers as peers, is a strategy of feminine style (Campbell 1989), as is his use of personal experience and anecdotes (17 percent) and expert authorities (17 percent), which first occurred in an ad that featured his wife talking about her husband's background and reason for entering politics.

Shallenburger employed logical appeals most frequently (100 percent) in his advertising (see Table 5.4) but also included emotional appeals in four of six ads (67 percent). He consistently structured his appeals inductively (100 percent) and typically used a female announcer as the dominant speaker in his ads (67 percent). Shallenburger did dress casually in all of the ads in which he was present (67 percent), which is typical of male candidate VideoStyle, but displayed a compact and closed posture (67 percent), considered feminine nonverbal communication.

Overall, Shallenburger most frequently mixed traditionally feminine strategies and traits with the challenger strategy of attacking the opponent throughout his advertising. Shallenburger began his ad campaign with two positive ads focusing on his platform and character traits. In these ads, he used the challenger strategy of being an action-oriented proponent combined with an incumbent style of discussing past performance that used feminine style strategies in proposing solutions to issues typically considered masculine. To further illustrate the difference in candidate presentation, in her ads Sebelius incorporated visuals depicting her in the role of governor while discussing her past accomplishments and vague plans for the future, whereas Shallenburger's ads portrayed him strictly as a candidate—at a rally, visiting people in the community, and giving speeches—even when discussing his past accomplishments.

Following these two initial ads, Shallenburger ran two negative ads. In these ads, he attacked his opponent on an issue seemingly unrelated to the campaign and issues of concern to voters (Moon 2002), Sebelius' votes on crime issues; regardless, this became the most discussed issue in his advertisements (50 percent; see Table 5.1). The fifth ad of the campaign featured Shallenburger's wife discussing why he entered politics and his caring nature. The ad dramatized his entrance into politics by showing his care and concern for children and indicated that concern for the people in his community served as the impetus for his entrance into politics. The final ad of his campaign was another completely negative ad, directly attacking a vaguely presented record of Sebelius' stands on crime and education. Ultimately, Shallenburger's lack of money precluded him from thoroughly developing a solid VideoStyle. Instead, as he was behind in the polls, Shallenburger devoted half of his advertising content to attacks and used a combination of predominantly challenger strategies and feminine traits. Doing so was an inconsistency that could easily have been perceived as too harsh and too soft. Certainly the use of a feminine style by male candidates is not unheard of (Campbell 1989); in fact, scholars argue that television requires more of this approach (Jamieson 1988). However, Shallenburger's negative advertising was not balanced by sufficient images of a positive, strong candidate who was willing to fight for his constituents as much as he was willing to fight with his opponent.

Conclusions

Ultimately, this study provides an in-depth analysis of how a female candidate ran a strategically successful ad campaign in a state assumed to inherently disadvantage her from a party perspective and from an issues perspective. It further highlights the importance of fund-raising, the ability to be on the air establishing a controlled image prior to one's opponent airing a contradictory ad campaign, the value of consistency, and the importance of establishing legitimacy.

6

Voter Reactions to Candidate VideoStyle

Descriptions of the styles of communication used by candidates in their televised campaign messages, or VideoStyles, have shown the differences and similarities in how male and female candidates present themselves to voters. In this chapter, the emphasis is on comparing how male and female voters respond to candidate presentations. The analysis provides two different approaches: (1) how male and female voters respond to male presidential candidate communications and (2) how male and female voters respond to female and male U.S. Senate and gubernatorial candidates.

The Gender Gap in Voter Reactions to Candidate Communications

The gender gap in voting for presidential candidates was described in chapter 1. This well-known phenomenon has been documented in voting behavior research at the presidential level and in many elections for statewide offices. Several reasons have been developed to explain these differences, including (1) different political knowledge levels of men and women voters, (2) emphasis by women voters on candidates' personality factors, (3) differences in issue concerns among men and women, (4) differing reactions of men and women to media messages, and (5) differences in the appeal of feminine and masculine communication styles (Banwart and Kaid 2003). The most important of these elements for the research presented in this chapter is the possibility that men and women voters react differently to media messages.

Gender Differences in Reactions to Political Media Messages

Responses to television advertising, in particular, have been considered a possible factor in gender candidate preferences because of potential differences in how men and women respond to aural and visual messages. With the dominance of television advertising in major campaigns today and the significant impact of these ads on voter information levels, attitudes toward candidates, and voting decisions (Kaid 1999), such differences between female and male voters in their responses should be considered important.

There is some evidence that suggests that men and women respond differently to this form of mediated message transmission. Studies on the effects of political advertising have found gender differences in the reactions to negative spots. For instance, women are more likely to blame the sponsor than the target of attack messages (Garramone 1984; Kern and Just 1997). Analyzing the formation of candidate images in this situation, Kern and Just (1997) attributed gender differences in image constructions to the different life experiences of women and men. In a multicountry comparison, Kaid and Holtz-Bacha (2000) concluded that women reacted differently than men to political advertising for male leaders.

For instance, women voters rated Bill Clinton (United States 1996) and Tony Blair (Britain 1997) much higher than they rated their opponents, Bob Dole and John Major. Overall, the gender comparisons across several countries suggested that "female voters are more likely to be affected by exposure to political spots; and, when they are, the spots are more likely to result in higher positive evaluations for the candidates than is true for male voters" (Kaid 1997: 20–21).

Beyond the presidential level, experiments conducted by Hitchon and Chang (1995) have documented that commercials for male and female candidates are processed differently by receivers. Ads for women candidates elicited greater recall of family and personal appearance, while recall was higher for men's ads when the content was political campaigning situations (Hitchon and Chang 1995). Men's negative ads against women elicited more emotional and negative responses than women's negative ads against men (Hitchon and Chang 1995). For women, neutral ads, as opposed to positive or negative ones, elicit more favorable responses from voters and are viewed as more socially desirable (Hitchon, Chang, and Harris 1997).

It is not entirely clear what it is about television advertising that gives male candidates an advantage with female voters, but some have suggested that women are more influenced by the visual nature and drama of the television medium (Banwart and Kaid 2003). Others attribute the difference in reactions to the fact that some issues in the content of political spots appeal to women more than men. Earlier research on the 1996 campaign, for instance, has noted the prominent use of women in Clinton's 1996 ad campaign as an invitation to identify with the issues, images, and the presidential candidate in the ad (Jamieson, Falk, and Sherr 1999). Banwart and Kaid (2003) have documented that Clinton sought to identify with women in his ads in both 1992 and 1996.

Other have suggested that the impact of political television on women is due to the tendency of women to react more emotionally than men and to focus more on candidate personality and image than on issues. Generalizations of early research on women's political orientations and behavior conceived women to be more candidate-oriented and thus more irrational than men in their assessments of presidential candidates (Hayes and McAllister 1997). In a recent international study comparing the interaction of gender and the images of party leaders in Australia, Britain, and the United States, the researchers concluded that although "there are comparatively few gender differences in how each of the leaders are viewed by the electorate," men and women "regard the leaders from different perspectives and see gender-specific qualities in them" (Hayes and McAllister 1997: 10, 21). In addition, they found that in Australia and in the United States, these different perspectives led to different election outcomes. Such work suggests that in electoral decision making, women are more likely to focus their attention on specific personal or image qualities of candidates and that these differences in focus may account for gender differences in voting behavior.

Responses of Male and Female Voters to Presidential VideoStyles

This chapter provides information on the responses of male and female voters to presidential candidate advertising in the 1996 and 2000 presidential campaigns. In each case, the research reports the results of experimental studies in which groups of voters were exposed to political television ads for each of the two presidential candidates in the general election. The attitudes of these voters were measured before and after the exposure to determine if viewing the television advertisements resulted in any differences in response to the candidates.

Voter Samples and Advertising Samples

In 1996, the sample of voters consisted of a total of 620 students from nineteen different universities through the United States.[1] These subjects were 47 percent male and 53 percent female; 33 percent were Democrats, 41 percent were Republicans, and 26 percent were independent or other. They viewed the sample spots in experiments on October 30–31, 1996. Each session proceeded identically, with basically the same questionnaires. The spots used in these 1996 experimental sessions contained four spots for each candidate (two negative and two positive each for Bill Clinton and Bob Dole), with the order alternated between candidates.[2]

The same procedures were used for the 2000 presidential campaign. Respondents viewed sets of spots produced by the Al Gore and George W. Bush campaigns (three negative spots and one positive spot for each candidate), with the order alternated.[3] These experimental sessions took place between November 1 and 3, 2000, just preceding election day on November 7. The respondents came from twenty-six different universities located throughout the United States, representing all regions and parts of the country.[4] A total of 906 respondents (39 percent male, 61 percent female; 36 percent Democrats, 39 percent Republicans, 25 percent independent or other) participated in the experimental sessions. Most of the participants were students; the mean age of the sample was twenty-one. However, this 2000 sample included some adults who participated in the study, and so the ages of participants in the sample ranged from eighteen to sixty; the mean number of years of education was fourteen.

Measurement of Effects

As mentioned above, respondents filled out a pretest questionnaire before viewing the spots, were shown a series of ads, and then filled out a posttest measure. The effect of the spots on images of Dole and Clinton in 1996 and Bush and Gore in 2000 were assessed in all sets of experiments with a series of twelve semantic differential scales used in the pre- and posttest questionnaires. These twelve adjective pairs were summed to provide an overall mean score evaluation of the candidate's image as well as analyzed individually through factor analysis.[5] These scales have been developed over a period of many years and are used frequently to measure candidate image with high reliability (Kaid 1995). The reliability (Cronbach's alpha) for these scales as used here on Clinton and Dole in 1996 ranged from 0.82 to 0.89; in 2000 the reliabilities for these scales on Bush and Gore were 0.65/0.85 in the pretest/posttest for Gore and 0.80/0.83 in the pretest/posttest for Bush.

Reactions to the candidates were also assessed by a "feeling thermometer" scale used by the National Election Studies to measure candidate favorability (Rosenstone, Kender, Miller, and National Election Studies 1997). The thermometer asks the respondent to place each candidate on a scale from 0 (cool) to 100 (warm). A cynicism scale that summed eight items used to determine the level of trust or confidence in government was also employed in this analysis.[6] The scale included efficacy items such as "Whether I vote or not has no influence on what politicians do" and distrust items such as "One cannot always trust what politicians say." Respondents were asked to agree or disagree on a five-point scale. These items were adapted from earlier studies using similar scales (Kaid, McKinney, and Tedesco 2000; Rosenstone et al. 1997) and achieved acceptable Cronbach's alpha levels for reliability.

Respondents also were asked to express the extent of their emotional responses to the candidates after viewing the spots. On these scales, the respondents marked whether, after viewing the spots for each candidate, they felt optimistic, concerned, angry, and other emotions.

Differences in Male and Female Voter Responses to Candidate Advertising in 1996

Differences in Image Ratings. The responses of male and female voters to the televised political advertising of both Clinton and Dole in 1996 are clear and consistent. Table 6.1 reports the before and after scores for both sexes on a summary image scale (the mean of the twelve semantic differential scales) and on the feeling thermometer (ranging from 0 to 100). Before watching the ads in the experiments reported here, female voters rated Clinton significantly higher than male voters on both image measures. The opposite seemed to be true for Dole. Table 6.1 shows that male voters rated Dole more positively than female voters both before and after viewing the televised spots. The only exception to the pattern was the finding that male and female voters rated Dole similarly on the pretest feeling thermometer. After viewing the spots, however, female voters became much more negative toward Dole, whereas male voters remained about the same in their ratings.

These data also indicate some interesting differences in the individual qualities of the candidates affected by the exposure to television advertising. These differences, as shown in Table 6.2, are much greater for Clinton than for Dole. For instance, women voters tended to perceive Clinton as significantly more qualified, more sophisticated, more honest, more sincere, and more active than did male voters. On the other hand, male voters saw Dole as more qualified, more believable, and more attractive.

TABLE 6.1 Images of Candidates before and after Viewing Political Spots 1996 and 2000

1996	Pre-Dole	Post-Dole	Pre-Clinton	Post-Clinton
Summary Image Scales				
Male (n = 294)	4.41	4.31	4.44	4.49
Female (n = 326)	4.23*	4.09*	4.58*	4.67*
Feeling Thermometer				
Male (n = 294)	50.4	49.0	47.6	46.8
Female (n = 326)	50.7	43.0*	52.0*	51.1*
2000	**Pre-Bush**	**Post-Bush**	**Pre-Gore**	**Post-Gore**
Summary Image Scales				
Male (n = 353)	4.67	4.70	4.52	4.48
Female (n = 553)	4.63	4.72	4.69*	4.78*
Feeling Thermometer				
Male (n = 353)	54.3	56.0	44.6	45.5
Female (n = 553)	52.9	54.1	51.4*	52.1*

* T-test indicates difference between male and female voters is significant at $p \leq .05$.

TABLE 6.2 Image Characteristics of Presidential Candidates before and after Viewing Ads

	\multicolumn{4}{c	}{1996}	\multicolumn{4}{c}{2000}
	\multicolumn{2}{c}{Dole}	\multicolumn{2}{c	}{Clinton}	\multicolumn{2}{c}{Bush}	\multicolumn{2}{c}{Gore}
	Pre	Post	Pre	Post	Pre	Post	Pre	Post
Qualified								
Male	5.31	5.21	4.74	4.72	4.56	4.93	4.36	5.18
Female	4.93*	4.76	5.03*	5.10*	4.82	4.80	5.44	5.49*
Sophisticated								
Male	4.85	4.68	4.67	4.62	4.53	4.61	5.13	4.92
Female	4.78	4.47*	4.87*	4.93*	4.73*	4.86*	5.03	5.17*
Honest								
Male	4.78	4.31	3.29	3.38	4.57	4.58	3.92	3.87
Female	4.44*	3.89*	3.64*	3.72*	4.42	4.46	3.98	4.49*
Believable								
Male	4.03	3.81	3.61	3.44	4.38	4.45	4.05	3.93
Female	3.75*	3.63*	3.87	3.57	4.30	4.57	4.18	4.24*
Successful								
Male	5.19	5.11	4.87	5.03	5.32	5.40	5.33	5.31
Female	5.09	4.93	4.93*	5.11	5.30	5.33	5.37	5.40
Attractive								
Male	3.39	3.49	3.72	3.77	4.28	4.17	4.34	3.97
Female	3.13*	3.16*	3.75	3.86	4.15	4.43*	4.26	4.27*
Friendly								
Male	4.19	4.05	5.41	5.25	5.30	5.20	4.24	4.55
Female	4.21	3.92	5.52	5.43*	5.41	5.34	4.82*	4.79*
Sincere								
Male	4.59	4.33	4.06	4.15	4.84	4.71	3.91	4.15
Female	4.39	3.97*	4.32*	4.37*	4.74	4.68	4.25	4.42*
Calm								
Male	3.63	3.73	3.85	3.90	3.93	4.16	6.02	3.99
Female	3.57	3.67	3.98	3.95	4.03	4.28	4.11	3.97
Aggressive								
Male	4.02	4.20	3.85	3.97	4.76	4.59	5.00	4.67
Female	3.88	4.08	3.86	4.18*	4.45*	4.49	4.85*	5.03*
Strong								
Male	4.10	4.02	3.71	3.94	4.66	4.67	5.64	4.49
Female	3.97	3.95	4.02*	4.12	4.50	4.55	4.74*	4.87*
Active								
Male	4.83	4.76	4.69	4.83	4.97	4.99	4.86	4.84
Female	4.66	4.63	4.98*	5.05*	4.97	5.01	5.23*	5.31*

* T-test indicates difference between male and female voters is significant at $p \leq .05$.

TABLE 6.3 Differences in Emotional Response Generated by Exposure to Presidential Ads

	1996		2000	
	Dole	Clinton	Bush	Gore
Optimistic				
Male	1.67	1.76	1.97	1.81
Female	1.59*	1.85	1.96	1.93*
Confident				
Male	1.75	1.77	2.02	1.87
Female	1.57*	1.85	1.98	1.93
Anxious				
Male	1.75	1.72	1.69	1.71
Female	1.88*	1.76	1.79*	1.74
Excited				
Male	1.63	1.59	1.71	1.54
Female	1.47*	1.62	1.68	1.65*
Secure				
Male	1.61	1.65	1.89	1.71
Female	1.47*	1.78*	1.97	1.83*
Fearful				
Male	1.73	1.78	1.59	1.68
Female	1.92*	1.72	1.62	1.58*
Bored				
Male	1.86	1.72	1.71	1.83
Female	1.79	1.56*	1.61*	1.67*
Patriotic				
Male	1.69	1.55	1.85	1.67
Female	1.59*	1.60	1.80	1.66
Concerned				
Male	2.15	2.14	1.99	2.07
Female	2.39*	2.16	2.07	1.99*
Angry				
Male	1.85	1.70	1.52	1.59
Female	1.96*	1.82	1.47	1.48*

* T-test indicates difference between male and female voters is significant at $p \leq .05$.

Differences in Emotional Responses. Given the suggestions by some observers that women voters may react more emotionally to candidates than male voters do, the experimental sessions also measured the voters' self-reported emotions generated by their exposure to the candidates' political advertising. After the viewing of spots for both candidates, voters were asked to indicate how much (a lot, a little, or not at all) they felt specific emotions had been engaged by each candidate's television spots. As shown in Table 6.3, there are several differences in men's and women's emotional reactions to the two candidates.

For female voters, exposure to the Dole spots made them feel significantly less optimistic, less confident, more anxious, more excited, less secure, more fearful, more concerned, and more angry than male voters felt after viewing the spots. Surprisingly, given Dole's war record, women viewers even felt less patriotic after viewing the spots. On the other hand, female voters felt that Clinton's spots had generated significantly more feelings of security and less boredom.

Differences in Levels of Cynicism. Many earlier studies of political advertising have suggested that exposure to advertising, particularly negative advertising, in campaigns may make voters more cynical and reduce feelings of political efficacy (Ansolabehere and Iyengar 1995; Ansolabehere, Iyengar, and Simon 1999; Ansolabehere, Iyengar, Simon, and Valentino 1994; Kaid, McKinney, and Tedesco 2000; Lemert, Wanta, and Lee 1999). Other studies have contested these predictions (Finkel and Geer 1998; Freedman and Goldstein 1999; Garramone, Atkin, Pinkleton, and Cole 1990; Kahn and Kenney 1999; Kaid 2002; Martinez and Delegal 1990; Pinkleton 1998; Pinkleton, Um, and Austin 2002; Schenck-Hamlin, Procter, and Rumsey 2000; Vavreck 2000). However, there have been no clear determinations of whether these cynicism or trust effects differ between male and female voters after exposure to political advertising messages. Table 6.4, in fact, suggests that there are very few differences in political cynicism attributable to gender.

In 1996, male voters seemed to have a significantly lower level of political efficacy, questioning whether their votes really made a difference. Female voters were less likely to think that their votes would not matter. However, female voters were significantly more inclined to agree that government is too complicated to understand and to feel that politicians could not be trusted to do the right thing.

Differences in Male and Female Voter Responses to Candidate Advertising in 2000

Differences in Image Ratings. The reactions to political advertising of the presidential candidates in 2000 was somewhat different than in 1996. As Table 6.1 shows, there were no significant differences between male and female respondents as a result of viewing George W. Bush's television ads. This was true both on the semantic differential scale measure of candidate image and on the feeling thermometer that rated candidate warmth.

Al Gore, on the other hand, was able to achieve some positive effects with his spots as perceived by female voters. Female voters rated Gore much higher than male voters in both the before and after testing sessions.

TABLE 6.4 Differences in Male and Female Levels of Political Cynicism after Viewing Political Ads, 1996 and 2000

	1996 Male	1996 Female	2000 Male	2000 Female
1. Whether I vote or not has no influence on what politicians do.	2.88	2.58*	2.58	2.36*
2. One never really knows what politicians think.	3.83	3.88	3.51	3.61
3. People like me don't have any say about what the government does.	2.58	2.49	2.37	2.11*
4. Sometimes politics and government seem so complicated that a person like me can't really understand what's going on.	2.87	3.12*	2.51	2.64
5. One can be confident that politicians will always do the right thing.[a]	4.19	4.31*	2.05	2.07
6. Politicians often quickly forget their election promises after a political campaign is over.	3.94	3.94	3.52	3.52
7. Politicians are more interested in power than in what the people think.	3.50	3.50	3.22	3.14
8. One cannot always trust what politicians say.	4.05	4.10	3.80	3.78

Note: Responses measured from 5, strongly agree, to 1, strongly disagree.
[a] The direction was reversed when scored, so all items go from 1, low level of cynicism, to 5, high level of cynicism.
* T-test indicates difference between male and female voters is significant at $p \leq .05$.

This was consistently true for both the semantic differential scale measure and for the feeling thermometer. Overall, then, women voters were more likely to be affected by the visual portrayals in Gore's spots.

However, there are some differences shown in Table 6.2 in male and female reactions to both candidates in regard to individual characteristics conveyed in the spots. For instance, after viewing the spots, female voters found Gore to be much more qualified than male voters. Compared to men, women also found Gore to be more sophisticated, more honest, more believable, more attractive, more friendly, more sincere, more aggressive, stronger, and more active. Thus, on almost every characteristic, viewing the spots had a positive effect for Gore. There are fewer differences for George W. Bush, but Table 6.2 does show that female voters found Bush more sophisticated than did male voters, in both the pretest and the posttest. After watching the spots, women also found Bush significantly more attractive than did male viewers.

Differences in Emotional Reactions. Like the 1996 television ads, the 2000 ads generated some significantly different emotions between male and female viewers. For instance, women found that, compared to men, Gore's ads made them significantly more optimistic, more excited, more secure, less fearful, less bored, less concerned, and less angry. The differences were less marked for Bush's ads. Women voters were significantly less anxious and less bored than men after viewing the spots, but there were no other significant differences in the emotions measured.

Differences in Levels of Cynicism. The trends in 2000 for levels of political trust and cynicism are also similar to those in 1996. Table 6.4 demonstrates that female voters are less likely to feel that their votes do not count or that they "don't have much say in government." No other differences between the sexes were apparent in 2000.

Voter Responses to VideoStyles of Male and Female Candidates

The analysis of reactions to presidential advertising offers some clear differences in how male and female voters react to presidential candidate VideoStyle but does not provide the opportunity to compare gendered reactions to male and female candidates. Of course, this is true because no female candidate has been able to secure the nomination of a major party in the United States. The discussion of the VideoStyles of male and female candidates at other electoral levels in the earlier chapters of this book suggests some similarities and some differences. One of the most interesting comparisons continues to be in the use of negative advertising as part of a candidate's VideoStyle. As women candidates often find themselves in the role of challenger, it has been impossible for them to avoid the use of negative advertising. But how do voters respond to negative advertising VideoStyles of male versus female candidates as well as to positive and mixed-message VideoStyles?

Experiments Exploring Voter Responses to Male and Female VideoStyles

To analyze the effects that advertising can have on how voters perceive male and female candidates, we review the findings from two studies examining gendered reactions to ads from mixed-gender races. The first study consisted of two experiments conducted in 1990 and 2000 that measured the difference in responses to negative ads used by U.S. Senate and gubernatorial candidates who ran for office between 1986 and 1996 (Banwart and Carlin 2001). In addition, a study was conducted to measure the gendered responses to positive, negative, and mixed-message campaign strategies of female and male U.S. Senate candidates in 2000 (Bystrom 2003).

In the Banwart and Carlin (2001) study, respondents were university students, 153 in 1990 and 118 in 2000, who were enrolled in large midwestern and southwestern universities. For this study, spot ads for the selected male/female races were obtained from the University of Oklahoma's Political Commercial Archive, which holds the largest collection of broadcast political commercials in the world (Kaid, Haynes, and Rand 1996). In the 1990 study, the races selected included the 1986 Missouri

U.S. Senate race between Harriett Woods and Christopher S. "Kit" Bond, the 1986 Florida U.S. Senate race between Robert Graham and Paula Hawkins, and the 1990 Texas Democratic gubernatorial primary race between Ann Richards and Jim Mattox. For the 2000 study, the races selected were the 1996 Kansas U.S. Senate race between Sam Brownback and Jill Docking, the 1996 New Hampshire gubernatorial race between Jeanne Shaheen and Ovide Lamontagne, and the 1994 Maine U.S. Senate race between Tom Andrews and Olympia Snowe. Spot ads with negative or comparative messages were first identified and then were randomly selected to compile six spot ads per race, three for each candidate.

In Bystrom's 2003 study, the participants consisted of 244 students enrolled in two courses—American government and advertising—at a large midwestern university in the fall 2002 semester. Television commercials from the female and male candidates running against each other for the U.S. Senate and governor in 2000 were obtained from "The Hotline," a political news and information subscription service offered by the *National Journal*. From the 168 ads obtained, ads from three races were selected for this study. In selecting the ads, care was taken to ensure that the commercials were similar in production quality and featured candidates not likely to be familiar to the participants.

Selected for Bystrom's 2003 study were the U.S. Senate races between Maria Cantwell and Slade Gorton of Washington and Debbie Stabenow and Spencer Abraham of Michigan and the gubernatorial race between Jeanne Shaheen and Gordon Humphrey of New Hampshire. Six television commercials—three for each candidate—were selected for each race.

Additionally, the ads selected were designed to explore reactions to certain communication styles and strategies and to mimic the course of an actual campaign. Four of the six ads selected from the Cantwell-Gorton race were positive messages, with a comparative ad from each campaign—Gorton's comparing the candidates on several issue stances and Cantwell's comparing her positive strategy with her opponent's attacks. The opening ads from both the Shaheen and Humphrey campaigns were positive, followed by two negative ads from each campaign—one using actual constituents to attack the opponent, the other using an anonymous announcer to make the attack. Ads chosen from the Stabenow-Abraham race included one positive ad from each campaign and two ads from each campaign that used mixed messages, either through comparison or through a blend of positive and negative themes in the same spot. To approximate an actual campaign, the first ad shown for each candidate summarized her or his background, image characteristics, and/or campaign themes. The second ad for each candidate focused on a campaign issue. The third ad for each candidate called for viewers' votes.

In these studies, respondents filled out pretest questionnaires with demographic information and were asked to evaluate the importance placed on the following variables when voting: issues, candidate's image, candidate's competency, candidate's qualifications, and candidate's gender. After viewing the spot ads from each respective race, the respondents then filled out ratings of each candidate on a semantic differential scale that contained ten items in the Banwart and Carlin (2001) study[7] and thirteen items in the Bystrom (2003) study,[8] and indicated which of the candidates they would vote for in each race.

Characteristics selected for the semantic differential scales were drawn from prior research on candidate image creation and perceptions of female candidates (Benze and Declercq 1985; Kaid et al. 1984; Wadsworth et al. 1987). Of the characteristics used in these studies, seven—qualifications, competency, assertiveness, aggressiveness, experience, activeness, and leadership—have been shown to be associated more with men, and eight qualities—honesty, believability, fairness, attractiveness, caring, sincerity, positiveness, and being personal—have been found to be more associated with women (Alexander and Andersen 1993; Huddy and Terkildsen 1993; Koch 1999; Leeper 1991; Rosenwasser and Dean 1989).

Comparing Voter Evaluations of Male and Female Candidate VideoStyles

In the 1990 study of viewer reactions to negative commercials used by female and male candidates from 1986 to 1990 (Banwart and Carlin 2001), the male candidate was consistently rated higher than the female candidate on most characteristics measured in the first two races, as shown in Table 6.5, but a directly opposite reaction occurred in the third race. In the first example (Harriet Woods versus Kit Bond, 1986 U.S. Senate, Missouri), the male candidate rated higher than the female candidate on all characteristics, including the more feminine traits of being caring, fair, and honest. In this series of spot ads, the male candidate used two strongly negative ads and was associated with one of the ads both verbally and visually. However, the male candidate also used images that emphasized his softer side by showing the candidate fishing with his son, visiting with the public, and hugging his wife and son, while also verbally and visually illustrating and reinforcing his leadership and experience.

In the second race (Bob Graham versus Paula Hawkins, 1986 U.S. Senate, Florida), the female candidate received slightly (but not significantly) better ratings than the male candidate on stereotypically feminine characteristics such as caring, fairness, and positiveness and was rated significantly higher on the characteristic of being personal. The female candidate used a one-on-one appeal that arguably influenced her caring and personal ratings. But, overall, the ratings were in favor of the male candidate, as was the subjects' vote choice.

The final example in the 1990 study was quite different. On all ten characteristics, the female candidate was rated significantly higher than the male candidate (see Table 6.5). This was a 1990 gubernatorial primary race

TABLE 6.5 Overall Subject Perception of Female and Male Candidates (Banwart & Carlin, 2001)

	Candidate					
	Race 1		Race 2		Race 3	
1990	Female	Male	Female	Male	Female	Male
Assertive	3.11	3.96*	3.50	4.03*	4.16	3.56*
Competent	2.99	3.83*	3.37	3.97*	3.71	3.01*
Experienced	2.76	4.26*	3.91	4.04	3.87	3.19*
Honest	2.97	3.41*	3.00	3.33*	2.99	2.12*
Caring	3.57	3.63	3.65	3.55	3.42	3.05*
Fair	3.07	3.37*	3.29	3.27	3.21	2.72*
Aggressive	2.99	3.99*	3.34	4.02*	4.17	3.65*
Strong leadership	2.81	3.91*	3.18	3.84*	3.76	3.01*
Positive	2.94	3.50*	3.43	3.35	3.14	2.56*
Personal	3.54	3.61	3.76	3.33*	3.41	2.83*
2000						
Assertive	4.04	3.87	4.03	3.62*	3.75	3.42*
Competent	3.60	3.81*	3.88	3.42*	3.64	3.19*
Experienced	3.22	4.04*	3.75	3.37*	4.26	3.04*
Honest	3.10	3.18	3.40	3.09*	3.15	2.86*
Caring	3.54	3.66	3.72	3.11*	3.24	3.03*
Fair	3.31	3.36	3.60	3.15*	3.14	3.07
Aggressive	3.91	3.69	3.94	3.57*	3.65	3.61
Strong leadership	3.42	3.66*	3.84	3.26*	3.59	3.10*
Positive	3.00	3.32*	3.62	2.70*	2.92	2.73
Personal	3.33	3.74*	3.78	2.86*	3.14	2.81*

* T-test indicates difference between male and female voters is significant at $p \leq .05$.

(Jim Mattox versus Ann Richards, governor, Texas) with more direct and personal attacks versus attacks on the opponent's record. In particular, the male candidate was directly accusatory and personal in his attacks on the female candidate. In her response, the female candidate was also accusatory toward the male candidate, but in a humorous manner that turned his efforts against him. For instance, in one of the female candidate's ads, the background featured a picture of the female candidate holding her granddaughter with an animated depiction of the male candidate throwing mud at the photo. At the conclusion of the ad, the mud was dumped back on the male candidate. The success of such an approach, although still couched in negative messages about her opponent, was illustrated not only in her higher character trait ratings but also in the subjects' vote choice in favor of the female candidate.

The three test races studied in 2000 from the 1994 and 1996 campaigns illustrate that the female candidates using attacks were able to compete much more evenly with their male opponents on the qualities measured. In the first example studied in 2000 (Sam Brownback versus Jill Docking, 1996 U.S. Senate, Kansas), the candidates were rated more similarly than in any other race, with the male candidate rated significantly higher on the dimensions of competency and experience (masculine traits) and positiveness and being personal (feminine traits) (see Table 6.5). Notably, the male candidate also used more comparative ads than the female candidate and thus had more of an opportunity to soften the blow and offer a positive alternative to the negative message used against his opponent. The study's subjects rewarded his efforts not only in higher character trait ratings but also in their vote choice.

In the second example studied in 2000 (Jeanne Shaheen versus Ovide Lamontagne, 1996 governor, New Hampshire), the female candidate was rated significantly higher than the male candidate on all ten characteristics, as shown in Table 6.5. Further, the female candidate received a majority of the respondents' votes (70 percent). This similarity to the success of the female candidate in 1990 in a gubernatorial race deserves future inquiry and analysis.

The third race used in the 2000 study was between Tom Andrews and Olympia Snowe (1994 U.S. Senate, Maine). The female candidate was rated higher on nine of the ten characteristics and rated significantly higher than the male candidate on the stereotypically masculine characteristics of assertiveness, competency, experience, and strong leadership, as well as the stereotypically feminine characteristics of caring and being personal (see Table 6.5). However, there were definite differences in the style of the negative ads used by these two candidates. Two of the male candidate's negative ads did not feature either candidate, but consisted primarily of ominous music, text, some black-and-white photos, and direct attacks on the female candidate followed by warnings to the voters of the negative consequences of reelecting the female candidate. The female candidate employed greater use of comparison ads, providing photos of both candidates and concluding the ads with a positive message, visuals, and music that again helped to soften the blow of her initial attacks. Consistent with their character trait ratings, the subjects were more likely to indicate they would prefer to vote for the female candidate.

Gender differences also were seen in Bystrom's 2003 study of viewer reactions to positive, negative, and mixed-message television advertising strategies. She found that both female and male voters were more likely to vote for a woman candidate in a positive-message campaign and for the male candidate in a negative-message campaign. In a mixed-message campaign, women voters voted for the female candidate, whereas men voters voted for the male candidate.

For example, after viewing the mostly positive ads from the Washington U.S. Senate race of Democrat challenger Maria Cantwell and Republican incumbent Slade Gorton, both women (67 percent) and men (54 percent) voted for Cantwell. Although both women and men preferred Cantwell, there was a thirteen-point gender gap in the support between women and men for each candidate.

On the semantic differential scales rating the candidates according to thirteen qualities (see Table 6.6), both women and men found Cantwell more honest, believable, attractive, caring, sincere, personal, and positive (all feminine characteristics) than Gorton, and Gorton more aggressive and experienced (masculine characteristics) than Cantwell. Though women and men were similar in their reactions to Cantwell and Gorton on these nine traits, there were significant differences in their reactions to Cantwell. Women found her significantly more honest, believable, attractive, caring, sincere, experienced, personal, and positive than did men (see Table 6.6).

Some gender differences between the respondents were noted on the four other qualities. For example, male respondents rated Gorton slightly higher on the characteristics of being qualified, competency, being active, and being a strong leader (masculine characteristics). On the other hand, female respondents found Cantwell significantly more qualified, active, and a strong leader than men and slightly more competent (all masculine characteristics).

After viewing the mostly negative ads from the New Hampshire governor's race between Democrat incumbent Jeanne Shaheen and Republican challenger Gordon Humphrey, both women (62 percent) and men (64 percent) voted for Humphrey, a gender gap of only two points.

On the semantic differential scales rating the candidates according to thirteen qualities, both women and men found Humphrey more honest, believable, caring, sincere, personal, and positive (feminine characteristics) as well as more qualified, competent, experienced, active, and a stronger leader (masculine characteristics) than Shaheen. Men found Humphrey more aggressive than Shaheen, and women found Shaheen slightly more aggressive than Humphrey. Men found Humphrey slightly more attractive than Shaheen, and women rated Shaheen and Humphrey equally on this quality (see Table 6.6).

Although both women and men rated Humphrey higher on eleven of the thirteen qualities, women rated Shaheen significantly higher than men did on five qualities: believability, attractiveness, competency, being active, and being a strong leader (see Table 6.6). Women rated Humphrey significantly higher than men did on four qualities—they found him more attractive, active, personal, and positive.

After viewing the mixed-message ads from the Michigan U.S. Senate race of Republican incumbent Spencer Abraham and Democratic challenger Debbie Stabenow, 60 percent of the women voted for Stabenow and 58 percent of the men voted for Abraham, a gender gap of eighteen points.

On the semantic differential scales rating the candidates according to thirteen qualities, both women and men found Stabenow more honest, attractive, caring, sincere, and personal (feminine characteristics) as well

TABLE 6.6 Semantic Differential Scale Scores by Campaign and Gender (Bystrom 2003)

	Positive						Negative				Mixed			
	Cantwell		Gorton		Shaheen		Humphrey		Stabenow		Abraham			
Trait	M	F	M	F	M	F	M	F	M	F	M	F
---	---	---	---	---	---	---	---	---	---	---	---	---
Qualified	4.84	5.15*	5.17	5.10	4.98	5.26	5.22	5.36	4.80	5.23**	5.14	5.22
Honest	4.87	5.25**	4.29	4.21	3.17	3.41	4.43	4.68	4.47	5.11*	4.45	4.51
Believable	4.77	5.24***	4.49	4.30	3.41	3.81*	4.57	4.75	4.33	4.94***	4.44	4.52
Attractive	4.81	5.28**	3.73	3.66	3.62	4.27***	3.91	4.27*	4.03	4.48**	3.69	3.84
Caring	5.12	5.68***	4.69	4.71	4.47	4.60	4.67	4.88	4.95	5.31*	4.69	4.86
Sincere	4.96	5.48***	4.50	4.38	4.09	4.27	4.64	4.93	4.65	5.15***	4.62	4.57
Competent	4.94	5.17	5.05	4.95	4.56	4.89*	4.99	5.18	4.60	4.99*	4.88	4.95
Aggressive	4.59	4.62	4.85	4.98	5.03	5.19	5.22	5.14	4.72	5.01*	4.92	4.98
Experienced	4.37	4.91***	5.19	5.09	5.03	5.27	5.29	5.34	4.54	5.10***	5.11	5.11
Active	5.10	5.40*	5.15	5.10	4.93	5.27**	5.07	5.39*	4.90	5.31**	5.04	5.17
Leadership	4.69	5.05*	4.79	4.87	4.32	4.91***	5.03	5.27	4.44	5.06***	4.97	4.99
Personal	5.07	5.64***	4.52	4.38	4.14	4.42	4.70	5.09*	4.76	5.44***	4.66	4.80
Positive	4.87	5.39**	4.17	3.97	3.55	3.87	4.01	4.46*	4.25	4.91***	4.33	4.42

* $p \leq .05$
** $p \leq .01$
*** $p \leq .001$

as more competent and aggressive (masculine characteristics) than Abraham. Both women and men found Abraham more experienced (though women just slightly so) than Stabenow. Women and men were split in their assessments of the candidates on the other five qualities—women found Stabenow more believable and positive (feminine characteristics) as well as more qualified, more active, and a stronger leader (masculine characteristics) than Abraham. Men found Abraham more qualified, more active, a stronger leader (masculine characteristics), more positive, and more believable (feminine characteristics) than Stabenow (see Table 6.6). Overall, women rated Stabenow significantly higher than men on all thirteen measures—they found her more qualified, honest, believable, attractive, caring, sincere, competent, aggressive, experienced, active, personal, and positive, and a stronger leader (see Table 6.6).

Taken together, these results measuring gendered responses to negative ads by female and male candidates in high-level races (gubernatorial and U.S. Senate) in 1986, 1990, 1994, and 1996 (Banwart and Carlin 2001) and to the negative, positive, and mixed-message strategies of female and male U.S. Senate candidates in 2000 (Bystrom 2003) suggest that there are still some strong stereotypes at work in judgments of women and men political candidates. Based on these results, it appears that women candidates may be most successful running a positive or mixed-message campaign emphasizing mostly feminine or a balance of feminine and masculine image traits.

Part III
Candidate Web Sites:
Gendered Messages, Reactions

7
WebStyle: *Communication Messages through Candidates' Web Sites*

By the end of the 1990s, the popularity of the Internet and its ability to provide a forum for distributing a controlled message to mass audiences—without interruption or interpretation by the media—had attracted the attention of political candidates. Political candidates running for office in 1996 were the first to make a concerted effort toward incorporating the Internet in their campaigns (Davis 1999), and by 1998, the Internet was viewed as a mass medium for political candidates' messages (Raney 1998; Glass 1998). Leading into the 2000 election cycle, the Internet was considered a "broad-based medium to be reckoned with" (Shiver 1999) and candidates' Web sites were advised to be "as fine-tuned as any TV spot or direct mail piece" (Jalonick 2000: 56).

This increase in attention by candidates was a clear reaction to voter use. Postelection polls in 2000 indicated that the number of Americans seeking election information on the Internet had more than quadrupled from 1996. In fact, 30 percent of American voters reported using the Internet to gather campaign news, "a threefold increase from 1996" (Pew Research Center 2000a: 2). Of those seeking election news, almost 70 percent indicated that they also "sought out information on the candidates' positions" (Pew Research Center 2000a: 2), and 28 percent reported visiting "the Web site of a candidate or campaign" to get their news (Pew Research Center 2000a: 5). The study concluded that "Campaign 2000 firmly established the Internet as a major source of election news and information" (Pew Research Center 2000a: 1).

As the Internet continues to emerge as a mass media tool for campaigns, it is important to understand how candidates are using it as a method to communicate with voters. As Davis has argued, "Since communication is so vital to a campaign, and candidates and voters are turning to the Internet to transmit and receive information, the Internet must be studied as a communication tool" (1999: 96). Selnow in particular highlighted the Internet's innovative mass communication potential for political candidates, as it utilizes "all the formats of the traditional media—text like a newspaper, audio like radio, and audio-visual something like TV or movies, and it can do them all at one time" (1998: 42).

With the Internet and its communication capabilities widely available, Davis argued that ultimately the Internet will not change who is elected but how candidates run their campaigns, and identified six functions that the Web sites served for candidates: "candidate symbol, information dissemination, opinion gauge, reinforcement of vote choice and GOTV (get out the vote), volunteer ID and fundraising, and interactivity" (1999: 97). He further situated campaign Web sites as a standard component in future campaigns, arguing that candidates will "need to place sites on the Web just as they need to raise minimum amounts of money and run television spots" (1999: 115). However, such sites will need to be armed with more information about issues, higher-quality graphics, greater interactivity, and attentive maintenance that updates the site as well as provides responses through the site's interactive capabilities.

Other researchers have also contributed to understanding the Internet's use in recent election cycles. Such analyses have found that the content in the 1996 presidential sites was "predominantly positive in its focus and primarily centered on campaign issue information" (Tedesco, Miller, and Spiker 1999: 62–63). Regarding the interactive nature of the 1996 presidential and gubernatorial sites, candidates' Web sites used far more media interaction (for example, hyperlinks, biographies, and issue information) than human interaction (for example, discussion boards, chat rooms, and the ability to send messages to the candidate) (Stromer-Galley 2000).

Similar to the presidential sites, the 1996 U.S. Senate candidates' sites also were found to predominantly provide issues sections, with the economy, education, and crime most commonly discussed (Klotz 1997). Such candidates frequently included personal information—marital status, children's names, and names of their parents—but less frequently included information about their religion, political affiliation, and hobbies. Thirty-four percent of Senate candidates mentioned their opponent in an unfavorable manner, with the attack almost always issue-focused (Klotz 1997: 484). One particular study advancing this line of research to the 1998 election focused on contribution solicitation (Dulio, Goff, and Thurber 1999) and found that 73 percent of candidates running for the U.S. Senate and in open races for the U.S. House solicited contributions on their Web sites. This is a substantial increase from 1996, in which only 46 percent solicited contributions in some manner (Davis 1999).

Advancing the study of candidates' Web sites through the 2000 campaign, researchers found that in the 2000 presidential primaries, candidates' Web sites correlated less with the voters' agenda than spot ads or the debates (Hansen and Benoit 2001). In 2000, U.S. Senate and gubernatorial candidates' Web sites provided more information, graphics, and interactivity than in 1998 (Greer and LaPointe 2001). When compared by level of office, Senate candidates provided more information—biographical details, issue-related information, details about voter interaction, general government information, and opponent information—as well as graphics than gubernatorial candidates, although by 2000 there was no difference in the amount of interactive features used by Senate and gubernatorial candidates (Greer and LaPointe 2001). No differences were indicated by gender in a comparison that included male candidates' sites from male versus male races as well as mixed-gender races (Greer and LaPointe 2001).

A study of U.S. Senate candidates' Web sites from campaign 2000 found that sixty of the sixty-eight candidates hosted campaign Web sites, all candidates included a biographical section, and the most frequently discussed issue was education (Puopolo 2001). This same study also offered a gender comparison, although the fifty-four Web sites of male candidates (from male vs. male races and mixed-gender races) were compared directly with the six Web sites of female candidates. However, the six female Senate candidates' sites were found to be more likely to discuss Social Security, taxes, senior citizens and retirement, technology, housing, abortion, immigration and borders, and foreign policy than male candidates' sites; the male Senate candidates discussed education, health care, prescription drugs, the environment, employment, gun control, crime, agriculture, infrastructure, public safety, campaign finance reform, veterans' affairs, the military, and welfare reform more than female candidates. Female and male candidates discussed the budget equally as often.

With regard to interactive capabilities in 2000, the six female Senate candidates were more likely to offer e-mail, solicit volunteers and campaign contributions, and provide voter registration, video files, audio files, newsletters, search capabilities, netcasting, and a town hall forum (Puopolo 2001). Male Senate candidates were more likely to offer links and the opportunity to purchase products such as T-shirts (Puopolo 2001). Although Puopolo's study does not distinguish by gender of opponent in analyzing the content, her attempt to segment differences in how female and male candidates have designed their Web sites was one of the first to incorporate gender as an analytical variable.

Research—particularly in the form of content analysis—is burgeoning in the study of the Internet, coinciding with the increase in Internet use by voters seeking new sources for political information and by candidates seeking unmediated communication channels for reaching voters. Although researchers have previously studied the content present on candidates' Web sites, Banwart's work was the first to analyze systematically the styles and strategies of candidate self-presentation on Web sites. In seeking to extend the VideoStyle framework (Kaid and Davidson 1986) and to use candidate gender as an analytical variable, Banwart (2002) constructed a WebStyle framework (see chapter 2) that this current study builds upon to examine the self-presentation strategies present on candidates' Web sites from mixed-gender races in election 2000 and 2002.

Candidates' Web Sites: U.S. Senate and Gubernatorial Races 2000–2002

In our analysis, forty-eight Web sites were examined from the 2000 and 2002 mixed-gender gubernatorial and U.S. Senate races.[1] Fifty-four percent of the Web sites were from female candidates' campaigns and 46 percent were from male candidates' campaigns; 48 percent were from gubernatorial campaigns and 52 percent were from U.S. Senate campaigns. A total of 52 percent of the Web sites represented Republican candidates, while 48 percent represented Democratic candidates. Fifty-two percent were created by candidates in open races, 29 percent were from challenger candidates' campaigns, and 19 percent were from incumbent candidates' campaigns.

Verbal Components in Candidates' Web Sites

Issues. A review of the issues discussed by female and male candidates on their Web sites indicates that viewers seeking issue discussion and information can find a substantial amount of it on those sites. However, although it is evident that candidates are willing to discuss a number of issues on their Web sites, candidates generally discussed the same set of issues, with education emerging as the most popular. Overall, education was the issue most frequently discussed on female and male sites, with 96 percent of female candidates' sites and 100 percent of male candidates' sites offering discussion of this topic (see Table 7.1). Other frequently discussed issues on female candidates' sites included health care, taxes, senior citizens' issues, and environmental issues. Male candidates also frequently discussed health care, environmental issues, taxes, and senior citizens' issues.

When the Web site issue discussion was examined by year, education remained the most frequently discussed issue in 2000 and 2002 on both female and male candidates' Web sites. Notably, candidates in 2002 seemed more likely to include a wider range of issues, with 56 percent of female candidates discussing more than ten issues and 71 percent of male candidates discussing between five and ten issues. A review of Table 7.1 also indicates that many issues received greater attention in 2002 than 2000. Further, many topics that were completely ignored in 2000 received attention in 2002, such as dissatisfaction with the government, international issues, and poverty, hunger, and homelessness for female candidates; gun control for male candidates; and ethics and moral decline, recession and depression, immigration, and homeland security for female and male candidates. Arguably the World Trade Center and Pentagon attacks on September 11, 2001, influenced the increased discussion of

TABLE 7.1 Issues Discussed by Gender on Candidates' Web Sites

Issue	Female (n = 26)	Male (n = 22)	Female '02 (n = 16)	Male '02 (n = 14)	Female '00 (n = 10)	Male '00 (n = 8)
Feminine Issues	96%	100%	100%	100%	90%	100%
Education/schools	96%	100%	100%	100%	90%	100%
Health care	81%	77%	75%	71%	90%	88%
Senior citizens' issues	65%	73%	81%	71%	40%	75%
Poverty/hunger/homelessness	8%	9%	13%	7%	0%	13%
Welfare/welfare reform	19%	14%	19%	14%	20%	13%
Environment/pollution	62%	77%	63%	79%	60%	75%
Drugs/drug abuse	23%	18%	31%	21%	10%	13%
Ethics/moral decline	15%	5%	25%	7%	0%	0%
Women's issues	42%	27%	44%	36%	40%	13%
Masculine Issues	96%	100%	94%	100%	100%	100%
Taxes	65%	77%	69%	71%	60%	88%
Budget/deficit	31%	41%	44%	50%	10%	25%
Unemployment/jobs	19%	9%	19%	14%	20%	0%
Cost of living	8%	5%	0%	7%	20%	0%
Recession/depression	4%	5%	6%	7%	0%	0%
Immigration	8%	9%	13%	14%	0%	0%
Economy in general	58%	50%	69%	64%	40%	25%
Crime/prison	31%	46%	44%	43%	10%	50%
Defense	31%	41%	38%	36%	20%	50%
International issues	8%	27%	13%	29%	0%	25%
Neutral Issues	69%	68%	75%	86%	60%	38%
Job growth	39%	36%	38%	50%	40%	13%
Dissatisfaction with the government	12%	0%	19%	0%	0%	0%
Gun control	39%	18%	38%	29%	40%	0%
Homeland security	31%	27%	50%	43%	0%	0%
Youth violence	12%	14%	6%	7%	20%	25%

Note: Percentages indicate frequencies within gender.

international issues and homeland security. For instance, Jim Talent (R-MO, U.S. Senate candidate, 2002) provided a specific issues section titled "Fighting for Our National and Homeland Security," in which he stressed his service on the Armed Forces Committee and his "plan [that] would strengthen our national defense, improve military readiness and ensure we have a coordinated homeland security system." Jeanne Shaheen (D-NH, U.S. Senate candidate, 2002) headlined "Enhancing Security" as an issue category, followed by the issue heading of "Ensuring Our Safety After September 11." The discussion indicated that in her past position as governor, Shaheen acted to secure the state by "stepping up patrols of our harbors and bridges and increasing inspections along our highways" and by creating a commission to "[protect] New Hampshire against terrorism."

A closer review by year and gender of the most frequently discussed issues (see Table 7.2) finds that, overall, female and male candidates have predominantly presented the same issue agendas on their Web sites. Further, most of the top issues have been traditionally considered feminine issues, such as education, health care, senior citizens' issues, and environmental issues. This agenda is further supported within each year, as education, senior citizens' issues, health care, and environmental issues were the most frequently discussed issues. In 2000, female candidates were also likely to include discussion of women's issues on their Web sites.

This prevalence of "feminine" issue discussion is of interest, as such issues have often been regarded as "compassion" or "domestic/social" issues, a category considered less important than "masculine" issues such as defense (Huddy and Terkildsen 1993). Further, these feminine issues have traditionally been associated with female candidates. Despite these findings, public opinion polling data show that issues such as education, health care, and senior citizens' issues have been frequently discussed by candidates in recent elections. Following the 2000 election, these issues emerged among the top issues for voters (Pew Research Center 2000b), and in 2002, voters cited education as the most important issue (Pew Research Center 2002b). Leading into the 2002 general election, domestic/social issues were more frequently mentioned as most important overall by the public, as opposed to economic issues or terrorism/foreign issues (Pew Research Center 2002b). Although the media do not seem to associate these issues with the candidates as frequently as the candidates are discussing them (Banwart, Bystrom, and Robertson 2003), it is clear that both female and male candidates are frequently discussing feminine issues—and, in turn, the public's top issue concerns—in the messages they *can* control.

Although the top issues discussed by female and male candidates were predominantly feminine issues, when all of the issues were combined into feminine and masculine issue categories, female and male candidates discussed both categories with similar frequencies (see Table 7.1). This similarity can be explained by the fact that although four of the top five issues

TABLE 7.2 Most Frequently Discussed Issues on Candidates' Web Sites by Gender

Overall

Female Candidates' Sites	*Male Candidates' Sites*
Education (96%)	Education (100%)
Health care (81%)	Health care (77%)
Taxes (65%)	Environmental issues (77%)
Senior citizens' issues (65%)	Taxes (77%)
Environmental issues (62%)	Senior citizens' issues (73%)

2002

Female Candidates' Sites	*Male Candidates' Sites*
Education (100%)	Education (100%)
Senior citizens' issues (81%)	Environmental issues (79%)
Health care (75%)	Health care (71%)
Taxes (69%)	Senior citizens' issues (71%)
Economy (69%)	Taxes (71%)

2000

Female Candidates' Sites	*Male Candidates' Sites*
Education (90%)	Education (100%)
Health care (90%)	Health care (88%)
Environmental issues (60%)	Taxes (88%)
Taxes (60%)	Senior citizens' issues (75%)
Senior citizens' issues (40%)	Environmental issues (75%)
Women's issues (40%)	
Economy (40%)	
Job growth (40%)	
Gun control (40%)	

Note: Percentages indicate frequencies within gender.

discussed were feminine, issues such as taxes, the budget, the economy, crime and prisons, and defense are recognized by candidates as important to voters and thus were frequently discussed on their Web sites. In 2002, the economy and taxes—traditionally considered masculine issues—were rated of high importance for voters (Pew Research Center 2002b), with the economy—inclusive of jobs, unemployment, and budget—mentioned by 55 percent of poll respondents in October of the midterm election cycle (Pew Research Center 2002a). In 2002, the importance of the economy was linked by the candidates to their state's budget and concerns over fiscal crises as well. In fact, the increased discussion of budget issues from 2000 to 2002 on candidates' Web sites can be directly correlated to the increased importance of the issue in the 2002 election cycle, particularly for gubernatorial candidates, with an increase in discussions of budget from 10 percent to 44 percent for female candidates and from 25 percent to 50 percent for male candidates.

Jennifer Granholm (D-MI, gubernatorial candidate, 2002) tied the issue of the economy to state budget problems and unemployment in a statement titled "Economics" on her Web site (www.granholmforgov.com):

> Last year, Michigan lost 86,000 jobs, and personal income grew slower than in any other state except one. At the same time, fiscal mismanagement in Lansing means that instead of having money set aside to help Michigan weather this storm, we find ourselves with a $1 billion budget shortfall.

Matt Salmon (R-AZ, gubernatorial candidate, 2002) also discussed his state's budget crisis on his Web site (www.salmonforgov.com). Under the heading "Leading Arizona Toward Prosperity," Salmon began a lengthy discussion of his plan by stating:

> Arizona is facing a state budget crisis that has the potential to overwhelm state government . . . there is no higher priority than resolving this problem.

Taxes also remained a consistently emphasized issue on candidates' Web sites for both female and male candidates overall and across both elections, although male candidates were slightly more likely to address the issue in their Web sites. Whether the candidates were discussing the need for eliminating taxes, reducing taxes, or providing tax incentives and credit (as on Judy Martz' [R-MT, gubernatorial candidate, 2000] Web site) or were discussing a plan to eliminate the state sales tax, provide tax relief to homeowners, institute a business equipment tax, or simplify the state income tax (as on Mark O'Keefe's [D-MT, gubernatorial candidate, 2000] Web site), the importance candidates placed on addressing taxes was evidenced by its frequent listing on candidates' Web sites as a main topic of discussion.

Character Traits. As with political television advertising, while candidates are concerned with including their issue positions on their Web sites, they are also concerned with conveying a particular image in the messages that they control. Quite dissimilar from televised political advertising is the emphasis by female and male candidates on masculine traits as compared to feminine traits on their Web sites (see Table 7.3). This finding offers several important indicators. First, this differential in emphasis suggests candidates recognize that the intimacy of television does require portrayal of a more feminine style (Jamieson 1988), with traits such as sensitivity, honesty, and cooperation accentuated in their messages. The lack of interactivity between different candidates' Web sites—as opposed to attack and rebuttal/response ads—also may decrease the need for candidates to counteract

TABLE 7.3 Character Traits Emphasized on Candidates' Web Sites

			2002		2000	
Issue	Female (n = 26)	Male (n = 22)	Female (n = 16)	Male (n = 14)	Female (n = 10)	Male (n = 8)
Feminine Traits	35%	59%	38%	64%	30%	50%
Honesty/integrity	15%	36%	19%	36%	10%	38%
Cooperation with others	23%	14%	25%	7%	20%	25%
Washington outsider status	0%	14%	0%	21%	0%	0%
Sensitivity/ understanding	4%	0%	0%	0%	10%	0%
Trustworthiness	4%	18%	0%	7%	10%	38%
Masculine Traits	100%	100%	100%	100%	100%	100%
Toughness/strength	39%	59%	19%	50%	70%	75%
Past performance/ success	100%	96%	100%	93%	100%	100%
Aggressiveness/being a fighter	54%	55%	38%	43%	80%	75%
Competency	58%	68%	50%	50%	70%	100%
Leadership	73%	96%	69%	93%	80%	100%
Experience in politics	89%	91%	88%	93%	90%	88%
Knowledge/ intelligence	39%	55%	44%	43%	30%	75%
Being action-oriented	62%	77%	56%	79%	70%	75%
Neutral Traits	85%	77%	81%	71%	90%	88%
Qualifications	69%	77%	56%	71%	90%	88%
Being of the people	23%	32%	38%	43%	0%	13%

Note: Percentages indicate frequencies within gender.

their tough and aggressive side, which may be highlighted in an attack ad, with a sensitive and honest side. We believe it premature to suggest that Web sites are a more masculine medium, although we argue that Web sites are still a neutral institution that call for the emphasis of traits commonly associated with political office—qualifications, experience in politics, leadership, and knowledge of the issues. This final point may in fact be closely associated with the audience. Ninety-one percent of those who recently received information online about the 2002 midterm elections reported that it did not cause them to decide to vote for or against a particular candidate, and 62 percent of those who specifically sought election news online reported it was not the cause of their decision (Pew Research Center 2002b). Thus, those seeking information online—and particularly from candidates' Web sites—may only be seeking clarification, reinforcement, or simply convenience. The self-presentation style of a candidate would then need to focus on the traits commonly associated with political office.

When individual traits were examined (see Table 7.3) on candidates' Web sites in 2000 and 2002, it is apparent that female and male candidates attempted to establish similar images, emphasizing performance and success, experience, leadership, and qualifications. Of note, however, is that performance and experience were typically discussed in the context of leadership, possessing qualifications for office, and/or being action-oriented. For example, Mitch McConnell (R-KY, U.S. Senate candidate, 2002) combined his past performance and experience with an emphasis on both his qualifications (his past record) and leadership in this statement (www.mcconnell02.com):

> Over the last seventeen years of public service in the United States Senate, Mitch McConnell has emerged as a national leader with strong Kentucky values. He has amassed an enormous amount of clout and used it to deliver for the Commonwealth like no other U.S. Senator in Kentucky history. In the last three years alone, he has brought home more than $500 million for Kentucky families. Mitch McConnell provides leadership that delivers.

The Web site of Jean Carnahan (D-MO, U.S. Senate candidate, 2002) (www.jeancarnahan.com) also emphasized her performance, experience, and qualifications (past record):

> Her success in building a broad base of support was evident when the Senate voted to include her plan in the Elementary and Secondary Education Act, the single most important education bill passed by the Senate in the last five years.

Jimmie Lou Fisher's (D-AR, gubernatorial candidate, 2002) Web site (www.jimmieloufisher.com) continued the trend:

> Jimmie Lou Fisher is the only person in the race for governor with this kind of experience.

And Spencer Abraham (R-MI, U.S. Senate candidate, 2000) offered the following on his Web site (www.abraham2002.net):

> Whether he's leading the charge to curb unfunded mandates and frivolous lawsuits, stiffening the sentences for the cocaine dealers who poison our kids, or keeping our Social Security dollars locked away from the big spenders, Spence Abraham fights hard for Michigan and he delivers.

Across all Web sites, male candidates more frequently emphasized character traits than female candidates, particularly in 2002 (see Table 7.3). Overall, the only traits female candidates were more likely to emphasize were past performance, cooperation with others, and being sensitive and understanding, although the differential was small for all but the emphasis on cooperation. Female candidates were most likely to differ in the frequency with which they emphasized their ability to cooperate (female, 23 percent; male, 14 percent) across both years combined, but in 2002, the differential was far more evident, with 25 percent of female candidates' sites and only 7 percent of male candidates' sites emphasizing the candidate's ability to cooperate with others. Mostly, however, the emphasis of cooperation was placed in a bipartisan context. For example, Maria Cantwell's (D-WA, U.S. Senate candidate, 2000), Web site (www.cantwell2000.com) stated, "She rapidly established a reputation as someone who could bring people together and make things happen." Jim Talent's (R-MO, U.S. Senate candidate, 2002) Web site (www.talentforsenate.com) emphasized his bipartisan efforts with such phrases as "original co-sponsor," "Jim succeeded in building bipartisan support," and "Congressman Talent was scrupulous in respecting the prerogatives of all the members of the Small Business Committee."

Appeal Strategies: Incumbent, Challenger, Feminine, Masculine

As explained in chapter 2, appeal strategies used in political advertising have been identified as gendered and relating to electoral status (incumbent or challenger). The presence of status strategies, as outlined by Trent and Friedenberg (2000), has been identified in both presidential advertising (e.g., Kaid and Johnston 2001) as well as advertising from mixed-gender races (e.g., Banwart 2002; Bystrom 1995; Bystrom and Kaid 2002). On the candidates' Web sites that we examined, incumbent appeals and challenger appeals were used at similar frequencies by male and female candidates (see Table 7.4). All of the female and male candidates' sites utilized incumbent strategies, with candidates most frequently emphasizing their own accomplishments. Such a result is consistent with the emphasis on the character trait of past performance and experience.

Female and male candidates also were likely to use endorsements—another incumbent strategy—that were generally from the news media

TABLE 7.4 Feminine, Masculine, Incumbent, and Challenger Appeal Strategies

			2002		2000	
Appeal	Female (n = 26)	Male (n = 22)	Female (n = 16)	Male (n = 14)	Female (n = 10)	Male (n = 8)
Feminine appeals	65%	64%	75%	71%	50%	50%
Masculine appeals	96%	100%	94%	100%	100%	100%
Incumbent appeals	100%	100%	100%	100%	100%	100%
Challenger appeals	89%	91%	100%	100%	70%	75%

Note: Percentages indicate frequencies within gender.

and political leaders. For example, Olympia Snowe (R-ME, U.S. Senate candidate, 2000) listed her most recent endorsements on her home page (www.olympiasnowe.org), which were from news media sources and a union group, but also included other endorsements in her "News" section. John Sununu (R-NH, U.S. Senate candidate, 2002) listed his endorsements under his "Team Sununu" section (www.teamsununu.org), detailing supportive political officials at the local, state, and federal levels.

In the use of challenger strategies, again, almost all female (89 percent) and male (91 percent) candidates' sites employed challenger appeals. Overall, male candidates employed the appeals at greater frequencies, except when emphasizing optimism/hope for the future. Yet the most frequently used challenger strategy for both female and male candidates was taking the offensive position on the issues. In other words, both female and male candidates were willing to compare or contrast their stands with those of their opponent and/or challenge their opponent's positions without offering specific solutions of their own. This strategy was closely identified with calling for change and attacking the record of the opponent. Of note, the strategy of attacking the record of the opponent increased in frequency on female candidates' sites from 2000 (10 percent) to 2002 (53 percent), while male candidates' sites decreased their use of the strategy (2000, 75 percent; 2002, 36 percent). Male candidates remained more likely to employ the strategy, but female and male candidates' use of it suggests that candidates overall may still be tentative about being too negative in this still developing medium.

When examining their Web site appeals within the categories of feminine and masculine, similar to character traits in their television ads, female and male candidates were more likely to emphasize masculine strategies than feminine strategies. The emphasis of one's own accomplishments has been identified as a masculine strategy as well as an incumbent strategy. Overall, this was the most frequent masculine strategy used by candidates and thus contributed to the higher use of masculine strategies overall. Half of male candidates' sites and 40 percent of female candidates' sites did incorporate the use of expert authorities, and almost one-quarter of both female and male candidates' sites used statistics. Although the use of statistics did not substantially change from 2000 to 2002, both female and male candidates were much more likely to use expert authorities to back up their positions in 2002 than in 2000. Such a change may well be attributable to candidates realizing the importance of legitimizing their claims and positions on the Web.

The most frequent feminine strategy used was that of inviting participation or action, with 50 percent of male candidates' sites and 42 percent of female candidates' sites doing so. Interestingly, many times candidates hesitated in asking viewers to participate or act in some manner, often using phrases such as "If you are interested in helping our campaign, please fill out the following form." Such a lack of call to action is distinctly different from statements such as the following, from the home page of Fran Ulmer (D-AK, gubernatorial candidate, 2002) (www.franulmer.com): "I have learned a lot from you, but now I have to ask you for something. I need your vote on November 5th." Bob Ehrlich (R-MD, gubernatorial candidate, 2002) (www.bobehrlich.com) went even farther in his opening letter to viewers, requesting that viewers participate in four specific ways and then concluding with the following: "Also, thank you in advance for all of your help in the days leading up to Election Day. I ask you one last time to do more than you ever have for this campaign. If you do, we will have an historic victory to celebrate on November 5th."

The actual lack of use of this strategy is surprising, considering that candidates can recruit volunteers, ask for monetary contributions, and introduce a variety of options for participation simply by incorporating the more obvious use of invitational and encouraging language, with little expense involved. The increased use of this strategy from 2000 to 2002 does perhaps suggest that candidates are exploring opportunities for their Web sites to more actively encourage viewer engagement.

Attack Appeals. The use of attacks in political advertising is well documented by prior researchers (e.g., Kaid 1998; Kaid and Johnston 2001) as well as earlier in this text. However, female and male candidates in 2000 and 2002 election cycles differed in the use of such an appeal when it came to their Web sites (see Table 7.5). When examining the 2000 Web sites, an attack was coded if it was included in the issues section, the section most logical for containing an attack if one was issued (compared to other common sections such as volunteer opportunities, campaign directory, or candidate bio). The results from the 2000 Web sites indicated that no female candidate issued attacks, while 38 percent of male candidates' sites did so. However, such candidates as Maria Cantwell (D-WA, U.S. Senate candidate, 2000) (www.cantwell2000.com) included a completely separate section in which she refuted claims made in her opponent's ads, stating, "Each of these ads distort[s] the record and purposefully mislead[s] voters."

Thus, in 2002, in response to the increasing diversity and complexity of Web sites, an attack was coded if it appeared at any place in the site. Our results concluded that 56 percent of female candidates' Web sites and 86 percent of male candidates' Web sites contained attacks. Yet less than 25 percent of either female or male Web sites actually featured the opponent's issue stands, although when such stands were presented, the candidates did so in a manner that compared their own stands with those of their opponent. Therefore, if the candidates are not featuring the opponent's issue stands, it is important to examine what the candidates are focusing their attacks on. Gloria Tristani (D-NM, U.S. Senate candidate, 2002) offered the following on her home page (www.gloriaforsenate.com):

126 • Gender and Candidate Communication

TABLE 7.5 Types of Verbal Appeals: Attack Appeals and Sectional Appeals

			2002		2000	
Appeal	Female (n = 26)	Male (n = 22)	Female (n = 16)	Male (n = 14)	Female (n = 10)	Male (n = 8)

Attack Appeals

Issues section only						
Opponent's issues stands featured	15% (n = 4)	23% (n = 5)	25%	14%	0%	38%
If yes, candidate's stands compared with opponent's?	75%	80%				
Attack present						
2000, issues section only			—	—	0%	38%
2002, anywhere on site			56%	86%	—	—
Strategy used when attack						
Humor/ridicule	33%	20%	33%	25%	0%	0%
Negative association	56%	53%	56%	42%	100%	100%
Name-calling	67%	33%	67%	42%	0%	0%
Guilt by association	11%	13%	11%	17%	0%	0%

Sectional Appeals

Home Page Section						
Identifies party	35%	50%	44%	43%	20%	63%
Identifies office	100%	96%	100%	100%	100%	88%
Intro with personal letter	39%	46%	38%	36%	40%	63%
New content						
Listed on home page	19%	9%	19%	14%	20%	0%
Available through link	4%	18%	0%	7%	10%	38%
Not listed/not available	77%	73%	81%	79%	70%	63%
Candidate Bio Section						
Candidate bio sheet	100%	100%	100%	100%	100%	100%
Personal note/letter	0%	9%	0%	0%	0%	25%
Personal info	92%	100%	100%	100%	80%	100%
Business info	85%	96%	81%	93%	90%	100%
Public service info	85%	91%	100%	100%	60%	75%

			2002		2000	
Appeal	Female (n = 26)	Male (n = 22)	Female (n = 16)	Male (n = 14)	Female (n = 10)	Male (n = 8)
Issues Section						
Position statements	96%	100%	100%	100%	90%	100%
Campaign Events Section						
Events open to public	35%	38%	50%	50%	10%	13%
Private political events	0%	14% *	0%	21%	0%	0%
Notice site updated	4%	5%	0%	7%	10%	0%
Past, current, and future events	15%	19%	25%	29%	0%	0%
Current, future events	19%	19%	25%	21%	10%	13%
Campaign directory						
List key contacts	19%	36%	19%	43%	20%	25%
Campaign HQ information	65%	73%	81%	86%	40%	50%
Full contact information	54%	59%	63%	57%	40%	63%
Partial contact info	23%	27%	38%	43%	0%	0%
Local campaign coordinators	15%	36%	19%	43%	10%	38%
Get-Involved Section						
Letter from candidate	15%	0%	19%	0%	10%	0%
Talking points	0%	0%	0%	0%	0%	0%
Info to contact people	12%	9%	19%	14%	0%	0%
General						
References for comments made by others	27%	27%	38%	29%	10%	25%

Note: Percentages indicate frequencies within gender.
* Significant at $p \leq .05$

Sadly, throughout the campaign Pete Domenici refused to discuss the issues publicly—opting to hide behind a multi-million dollar advertising blitz, scripted appearances, and the entrenched power of incumbency. Domenici's inaccessibility deprived New Mexico voters of the opportunity to compare their senatorial candidates.

Mitt Romney (R-MA, gubernatorial candidate, 2002) (www.romney-healey.com), launched a similar attack, although it was shrouded within the context of an issue: "This is the arrogance of Beacon Hill and it shows yet again why Shannon O'Brien cannot be trusted when it comes to fixing our schools, or running our state." Therefore, although most of the candidates were not taking the opportunity to provide direct issue comparisons, they were finding Web sites as an avenue in which to launch attacks similar to those found in political advertisements.

Group and Sectional Appeals. Although advertising may primarily seek to appeal to a broad audience for the greatest impact per dollar spent, Web sites provide the uniquely inexpensive option of adding special sections for demographic groups to which the candidate may seek to appeal. For the most part, however, female and male candidates in 2000 and 2002 did not choose to take advantage of this opportunity. Although the candidates were most likely to include special sections that would appeal to young voters, only 12 percent of female and 18 percent of male candidates' sites did so. Of interest, male candidates did provide a special section or page for women voters in almost one-quarter of the sites. For example, Jim Talent (R-MO, U.S. Senate candidate, 2002) (www.talentforsenate.com) included a link for Women for Talent, at whose site viewers were encouraged to join the group, review comments from other women supporting Talent, and view photos from the "kickoff Women for Talent events." Hispanic voters were the other demographic group that caught some of the candidates' attention. Eight percent of female and 14 percent of male candidates' sites offered either special sections for Hispanic voters or a Spanish version of the site.

Web sites also offer the uniqueness of multiple sections through which to communicate a variety of messages and appeals. Sections common to the candidates' Web sites included the home page, candidate biography, issues, campaign events, campaign directory, a get-involved section, and links (the content of which will be discussed later). In the home page section (see Table 7.5), candidates were very likely to identify the office being sought; however, candidates were much less likely to identify their party affiliation. Specifically, female candidates' sites (35 percent) were less likely to identify the candidate's party than male candidates' sites (50 percent). Neither party nor level of office provides any explanation, although male gubernatorial candidates were more likely to identify their party affiliation (female, 39 percent; male, 60 percent) than were male challenger candidates (female, 38 percent; male, 67 percent). Overall, this does suggest that candidates are seeking to appeal to a broader audience of voters instead of limiting their appeal to their party, although female candidates might be more cautious in doing so in order to escape the appearance that they are beholden to party platforms and positions, choosing instead to promote the idea that they are legitimate enough to have developed their own positions.

Less than half of either female or male candidates introduced their Web site with a personal letter, and even fewer directed viewers to any new content posted on the site. Therefore, there was little guidance for frequent viewers who might want to find out what had been added since their last visit to the site, and consequently little indication that the site was being updated and attended to on an ongoing basis.

All candidates were diligent in providing a biography section, used to introduce the candidate to the viewer, but few included a note or letter welcoming the viewer to this section. In fact, only 9 percent of male candidates' sites and no female candidates' sites provided a note or letter to the viewer in this section. However, almost all female candidates' sites (92 percent) and all male candidates' sites (100 percent) provided personal information, including information about their family, youth, and education. With candidate biographies (Davis 1999; Greer and LaPointe 2000; Puopolo 2001) virtually standard on candidates' Web sites, it is not unusual to expect that the candidates studied here—both female and male—would provide that feature. However, the way the most personal of information—marital status and family—was handled is notable, as it was typically minimized. For instance, with most candidates marriage and family was mentioned in a single sentence at the end of their biography.

Kathleen Kennedy Townsend (D-MA, gubernatorial candidate, 2002) (www.friendsofkathleen.com) was an exception. Within her biography, not only did she include one entire section on "Going to College, Falling in Love," where she detailed developing a crush on and attracting the attention of her future husband, who was also one of her teachers and a Ph.D. candidate at the time, but continued on with sections titled "Going to Law School, Starting a Family" and "The Townsends: A Tight-Knit Family." Such an overt emphasis on family and marital status remains rare for a female candidate, as most of their biographies placed greater emphasis on their public service, experience, and qualifications. As such, 85 percent of female and 96 percent of male candidates' sites provided information about their business experience, and 85 percent of female and 91 percent of male candidates' sites provided information about their public service history.

In the section including information about campaign events, few appeared likely to post information about events open to the public. Specifically, 35 percent of female and 38 percent of male candidates' sites posted such information in both years combined, with half of female and male candidates doing so in 2002. Less than 20 percent of either female or male candidates posted information about current and future events, although more candidates posted such information in 2002 than in 2000. Therefore, in an era when we are typically unable to meet our candidates face-to-face but instead get to know them via television, candidates in 2000 and 2002 did not utilize Web sites as an information source for encouraging voters to attend campaign events.

The most interesting finding with regard to the campaign directory information was the overall lack of candidates' Web sites providing such information. Across all variables, male candidates were more likely to provide campaign contact information, with the greatest difference occurring in the provision of local campaign coordinator information followed by a listing of key campaign contacts. Only 15 percent of female candidates' sites and 36 percent of male candidates' sites provided local campaign coordinator information, and only 19 percent of female candidates' sites and 36 percent of male candidates' sites provided information about key campaign contacts. Candidates' Web sites were most likely to provide campaign headquarters information (female, 65 percent; male, 73 percent), and 59 percent of male candidates' sites and 54 percent of female candidates' sites provided full contact information, including mailing address, phone number, fax number, and e-mail address. This lack of willingness to provide contact information seems surprising, particularly since one advantage of Web sites has been the ability to disseminate information in an attempt to involve voters and encourage interaction. What emanates from this dearth of information is a lack of desire on the candidates' behalf that interested viewers be able to access them through a variety of contact options. This appearance of inaccessibility runs counter to expectations.

Also of interest was the lack of personalization in the get-involved section of the candidates' sites. Only 15 percent of female candidates and no male candidates introduced this section with a personal letter or note. Candidates primarily used this section as a place for would-be volunteers to submit their information to the campaign and, in some instances, to contribute. Unfortunately, the messages on the Web sites at times did not provide much encouragement for viewers to get involved. For instance, the introduction to the volunteer section of Frank Murkowski's (R-AK, gubernatorial candidate, 2002) (www.frankmurkowski.com) site said: "If you would like to assist Frank's campaign, please let us know your name, contact information and areas of interest. We'll contact you when Frank needs help in your area." Pete Domenici's (R-NM, U.S. Senate candidate, 2002) (www.domenici.org) site included this statement: "If you would like to get involved with the campaign, please complete the form below. Make sure to click the 'Submit' button at the bottom of the page." Other candidates, such as Myrth York (D-RI, gubernatorial candidate, 2002) (www.myrthyork.com), were far more inviting and expressed thanks to her volunteers, stating, "Volunteers really do make the difference and I am grateful to each and every one of you for your help." Mitch McConnell's (R-KY, U.S. Senate candidate, 2002) (www.mcconnell02.com) Web site also communicated more interest in encouraging the viewer to get involved:

> Without the help of individuals like you, it would be impossible to operate a successful statewide campaign. Senator McConnell is

depending on you to help him return to Washington and continue fighting for the citizens of Kentucky. Please take a moment and fill out the information below, and someone will contact you soon!

Nonverbal Content in Campaign Web Sites

As with televised political advertising, candidates' use of nonverbal cues on their Web sites aid in communicating their message through a visual channel. For example, photos reveal a candidate's dress, facial expressions, and posture as well as the settings in which the candidate is featured. In the 2000 and 2002 female and male candidates' Web sites, the candidates offered a mix of formal and informal nonverbal communication (see Table 7.6).

For instance, when female candidates were featured in the photos on their Web sites, they were frequently seen in formal attire (92 percent). Differing from their televised advertising, however, male candidates were more likely to be seen in formal attire (71 percent) on their Web sites. This dominant use of formal attire for female candidates continues to confirm that it is a characteristic of female candidate self-presentation. Scholars have argued that women have chosen formal attire in order to establish a professional, businesslike appearance that emphasizes their competence and the seriousness of their candidacy in order to "convince voters of their legitimacy" (Kahn 1996: 32). However, on the medium of a Web site—as opposed to television—male candidates clearly feel the need to appeal to more traditional political expectations, establishing an image of a serious, viable political candidate.

In their photos, 62 percent of female candidates and 59 percent of male candidates established eye contact sometimes, and 23 percent of female candidates and 41 percent of male candidates established eye contact almost always. Such a differential is not surprising, however, as many candidates sought to provide insight into their personal lives through photos of the candidate with family and/or friends, or to provide a bandwagon effect through photos of the candidate on the campaign trail, talking to constituents, or speaking at a rally. In such instances, a candidate is unlikely to have eye contact with the camera. However, most candidates featured a photo on the home page—which also often replicated via the banner on each page of the site—that featured a head and shoulders shot of the candidate looking directly at and welcoming the viewer to the site.

Overall, female and male candidates were more likely to smile in their Web site photographs, a cue that one would assume is necessary when welcoming visitors—and potential voters—in search of information to a campaign site. Because many of the photos sought to present a successful candidate, one worthy of votes, contributions, and other forms of support, it is logical that the candidate would provide those cues through positive, upbeat facial expressions.

132 • Gender and Candidate Communication

TABLE 7.6 Nonverbal Strategies Used on Candidates' Web Sites

	\multicolumn{2}{c}{}	\multicolumn{2}{c}{2002}	\multicolumn{2}{c}{2000}
Strategy	Female (n = 26)	Male (n = 22)	Female (n = 16)	Male (n = 14)	Female (n = 10)	Male (n = 8)
Candidate Dress						
Formal	92%	71%	94%	85%	89%	50%
Casual	8%	29%	6%	15%	11%	50%
Eye Contact						
Almost never	15%	0%	19%	0%	10%	0%
Sometimes	62%	59%	56%	71%	70%	38%
Almost always	23%	41%	25%	29%	20%	63%
Facial Expressions						
Smiling	92%	95%	94%	100%	89%	88%
Attentive/serious	8%	5%	6%	0%	11%	13%
Candidate Posture						
Compact/closed	50%	73%	25%	64%	90%	88%
Expansive/open	23%	14%	19%	7%	30%	25%
Combination	46%	18%*	56%	21%	30%	13%
Photographs						
Home Page						
Candidate only	27%	32%	25%	21%	30%	50%
Candidate with others	27%	18%	19%	14%	40%	25%
Combination	46%	41%	56%	50%	30%	25%
Candidate Bio Section						
Candidate only	54%	68%	63%	64%	40%	75%
Candidate with others	73%	64%	75%	64%	70%	63%
General						
Others shown in photos						
Men	92%	64%*	100%	71%	80%	50%
Women	85%	68%	94%	79%	70%	50%
Candidate family	46%	59%	63%	64%	20%	50%
Children	58%	50%	75%	57%	30%	38%
Senior citizens	69%	46%	81%	64%	50%	13%
Ethnic minorities	58%	55%	81%	71%	20%	25%

Note: Percentages indicate frequencies within gender.
* Significant at $p \leq .05$

Although the most frequent posture for female and male candidates—compact/closed—might seem counterintuitive, it is important to consider how the candidates were portrayed in their photos. For instance, Lois

Combs Weinberg (D-KY, U.S. Senate candidate, 2002) posted many photos on her Web site in which she was seen standing with supporters and posing for the camera, listening to supporters, speaking with the media, receiving a check from a supporter, and speaking while holding a microphone. Bob Ehrlich (R-MA, gubernatorial candidate, 2002) was featured on his site standing beside a police officer to indicate the support of a county police department, was seen holding his child, and was photographed while speaking at a podium with his hand gripping the side of the podium. Typically the candidates posted photos of themselves that showed them in control of the situation and of their body language; when they were portrayed with an open posture, they were waving or had their arm around someone to pose for the photograph. In other words, instead of claiming large amounts of space, candidates were portrayed as comfortable, at ease with others, and thus more likely to share personal space with supporters.

Most of the photographs on the candidates' sites, whether located on the candidates' home pages or in their biography sections, included the candidate and other people. Male candidates were slightly more likely (68 percent) than female candidates (54 percent) to include pictures of just themselves in their candidate biography section, while female candidates were slightly more likely (73 percent) than male candidates (64 percent) to include pictures of themselves with other people, perhaps seeking to illustrate that their campaigns draw wide support. When others were shown in the photos, female candidates were significantly more likely (92 percent) than male candidates (64 percent) to have men in their photos, and in many instances, these were men in positions of power and prestige, a strategy that undoubtedly sought to lend legitimacy to the female candidate's campaign.

For instance, Jennifer Granholm (D-MI, gubernatorial candidate, 2002) (www.granholmforgov.com) featured photos on her site of Al Gore appearing with her at a rally; of Granholm with Muhammad Ali, who was noted as "helping [her] get out the vote"; and of Granholm with Teamster president James P. Hoffa and with Senator Carl Levin from Michigan. Dianne Feinstein (D-CA, U.S. Senate candidate, 2000) included photos on her site of her with President Bill Clinton, as well as President Clinton signing a bill while Feinstein and a group of male legislators looked on. Alternatively, Olympia Snowe (R-ME, U.S. Senate candidate, 2000) did not feature a wide array of photos with powerful men, but instead posted photos including men who appeared to be part of her constituency. Although one photo showed Snowe speaking to a group of senior citizens, both male and female, another showed Snowe with an all-male color guard at a campaign appearance.

Female candidates were also more likely to feature women in their photos (85 percent) than male candidates (68 percent), and children and senior citizens were commonly featured as well. Female and male candidates also sought to foster diversity in the photos on their sites, as over half of the sites included ethnic minorities in the photos.

Although 59 percent of male candidates' sites included photos of their families, only 46 percent of female candidates' sites included such images. Female candidates have chosen not to represent themselves with their families in their advertising in the hope of not being associated with motherhood and domestic responsibilities, which can "drown out [their] political experience" (Witt et al. 1995: 116). For male candidates, however, the presence of family can evoke notions of stability and tradition, suggesting that because he has a family to protect, he will govern in ways that will protect the viewer's family as well. Because family photos have typically been present in the candidate biography section, an expectation has arisen that this is part of the type of information shared in this section (Davis 1999). Thus perhaps because the institutional expectation is present—and because a still photo can be less evoking of emotion than visual footage of the candidate interacting with her family—female candidates find it more important to meet the expectation than leave viewers in question.

Production Content in Candidates' Web Sites

The continuing advancement of Web site design is evident in the increased use of graphics from 2000 to 2002, with all of the candidates in 2002 using graphics on their Web sites (see Table 7.7). Candidate graphics were the most common graphics used by both female (74 percent) and male (79 percent) candidates; the candidate's photo and the campaign's logo were often combined in a banner used on every Web page.

Graphics depicting the candidate's state were also often incorporated. For instance, Jennifer Granholm (D-MI, gubernatorial candidate, 2002)

TABLE 7.7 Production Strategies Used on Candidates' Web Sites

Strategy	Female (n = 26)	Male (n = 22)	2002 Female (n = 16)	2002 Male (n = 14)	2000 Female (n = 10)	2000 Male (n = 8)
Graphics on Home Page						
Presence of graphics	73%	86%	100%	100%	30%	63%
	(n = 19)	(n = 19)	(n = 16)	(n = 14)	(n = 3)	(n = 5)
Party graphics	5%	11%	6%	14%	0%	0%
Candidate graphics	74%	79%	81%	86%	33%	60%
District/state	53%	74%	63%	93%	0%	20%
Election/campaign	58%	37%	63%	29%	33%	60%
Generic	53%	47%	56%	50%	33%	40%
Issue Comparison	(n = 4)	(n = 4)	(n = 4)	(n = 1)	(n = 0)	(n = 3)
By text only	50%	50%	50%	100%	0%	33%
Combination of text and graphics	50%	50%	50%	0%	0%	67%

Note: Percentages indicate frequencies within gender.

cropped her photo in the shape of the state of Michigan and periodically placed the graphic throughout her Web site. Janet Napolitano (D-AZ, gubernatorial candidate, 2002) placed a graphic of the state of Arizona, divided by counties, on every page of her site so that at any time a viewer could click on his or her county and find out where polling places were located, how to vote early, and names of the local campaign representatives. Tim Shallenburger (R-KS, gubernatorial candidate, 2002) used a graphic of the state seal on his home page, and Frank Murkowski (R-AK, gubernatorial candidate, 2002) (www.frankmurkowski,com) featured a graphic of his state as well as photos indicative of his state's landscape and wildlife. Campaign- or election-related graphics, such as flags, campaign buttons, or background images of a statehouse, were also used frequently on female and male candidates' sites, although slightly more so on female candidates' sites. The combination of campaign- or election-related graphics and district or state graphics was also popular with some candidates. The Web sites of Erskine Bowles (D-NC, U.S. Senate candidate, 2002) and Lois Combs Weinberg (D-KY, U.S. Senate candidate, 2002) both featured the outline of their respective state filled with an American flag as part of the banner for every page.

As has already been discussed, female and male candidates did not frequently feature their opponent's issue stands on their sites; when they did, they were very likely to compare their opponent's issue stands with their own. However, the techniques by which such comparisons were offered varied (see Table 7.7). Half of the female and male candidates made such comparisons by text only, whereas the other half presented the comparisons through a combination of text and graphics, such as a table. Although some candidates approached the act of comparison carefully, others treated the presentation as they might have a negative political advertisement or a direct mail piece, suggesting that the issue of comparison and opponent attacks on Web sites remains without established norms.

For instance, on his Web site (www.frankmurkowski.com), Frank Murkowski (R-AK, gubernatorial candidate, 2002) highlighted four specific issues in tabular form, with the top row summarizing his general approach to the issue (e.g., "Will control state spending and make government live within its means.") and the second row summarizing the stands of Fran Ulmer, his opponent (e.g., "Supported spending increases for the last eight years totaling more than $865 million"). It is interesting to note that although Murkowski placed his color picture to the left of his issue stances, he used a black-and-white standard campaign photograph of his opponent that did not feature her in any particularly negative manner.

Using a different approach, Kathleen Kennedy Townsend (D-MD, gubernatorial candidate, 2002) (www.friendsofkathleen.com) far more extensively utilized the capabilities of the Internet by posting two brochure-style documents that were clearly originally designed to be sent via the U.S. mail. Both brochures were in full color and hosted a variety of graphics and photos to emphasize the differentials in the comparisons. For instance, one of the documents, titled "Who's Fighting for Maryland's Future?" displayed a back cover that touted Ehrlich's "failing record" through a series of report cards. The inside pages of the brochure featured one page that highlighted Townsend as "the only candidate for Governor with a detailed blueprint for education" and noted that she was focused on health care and prescription drug coverage. The opposite page, headlined "[Bob Ehrlich's] Votes Hurt Our Families and Endanger Our Future," indicated that Ehrlich had voted to cut education funding and privatize Social Security, was against the Patients' Bill of Rights, and supported cuts in Medicare. The textual descriptions were supported with a photo, a graphic of a newspaper, and a graphic of a pair of scissors cutting across a document representing Medicare.

Although the use of production strategies seems similar between female and male candidates, this example illustrates the importance of examining the context and presentation of such strategies on campaign Web sites. Doing so will not only more accurately depict potential differences in the techniques employed, but also show the willingness to be more technologically advanced and sophisticated in message presentation.

Interactive Content on Candidates' Web Sites

The ability to use interactive content has been an advantage that could allow candidates to be—or at least seem—more personal (Selnow 1998). Female and male candidates seem to be trying to take advantage of the opportunity for interactivity, although in rather limited forms (see Table 7.8). The female and male candidates in 2002 did attempt to include more links from the home page, although male candidates were more likely to offer more links overall than female candidates. Almost all candidates provided a link from their home page to a candidate biography section, issues section, contribution section, and get-involved section. Excluding a links section and a site search engine, male candidates seem to establish a wider variety of Web site sections than female candidates. Male candidates, in particular, were more likely to link to a calendar of events. Such a section requires more frequent updates and attention than a well-established biography section, contribution section, or even issues section. Such a difference may suggest that male candidates' campaigns, at least in 2000 and 2002, have been more in tune with the necessity of a site appearing to be current and up to date, or they may simply have the financial ability to pay someone to do so. It is clearly evident, however, that the media are not of central importance in candidates' Web site development. Only 4 percent of female candidates' sites and 14 percent of male candidates' sites provided a specific link to a media section.

TABLE 7.8 (continued) Interactive Strategies Used by Gender on Candidates' Web Sites

	2002		2002		2000	
Strategy	Female (n = 26)	Male (n = 22)	Female (n = 16)	Male (n = 14)	Female (n = 10)	Male (n = 8)
Home Page						
5–10 links	62%	36%	56%	29%	70%	50%
10+ links	39%	64%	44%	71%	30%	50%
Link to candidate bio section	96%	100%	94%	100%	100%	100%
Link to new content	12%	24%	0%	15%	30%	38%
Link to issues section	92%	96%	94%	93%	90%	100%
Link to calendar of events	23%	56%*	31%	57%	10%	50%
Link to contribution section	85%	96%	81%	93%	90%	100%
Link to campaign directory	69%	77%	81%	93%	50%	50%
Link to get-involved section	92%	100%	88%	100%	100%	100%
Link to breaking news	27%	36%	19%	21%	40%	63%
Link for media	4%	14%	6%	14%	0%	13%
Links section	31%	23%	25%	14%	40%	38%
Site search engine	27%	18%	25%	21%	30%	13%
Candidate Bio Section						
Link for feedback	50%	36%	69%	57%	20%	0%
Issues Section						
Link to detailed information	54%	55%	56%	50%	50%	63%
Link to press coverage	12%	0%	19%	0%	0%	0%
Link to legislation	0%	5%	0%	0%	0%	13%
Link for feedback	50%	46%	69%	57%	20%	25%
Calendar of Events Section						
Link for feedback	23%	33%	38%	43%	0%	13%
Campaign Directory						
Links to campaign coordinators in a specific area	15%	14%	19%	7%	10%	38%
Link for feedback	69%	76%	88%	86%	40%	50%

138 • Gender and Candidate Communication

TABLE 7.9 (continued) Interactive Strategies Used by Gender on Candidates' Web Sites

			2002		2000	
Strategy	Female (n = 26)	Male (n = 22)	Female (n = 16)	Male (n = 14)	Female (n = 10)	Male (n = 8)
Get Involved Section						
Form for contributing	65%	64%	81%	79%	40%	38%
Form for volunteering	69%	59%	81%	71%	50%	38%
Form to get involved	62%	64%	56%	50%	70%	88%
Link for feedback	35%	50%	56%	64%	0%	25%
Download letter to the editor	0%	0%	0%	0%	0%	0%
Download door to door flyers	4%	0%	0%	0%	10%	0%
Download phone bank information	0%	0%	0%	0%	0%	0%
Download press releases	46%	36%	75%	57%	0%	0%
Download media kit	4%	5%	6%	7%	0%	0%
2002 only						
Desktops			13%	21%		
Screensavers			6%	7%		
Bumper stickers			6%	7%		
Links Section						
National party link	15%	9%	13%	7%	20%	13%
State party link	39%	18%	31%	14%	50%	25%
Other candidate links	4%	0%	0%	0%	10%	0%
Special-interest links	15%	5%	13%	7%	20%	0%
Governmental sites	23%	18%	25%	14%	20%	25%
Media sites	12%	9%	6%	7%	20%	13%
General						
Videos of speeches	4%	14%	0%	0%	10%	38%
Videos of ads	50%	46%	56%	43%	40%	50%
Videos of debates	0%	14%	0%	7%	0%	25%
Videos of news conferences	0%	5%	0%	0%	0%	13%
Transcripts of speeches	27%	18%	69%	93%	80%	63%
Link to sign up for e-mail updates	77%	86%	88%	86%	60%	88%

Note: Percentages indicate frequencies within each subcategory.
* Significant at $p \leq .05$

The link for feedback throughout each section was also not a high priority. Not surprisingly, the most frequent presence of a link for feedback could be found in the campaign directory section, which, because it provides contact information, would seem to be a natural place for it, yet not all sites even provided that option.

In the issues section, just over half of female and male candidates' sites provided additional links to detailed information about their stands on the issues. Although 20 percent of the candidates whose Web sites were included in this study were incumbents, no female candidates and only 5 percent of male candidates offered links to legislation the candidate had sponsored or cosponsored.

Although the sites analyzed were from statewide races, candidates did not seem willing to enable immediate contact with campaign coordinators in specific areas of the state, though it is not clear whether this indicates a lack of organization on behalf of the campaign or a desire to control the flow of information and inquiries. Still, it is evident that candidates make little use of the unique features of this channel and the resulting ability to reach out and appear eager for contact.

From 2000 to 2002, the use of forms on candidates' Web sites for volunteering and contributions increased, most certainly a result of advancements in Web site design and functional capabilities. Approximately 80 percent of female and male candidates' sites made use of contribution forms in 2002, and 81 percent of female and 71 percent of male candidates included forms for volunteering, ultimately making it easier to develop a database for corresponding with volunteers and to use in solicitation efforts. As the success of online fund-raising increases with each election cycle, incorporating the contribution function within all candidates' sites will be imperative; to do otherwise means the loss of a potential donor pool.

The ability to download additional materials—particularly promotional materials—is yet another decided advantage Web sites offer to political campaigns, but it remains underused. Research from an analysis of presidential and gubernatorial candidates' Web sites in 1996 argued that campaigns limited interaction due to the risk of losing control of the messages or other information posted on the sites (Stromer-Galley 2000), an argument that must have been salient in 2000 and 2002 as well. Neither male or female candidates made available template letters to be sent to local newspaper editors by candidate supporters, door-to-door flyers, or information for contacting people on behalf of the candidate's campaign, although a few female candidates (4 percent) and male candidates (5 percent) made media kits available online. The most frequent items available to download were campaign press releases (female, 46 percent; male, 36 percent), but such information does not pose a risk if an opponent happens to find it, as it has already been released to the public. In analyzing the 2002 Web sites, the ability to download desktops, screensavers, and bumper stickers was coded; of the three options, desktops were the most frequently available item offered by technologically advanced Web sites.

When candidates did provide links to other sites and information in a links section, state party and governmental sites were the most frequently provided links. Female candidates were most likely to provide links to all outside sources coded, a finding consistent with female candidates simply being more likely to actually offer a links section on their Web site. Media and other candidates' sites received little attention from candidates; special-interest and national party links were each provided on only 15 percent of female candidates' sites as compared to only 5 percent and 9 percent, respectively, of male candidates' sites.

The ability to post a variety of messages originally created to be delivered through other channels—speeches, ads, debates, news conferences—on their Web sites is yet one more important advantage that enables candidates to reach a wider audience with an unmediated message. However, candidates are unlikely to take full advantage of this potential benefit. Fifty percent of female candidates and 46 percent of male candidates did make their advertising available on their Web sites, although perhaps not their entire compilation of positive and negative spot ads. In the Kansas 2002 gubernatorial race, Tim Shallenburger (R) did make his entire compilation of spots available, as did his opponent, Kathleen Sebelius (D). Elizabeth Dole (R-NC, U.S. Senate candidate, 2002) chose to make only her positive spots available, whereas others were likely to only post their most recently aired spot ad.

In 2000, candidates were more likely to post videos of their speeches on their Web sites than candidates in 2002, and male candidates have been more likely to post videos of campaign debates. Both female and male candidates apparently find value in e-mail updates, as 77 percent of female candidates and 86 percent of male candidates made a sign-up process available for the viewer to be able to receive these messages.

Conclusions

The WebStyles of candidates running in U.S. Senate and gubernatorial mixed-gender races from 2000 to 2002 overall were vastly similar. Candidates are using their Web sites not only to discuss issues, but also to establish an image of a viable political candidate through verbal, nonverbal, production, and interactive content. Yet it is disappointing that candidates appear to be underutilizing dramatically the opportunities the Web provides to interact with potential voters. Perhaps as the use of candidates' Web sites by potential voters continues to grow, campaigns will be called upon to provide more opportunities for interactivity and respond in kind with advancements in their Web communication. Unfortunately, it appears that the candidates are not willing to initiate this development.

We argue that as campaigns design their Web sites—and thus the images of their candidates—the strategies currently used are in response to expectations for the medium instead of expectations based on the candidate's gender. Thus, the combination of Web stereotypes—instead of gendered stereotypes—and the ability to present an unmediated message to a potential voter makes the campaign Web site an appealing venue for female candidates in particular.

8
WebStyles in a North Carolina U.S. Senate Race and a Montana Gubernatorial Race: *A Case Study*

In 2000, five women ran for their state's governorship; three female candidates were successful in their bid, and two of those women represented the Republican Party—Judy Martz (R-MT) and Ruth Ann Minner (R-DE). In 2002, eleven women ran to represent their state in the U.S. Senate; three of those women won, and two of those three were Republicans—Elizabeth Dole (R-NC) and Susan Collins (R-ME).

Of these successful Republican women, two in particular made history in their state through their skill, tenacity, and success. When Martz was elected governor of Montana in 2000, she became the first woman elected to her state's highest executive post. When Dole was elected to the U.S. Senate from North Carolina in 2002, she became the first woman to hold a U.S. Senate seat from her state. Both faced tough opponents, both campaigned tirelessly, and both of their races offer excellent case studies for examining the diversity in candidate self-presentation on the Internet.

This case study will provide a more detailed examination of the WebStyles of two important races. Although chapter 7 pointed out the limited differences that have been found in the WebStyles of female and male candidates running in mixed-gender races, this detailed analysis will bring to light ways in which candidates are using the same technology, but with a different purpose. The case study, unfortunately, also brings to light the candidates' inability to use the technology to its full potential and as a means for reaching citizens seeking e-interaction. First, however, this chapter will provide a brief background on each race.

2000 Montana Governor's Race

In July 1999, Judy Martz became the first Republican to declare her candidacy to become Montana's next governor (Laceky 1999). At the time, she was the state's lieutenant governor—the first woman to serve in that role for Montana. Martz also had worked in politics for more than twenty years, had helped her husband run their family business, and had competed in speed skating at the 1964 Olympics. A few months prior, on May 10, 1999, Mark O'Keefe, the state auditor, had thrown his hat in the ring. O'Keefe was finishing the second of two four-year terms as state auditor, had served in the state House of Representatives, and had held a variety of other public and private business roles. Both faced tough primary battles, with O'Keefe running against two other opponents—Mike Cooney, secretary of state, and Joe Mazurek, attorney general—and Martz running against Rob Natelson, a University of Montana law professor (Johnson 2000b).

Although they faced opponents within their own party for the June primary election, the negative messages began early between O'Keefe and Martz. A February 2000 newspaper article indicated that O'Keefe suspected Martz of hiring someone to look into travel- and reimbursement-related documents from his office as well as personal information such as house plans (Anez 2000a). Martz denied the accusation. In June, she won her primary race with 57 percent of the vote. O'Keefe won his primary race with 48 percent of the vote to Mazurek's 36 percent and Cooney's 16 percent.

As the general election heated up, the candidates sought to emphasize their differences. Martz argued that her leadership was more inclusive, that she was more supportive of business in the state, that she was for removal of the business equipment property tax, and that she offered a less costly approach to improving education (Johnson 2000c). O'Keefe argued that his plan of using improvements in education and recruitment of businesses to increase the state's economy was far more positive for Montana, that he was for an increase of public lands, that he supported enhancing the role of technology in education, and that he differed significantly from his opponent on abortion (Johnson 2000c).

Another difference between the candidates in the general election was fund-raising. In September 2000, O'Keefe was reported to have raised more than $900,000, whereas Martz had raised just over $500,000 (Johnson 2000d). Of the money that O'Keefe had amassed, more than $350,000 was reportedly a loan from O'Keefe himself (Lutey 2000). Following the uproar over O'Keefe's large personal campaign loan and an $88,000 advertising blitz that aired from September 15 to September 26, the Stall party spent the same amount on an ad campaign on behalf of Martz that ran from September 22 to October 4. Still, Martz significantly lacked funds throughout the campaign. By the end of October, O'Keefe had raised almost $3 million, just over $2 million of which was his own money, and had spent more than $2.5 million. By that time, Martz had raised about $800,000, only $325 of which was her own money, and had spent just over $740,000 (Johnson 2000e).

However, through contentious debates (Anez 2000b), accusations, the spending of "unprecedented amounts of money" by the parties and special-interest groups, and a race that was tight up until the final day (Anez 2000c), Martz emerged as the winner, with 51 percent of the vote to O'Keefe's 47 percent. Martz' success seems to defy logic just by the disparity of funds alone. Further, she had to overcome attacks on her qualifications to be governor in a race where she was attacking her opponent's stands on the issues (Anez 2000c). Her victory was considered a "major upset," and some credit was given to Republican George W. Bush's large win in the presidential race over Democrat Al Gore in that state (Johnson 2000f). Regardless, Martz was successful in appealing to voters ages eighteen to forty-four and to those over sixty as well as to high school and college graduates (Associated Press 2000). Further, whereas Martz was able to secure those voters concerned about jobs and the economy, signature issues for her campaign, voters concerned about education, O'Keefe's signature issue, divided their vote (Associated Press 2000). Thus, with her strong message and party support, Martz made history in 2000.

2002 North Carolina U.S. Senate Race

In September 2001, Elizabeth Dole officially announced her candidacy for the open U.S. Senate seat in her home state of North Carolina. Another North Carolina native, Erskine Bowles, joined the race in October 2001, setting the stage for an expensive and bitter fight between two well-versed public officials. Dole was known for her term as president of the American Red Cross and her work in five presidential administrations, including serving as secretary of transportation in Reagan's administration and secretary of labor in the elder Bush's administration. Dole also was known for her campaign efforts on behalf of her husband, former senator Bob Dole, during his 1996 presidential bid, as well as her own bid for the 2000 Republican presidential nomination. Bowles was known for his success as an investment banker, his term as head of the Small Business Administration in the Clinton administration, and, perhaps most of all, from his term as chief of staff to President Clinton. Thus, North Carolina was faced with two high-profile candidates running in a high-profile race.

The political savvy of the candidates was immediately put to the test, and both appeared to rise to the expectations. Dole began running television advertising in June, just as Bowles, even without a primary victory yet in hand, turned his attacks toward Dole and began ignoring his primary rivals (Dyer 2002a). By July 2002, with the primary election still months away, Dole had raised $8.2 million and Bowles had raised $4.2 million (Dyer 2002b).

In the September primary election, which was delayed by redistricting issues, Dole competed against six opponents for the Republican bid, and Bowles ran against eight opponents for the Democratic ticket. Although Dole's opponents were largely considered "lesser-known and lesser-financed" (Shepard 2002: 6A), Bowles faced two tough competitors in State Representative Dan Blue and Elaine Marshall, North Carolina's secretary of state. The result was that Dole captured the Republican nomination with approximately 80 percent of the vote, and Bowles picked up the Democratic nomination with approximately 44 percent of the vote, with 28 percent and 15 percent of the vote carried by his two closest competitors (Damico and Rice 2002).

After the primary, Dole held the lead over Bowles. A poll published shortly following the primary election found that 49 percent of likely voters favored Dole and 35 percent favored Bowles (Rice 2002). Appeals to female voters, NASCAR fans, and basketball fans fueled the heated race throughout the fall. Dole added to the fire when she used ads and press releases to openly criticize Bowles for the North Carolina job layoffs made by his wife's company, which was keeping open factories in Mexico and other countries (Mooneyham 2002). Bowles incessantly attacked Dole for what he considered to be the shortcomings of her plan for Social Security and for her liberal trade policies through an ad campaign funded, at least in part, by his own $3 million (Broder 2002). Such money was well spent from Bowles' perspective, as polls taken just days before the general election indicated that 48 percent of the voters supported Dole and 42 percent favored Bowles (*Virginian-Pilot* 2002). The poll further reported that Bowles' "attack ads" were to blame for the increase in Dole's unfavorable ratings (*Virginian-Pilot* 2002).

At the end of the "most expensive senate race in the country" in 2002 (Kondracke 2002), Dole won with 53 percent of the vote; Bowles received 45 percent. Dole raised and spent $13 million in her bid for the U.S. Senate seat, with Bowles spending $11.5 million (Kondracke 2002), $4 million of which consisted of personal loans to his campaign (Theimer 2002). Not necessarily the major upset seen in the 2000 Montana gubernatorial race, the North Carolina race was undeniably well funded, and the candidates spent much money in an effort to spread their message and win the voters' support.

In North Carolina in 2002, the use of the Internet was an important part of that effort. For instance, by taking advantage of advanced technology, Dole's campaign was reported to have accumulated forty thousand e-mail addresses (Jesdanun 2002) to which they could send immediate messages to rally and persuade voters. Potential voters were not necessarily the only ones who used campaign Web sites in this race, as the media utilized information from the candidates' sites to supplement news articles. For instance, in at least one news article, the issue stance posted on Dole's Web site was compared against—and used to offer an alternative to—an attack personally issued by Bowles on Dole (Turnbull 2002). With candidates and others placing more emphasis on actively using the Web sites, this case study explores just how active and innovative the North Carolina U.S. Senate candidates truly were.

WebStyle: Web Content in 2000 and 2002

The four candidates on which this case study focuses all posted and maintained a Web presence throughout their general election campaigns and most, if not all, of their primary campaigns. Similar to the method used in chapter 7, this analysis will focus on the Web sites of each of the candidates in their general election campaigns, when they were running directly against one another. Further, the study will analyze the Web sites as they appeared in the final week of the campaign. Choosing only one point in time is important for our purposes because we want to capture the WebStyles of the candidates at a moment in which their presentations as viable contenders should be at their peak.

Verbal Content

As explained in chapter 7, the verbal content of a candidate's WebStyle includes issue discussions, emphasis on certain character traits, appeal strategies, attacks, and demographic group and sectional appeal strategies. The following discussion compares the verbal content of each category within each race.

Issues, Montana 2000. At first glance, Judy Martz' Web site appeared to be far less advanced than her opponent's, and therefore appeared to offer far less information. Martz' site did not feature a specific section for issues, but instead provided three links from the home page to additional information on her three issue plans, which focused on cooperative labor relations, education, and jobs. Once a viewer clicked on each plan, each presented a similar layout. A series of priorities was listed first, with bullet points providing minimal elaboration. These were followed by an extensive narrative (ranging from 1,100 to 2,800 words) that discussed Martz' vision for Montana based on that particular issue focus. Such a design provided viewers with a quick overview by listing priorities—important points, phrases, or words were placed in bold to further enhance a quick scan of the information—as well as more elaborate and expansive information, although the text-heavy narratives required a viewer's patience and focus.

Within these narratives, however, Martz would mention a variety of additional issues. For instance, within her jobs plan, she addressed telecommunications, electronic commerce, natural resources, tax reform, education, transportation, job opportunities, job loss, economic growth, and agriculture. The education plan primarily focused on educational issues, including character education and mentoring, and her labor relations plan included economic growth, job creation, environmental standards, tax reform, and educational issues such as high-tech scholarships, a high-tech curriculum, and workforce training.

O'Keefe's Web site, featuring a more professional and elaborate design, listed all of his issue concerns under the title "Our Plan." Viewers could then explore O'Keefe's stands on education, a "child-friendly Montana," taxes, senior citizens' issues, higher education, health care, tourism, public access, a "livable Montana," and a "rebuild Montana plan." O'Keefe's issue stands were presented in narratives (ranging from 497 words on higher education to 1,500 words on education in general), although the discussion on taxes included graphs and more elaborate headings.

O'Keefe outlined a larger number of topical issues than Martz but, like his opponent, incorporated a wide variety of issues within each topic. For example, under his discussion of education, O'Keefe's narrative included general education measures such as increasing teacher pay, supporting their professional development, and encouraging gifted student education as well as new technology, safer schools, the importance of volunteering, loan assumption for teachers taking jobs in hard-to-recruit areas, health care for teachers and students, and funding for inclusion of American Indian culture. Within the topic of rebuilding Montana, O'Keefe discussed the recruitment of new businesses, infrastructure development, and aiding small business as well as the importance of education, technology, and agriculture.

Not only did both candidates cover a variety of issues, but both also actually covered similar issues throughout their discussions. A striking difference between the discussions on the two sites was in the rhetorical presentation of the message. When Martz outlined the priorities of each plan, she briefly described her priorities in the third person. When she discussed the plan in detail, she used the first person. For instance, in her labor plan, one bullet point stated, "Judy Martz supports environmentally safe mining, timber harvest and oil and gas production." In her detailed discussion, Martz assumed ownership of the plan, stating, "I will demand that our forests are made healthier with responsible, best management practices to reduce fuels, disease and overcrowding in our forests, while providing the resources we need to employ union workers and protect our communities."

O'Keefe, however, did not have a consistent style in presenting the discussion of the various issues on his site. For example, when discussing education, public access, and a livable Montana, the ideas were presented by a generic "we," such as, "We need to work for good jobs and a livable environment." When discussing senior citizens' issues, higher education, health care, a child-friendly Montana, and the plan for rebuilding Montana, the material was presented in the third person: "O'Keefe noted that . . ." No one claimed ownership of the issue discussion under tourism, although O'Keefe himself claimed ownership of the ideas and material presented under the topic of tax fairness, stating, for example, "I oppose a statewide sales tax, and will veto one if it gets to my desk."

This lack of consistency on O'Keefe's site and the consistency on Martz' site with regard to issue discussion suggests that Martz was far more personal and that she actually had a role in creating the information—in this case, the issue statements and stands—presented on the site. Although O'Keefe's visual presentation was more sophisticated, the lack of personalness left a lingering question as to who really authored the ideas.

Issues, North Carolina 2002. Unlike the two Montana gubernatorial sites, Elizabeth Dole's site in 2002 included a specific issues section available from her home page. The link took a viewer directly to a page listing four issue topics with a brief description of each issue underneath, and a link for viewers who wanted to read more. The four issue topics included "tax relief," "jobs and the economy," "strengthening the national defense," and "education—local control." Although the issue discussion was not lengthy when a viewer clicked to read more—usually a three- to five-sentence discussion—Dole stayed focused on the topic in her discussion. She also assumed ownership of the ideas, presenting each in the first person and explaining what she would do or what she believed in. For viewers who wanted additional information, the site provided a link, "Click here to see more of what Elizabeth Dole is saying about the issues," that took the viewer to a page listing press releases created by the campaign.

Erskine Bowles chose a different format for presenting his issues, listing eight issue topics in a box at the bottom of his home page with links to further information: jobs and economy, national security, health care, education, retirement security, the environment, energy, and foreign policy. Similar to Dole's issue discussion, the elaboration on issue stands was minimal (ranging from three to eight sentences), although focused on the topic. Unlike Dole, Bowles' issue messages were presented in the third person, such as "Erskine believes . . ." and "He will support efforts . . ." In most of his issue statements, Bowles included links to direct the viewer to press releases or news articles that were related or distantly related to the issue topic. For instance, in the national security statement, the link "North Carolina Firefighters Endorse Erskine Bowles" sent viewers to a campaign press release, and another link, "Bowles Casts Differences with Dole," sent viewers to a news article. The latter link was included on seven of the eight issue topic pages.

Character Traits, Montana 2000. The WebStyle analysis of Judy Martz' site identified character traits that created a role as the incumbent and her presence as a leader. Martz' site emphasized her past performance, experience in politics, leadership, and competency, and that she was qualified and action-oriented. In addition, her site emphasized her trustworthiness and ability to cooperate with others. Martz' record as "Montana's first female Lieutenant Governor" was particularly emphasized in her biography, as well as her community leadership. The issue-related plans that

Martz included on her site presented her as a candidate who had a clear and developed plan of action for her term in office.

O'Keefe's site presented a candidate with strong "masculine" traits, such as toughness and strength, aggressiveness, and being a fighter. O'Keefe's site also emphasized his past performance, competency, leadership, experience in politics, knowledge and intelligence, and that he was action-oriented and qualified. On his biography page, O'Keefe titled one column "Fighting for Montana Families," under which he discussed his consumer advocacy approach when serving as state auditor and noted that he had used an "aggressive public relations program" and "aggressive public outreach." Within his biography, O'Keefe listed and elaborated on his past experience in public office, and even stated that his "background has made him one of the most experienced and dynamic candidates in the race for Governor." The site also hosted an "accomplishments" page that listed "a few of the awards Mark has received" and provided brief synopses of his work with consumer protection, public outreach, public lands, and limiting insurance fraud, to name a few.

Character Traits, North Carolina 2002. Elizabeth Dole and Erskine Bowles also emphasized similar traits on their Web sites, most of which were traditionally masculine traits and focused on establishing their credibility to serve as a high-ranking public official. For instance, Dole's biography highlighted her past experience, performance, and leadership in public service as president of the American Red Cross. She then described her work in government public service, from serving as deputy assistant for consumer affairs under President Nixon to her cabinet position as secretary of labor under the first President Bush. In her issue discussion, Dole also established that she was action-oriented as well as strong and willing to fight for her constituents. Dole offered such statements as "I will fight for higher pay and better benefits," "My guiding principles are . . . ," "I'll fight for North Carolina jobs," and "In the Senate, I will vote to make all of President Bush's tax relief passed last year permanent."

Bowles sought to emphasize his past performance, leadership, and experience in politics through his biography, titled "Bringing People Together and Getting Results." The biography highlighted his public service and private sector work and his leadership positions within both, and concluded with discussions of his service as chief of staff to President Clinton. Bowles' ability to organize, restructure, and create organizations for greater efficiency seemed to be a common theme throughout this section of the site. The site also emphasized his willingness to be aggressive and a fighter, with statements such as "He will push for strict enforcement" and "[H]e will fight to restore . . ." Bowles' attempts to appear action-oriented through his issue discussion were much more vague than Dole's issue stands, largely due to the use of the third person. Statements such as "Erskine favors legislation . . . ," "Erskine will work to encourage . . . ," and

"Finally, he will work to propose . . . ," illustrated a lack of aggressiveness and strength. In his discussion of the economy and health care, he did present more forceful, action-oriented positions, stating, for example, that he "will fight to pass a Patients' Bill of Rights." Yet his lack of specificity within the other issue positions suggested that he was more prepared to be action-oriented on these latter two issues than on the other concerns listed. Finally, Bowles did emphasize throughout the Web site that he was cooperative, was willing to work across the aisle (i.e., with members of the other party), and had a record to support that trait.

Appeal Strategies, Montana 2000. In 2000, the Montana gubernatorial race was an open race—neither candidate was an incumbent. Because the sitting governor could not run again due to term limits and Martz was the sitting lieutenant governor, she could have theoretically claimed the role of an incumbent. Although O'Keefe did arguably assume a strong challenger position through his use of strategic appeals, Martz employed a mix of strategies instead of assuming the full role as an incumbent.

One of the more distinguishing appeals used by Martz' Web site was that of addressing the viewers as peers, traditionally considered a "feminine" strategy. Throughout Martz' Web site, she personalized her message and spoke directly to her viewers as their equal, frequently using the terms *we* and *our*. Statements such as the following provide an illustrative example: "Too often our children are forced to move out of state to find better jobs. We need them starting businesses here. We need them raising families here. We need to bring our young people home—and we will." Martz also stressed on her Web site that, with her administration leading the way, the future was bright for Montana, even titling one of her links "A Promising Future." Martz also emphasized her own accomplishments, particularly in her biography section, and listed her endorsements from party and other political leaders on her home page.

O'Keefe predominantly displayed a challenger style on his Web site by using such appeals as calling for change, taking the offensive position on issues, and attacking the record of the opponent. For instance, in one press release posted in the upper center of his site, O'Keefe was quoted as saying, "It's time for a change. The failed policies of the last 12 years aren't working. We need a new direction, we need new leadership, and we need new ideas." O'Keefe also featured a section on his home page titled "Recent Opinion Editorials by Mark O'Keefe," in which he made such statements as "We're going backwards, and need a change in leadership and direction. Montana can't afford to slip any further." In an editorial concerning job growth, O'Keefe stated, "Montana needs new ideas and innovative solutions to bring good-paying jobs to the state." O'Keefe also often attacked his opponent's record and challenged her positions, assuming an offensive position, but did not offer any specific solutions of his own. For instance, in one press release that was representative of several posted on his site,

O'Keefe criticized what he called Martz' "lack of leadership" in regard to a water quality program; however, he did not suggest what he would have done or the stand he would take if he became governor.

Appeal Strategies, North Carolina 2002. Throughout the North Carolina U.S. Senate candidate sites in 2002, the candidates used a mix of strategic appeals on their sites, providing an interesting comparison. For example, Dole employed the challenger strategy of calling for change, but she also used two interesting incumbent strategies. Not only did Dole emphasize her own accomplishments from prior leadership positions as an incumbent strategy, but she also used an "above-the-trenches" strategy. The use of this latter strategy—which was in stark contrast to her opponent—is perhaps an unusual one for a Web site. Theoretically, Web sites could provide a forum through which candidates could respond directly to attacks, post differences and points of contention, and launch one's own attacks, particularly if the audience is, as is assumed, primarily already interested voters seeking reinforcement. However, Dole did not choose this approach.

In fact, throughout most of Dole's site there was little indication that she was part of a hotly competitive race; instead, the site assumed the tone of a candidate who was focused on getting her message to the voters. Once a viewer reached the press release section of Dole's site, however, it was apparent that she could be critical of her opponent. Dole posted a press release titled "Bowles' Family Company Exports Hundreds of North Carolina Jobs to Mexico and China" and another titled "Bowles Campaign Overreaches in New Ad." Dole's spokesperson stated in the release, "In his ads, Erskine Bowles says he cares about North Carolina workers, but the facts tell a different story. Erskine Bowles will say anything to get elected." Notably, however, Dole herself did not make any statements—negative, positive, or neutral—in the press release, allowing her surrogate to level the charges.

As part of her strategic mix, Dole also frequently employed strategies considered elements of the "feminine style" (Campbell 1989). For instance, Dole invited viewer participation by asking that they become "E-Leaders" and "help spread the word"; she invited them to "join Elizabeth on the campaign trail," and further encouraged their action through nine activities posted in the volunteer section. Dole also addressed her readers as peers, calling military personnel "our young men and women," commenting that "our taxes are too high," and sharing concern for "our children." Such strategies allowed Dole to seem more in tune with voters and focused on their needs and concerns.

Bowles, on the other hand, used a solid mix of incumbent and challenger strategies throughout his site. He capitalized on the incumbent strategies of emphasizing his own accomplishments and highlighting the endorsements he received from party and political leaders as well as expert authorities. For instance, in the lower left-hand column on his home page, he listed endorsements from a state representative, city mayors, North Carolina's governor, and various newspapers. On the right-hand side of his home page, he posted a photo with the caption "Erskine receives an enthusiastic endorsement from U.S. Senator Blanch Lincoln (D-Arkansas) who came to Charlotte to show her support for Erskine."

Bowles also employed the challenger strategies of calling for change, taking the offensive position on issues, and attacking the record of his opponent. On his home page, Bowles placed such statements as "Find out why Dole's plan to privatize Social Security will hurt North Carolina's working families." Bowles also used such rhetorical strategies in his press releases, all of which were posted on the site. In one release titled, "Bowles Blasts Dole for Flip-Flop on Family and Medical Leave," Bowles called her support of the act a "last minute conversion" and a "weak attempt to hide her real positions on issues affecting North Carolina's working families." In yet another press release, Bowles called Dole's prescription drug benefit plan a false promise, her plan for Social Security "risky," and her campaign "out of touch." On his home page he even promoted a Web site, bowlesvsdole.com, that was created so that the viewer could "see how Erskine Bowles will protect your interests." Overall, Bowles appeared to be the trailing candidate seeking to undermine the success—and image—of his opponent, and unlike his opponent, he leveled the attacks himself.

As is evidenced, both of the male candidates more readily assumed challenger roles in these races—they were more likely to attack their opponent and directly challenge her candidacy. The female candidates both used incumbent strategies more effectively and frequently and successfully coupled them with feminine style strategies, which allowed them to appear more personal. Viewers often seek out a candidate's Web site for learning purposes, but a site that appears distinctly separate from the candidate certainly does not encourage identification between the viewer and the candidate nor support of the candidate.

Group and Sectional Appeals, Montana 2000. Candidate Web sites also offer the unique opportunity to post specific pages for targeted demographic groups while keeping the larger message focused on the general bloc of voters. Further, Web sites allow candidates to organize their information into specific content sections and to develop the rhetoric based on the viewer's purpose for seeking that information. However, the specific group and sectional appeals in the 2000 Montana gubernatorial sites were minimal. O'Keefe did include a children's page that provided factual information about the state and links to various maps of interest, but beyond that, neither candidate created sections on their Web site to specifically appeal to a targeted demographic group, such as women, veterans, or senior citizens. Both candidates did identify the office they were seeking on their home page, although neither candidate posted a personal letter welcoming the viewer to the site.

Both candidates provided biographies on their Web sites and biographies for their lieutenant governor candidates. Both included public service information in their biographies, as well as information about their involvement in private businesses. Both also provided personal information, such as information about their parents and marital status, although the placement of this information was vastly different. Martz listed the following sentences at the bottom of her biography: "Martz and her husband have two children, Justin, 29, and Stacey, 25. They are both married; Justin lives in Butte and works with the family business, and Stacey is a student in Laramie, Wyoming." O'Keefe, on the other hand, opened his biography with the following sentences: "Mark O'Keefe is married to Lucy Dayton, and they have three children: Maggie [15], Gus [12], and Greer [8]. All 3 attend public schools, reinforcing O'Keefe's commitment to making Montana a better place for families to live." Such a difference in presentation of the information—and one candidate's willingness to highlight the material and another candidate's choice not to highlight it—reinforces the research that suggests female candidates seek to minimize the attention placed on their additional roles as mothers and wives. Such roles do not carry the same advantages for female candidates seeking public office as do the roles of husband and father for male candidates.

Neither Martz nor O'Keefe provided information about campaign events so that viewers could attend gatherings or rallies. However, both candidates expressed interest in allowing interested citizens to contact them. Martz provided a separate section titled "Contact the Campaign," in which she included the campaign's mailing address, physical address, phone number, fax number, and e-mail address. O'Keefe listed the mailing information for his campaign headquarters, phone, and fax on his home page, along with a link titled "Field Offices." On the field offices page, he again listed the mailing address, phone and fax numbers, and e-mail address of his campaign headquarters as well as contact names, physical locations, phone numbers, and e-mail addresses of offices in Billings, Great Falls, and Missoula. O'Keefe did not list a physical address for his campaign headquarters in Helena.

Martz and O'Keefe both included a get-involved section and a form through which viewers could submit information. Martz' information was far less elaborate and sophisticated. At the top of her page, she listed seven ways that a viewer could help her campaign (display a bumper sticker, host a fund-raiser, donate to the campaign fund, and so on). This listing was followed by a short paragraph that provided directions if the viewer would "like to volunteer for the campaign," and stated that "someone from campaign headquarters will contact you to talk about your ideas." The form posted on the page resembled an e-mail message, wherein the viewer listed contact information, simply typed in a message, and then sent it electronically to the campaign.

O'Keefe's get-involved page included three columns: "Ten Ways You Can Help!" "Sign Me Up!" and "Volunteer Opportunities!" The first column included five of the ten ways in which a volunteer could help, and column three contained the remaining five ways. Each suggestion provided a short narrative on how the viewer could help "Mark and Carol," the gubernatorial candidate and his running mate, Carol Williams. The middle column contained a form that the viewer could fill out, select options for volunteering (putting a sign in a yard, putting a bumper sticker on a car, contributing to the campaign), and then send electronically to the campaign. In this format, the sender could not include a narrative message.

Martz did not have an option for contributing to the campaign online, nor even a form that could be printed and mailed to the campaign with a check. O'Keefe, however, did have a link available through his get-involved section through which a viewer could contribute online or print a form to be mailed to the campaign. There were no contribution guidelines or regulations posted on either candidate's site.

Group and Sectional Appeals, North Carolina 2002. Elizabeth Dole provided the most extensive group and sectional appeals in her 2002 U.S. Senate Web site as compared to her opponent, Erskine Bowles, who did not target any particular demographic group with a special section. Dole, on the other hand, provided a "Students for Dole" section that opened with a letter from the candidate and offered a trivia challenge, photo gallery, university contacts, fun facts, campaign news, quotes, and the opportunity to post messages.

Regarding other sections on their sites, both Dole and Bowles offered similar sections when it came to campaign news, contributing, volunteering, and a biography. On the home page, Dole did not make her party affiliation known, and both listed the office they were seeking. Neither candidate opened with a personal letter or welcomed the viewer to the site.

Both candidates featured a biographical section detailing their background and history and generally provided similar information. Although Bowles' biography included a lengthy section about his family—parents, wife, and children—Dole only briefly mentioned her husband in her biography. The reference made note that she had taken a leave of absence from her role as president of the American Red Cross to campaign for her husband in his 1996 presidential bid.

Both candidates included a volunteer section, inclusive of forms for the viewer to complete. Dole's site encouraged the viewer to help and to "shape a brighter future for North Carolina." Bowles' get-involved section was less inviting, beginning with a simple statement: "Come join the Erskine Bowles for Senate campaign." Compared to the idea of being able to shape North Carolina's future, little effort had gone into Bowles' encouragement and persuasion of viewers to become volunteers.

Both candidates also provided campaign contact information, although Bowles featured a separate section devoted to this information. On his site he included campaign headquarters information at two locations, driving directions, and telephone and fax numbers. In a strikingly different manner, Dole simply listed at the bottom of every page on her site her campaign headquarters' mailing address, along with a phone number; no physical address or e-mail address for the campaign headquarters was included. Although Dole did have a contact link on all of the pages on her site, the section was designed to serve as a way for a viewer to contact the campaign electronically and to send in comments. The site also listed the contact person for issuing invitations and requests for Dole to participate in an event, but requested that these be sent via mail. Dole also included campaign events information, including time and location, so that viewers could attend rallies and gatherings throughout the state—something unavailable on Bowles' site.

The contribution sections available on both candidates' sites provided forms for the viewer to complete and send either by mail or electronically. Both sites highlighted the security of making an online contribution and, importantly, provided detailed information as to contribution limitations. This portion of Bowles' site was more rhetorically persuasive than that of Dole's, however. Bowles' introduction urged:

> Please join us in making Erskine Bowles our next United States Senator. Every contribution—no mater how small—can help. Your financial support will help Erskine pay for the television time, literature, campaign rallies and all the other things that are so important in mounting a successful campaign.

Dole, on the other hand, began by thanking the viewer for the contribution, but then immediately began to explain that the server was secure and how much could be given. On a site where so much emphasis was placed on persuading volunteers, it is surprising that so little rhetorical attention was given to persuading—or at least reaffirming—the online contributor.

Overall, the North Carolina candidates made better use than the Montana candidates of the expansive capabilities of the Web site to provide the viewer with specialized and organized information as well as specialized rhetorical appeals based on the content of the section. However, this analysis reveals that there is more work to be done to make the most effective use of the space a Web site offers.

Nonverbal and Production Content

Nonverbal and Production Content, Montana 2000. As in the traditional framework of WebStyle, the nonverbal content in Judy Martz' and

Mark O'Keefe's campaign Web sites was analyzed through the photos placed on the site. The nonverbal communication displayed by Martz in her photos presented a professional, businesslike woman. Martz was generally shown in photos with her running mate, either standing outside of the Capitol building talking or in a head-and-shoulders portrait style shot in which they were smiling at the camera. Martz did feature a "snapshots" page that contained photos of Martz with supporters at a picnic, at a fundraiser, and when she filed to run for office.[1]

O'Keefe also used a portrait-style shot of himself and his running mate throughout his Web site. The photo was used in conjunction with his logo and featured the two candidates smiling at the camera. The site also included a single head-and-shoulders shot of O'Keefe smiling at the camera in an outdoors setting; there were others of him with his family, outdoors by a pond with two of his children, with his father, and reading to children, and also a military photo. Corresponding to his emphasis on his family in his biography section, the photo of O'Keefe with his entire family was featured at the top of his biography page. Martz' Web site did not include a photo of Martz with her family. Both Martz and O'Keefe were most likely to be shown in formal attire, almost always having eye contact with the camera, and smiling. Neither candidate was frequently shown interacting with constituents or voters in their photos

In regard to production content, Martz' site incorporated far fewer graphics and attention-capturing design techniques when compared to her opponent's. The only photo on either Martz or O'Keefe's home page was a joint photo of the candidates for governor and lieutenant governor. Martz used virtually no graphics on her home page but did feature her campaign logo, which included a small version of the Republican elephant. In the sections that discussed her issue-related plans, Martz incorporated some topic-related graphics but no photos. For example, on the education plan page, the graphics included an apple, a pencil sharpener, and a school crossing sign placed sporadically down the page.

O'Keefe's Web site contained more graphics. On his home page, he included his logo, which used an American flag in the design, a partial outline of the state, the word *Democrat* in small letters, and the photo of O'Keefe and his running mate. His home page also included character graphics to grab the viewer's attention, such as cartoon-style drawing of a voter placing a ballot labeled "O'Keefe" into a ballot box, a paperboy holding up a newspaper near the "Press Archives" link, and a donkey flexing its arm muscle with "We Can Do It!" as the caption. The most prevalent use of graphics occurred on his "Kids Page," where flags waved; photos of Montana animals were used; and the state seal, a map, and a chart all drew attention to various facts. In his issues discussion, O'Keefe employed graphics only when discussing education, using apples as bullets to highlight the main points of his plan.

Neither Martz nor O'Keefe provided a visually stimulating or attention-grabbing Web site. Clearly, both of these candidates were focused on providing far more textual and detailed information about their stands on the issues.

Nonverbal and Production Content, North Carolina 2002. In the 2002 North Carolina U.S. Senate race, Dole and Bowles were far more active in posting photos throughout their Web sites, particularly photos of citizens, supporters, and of the candidate during the campaign. Both candidates had links leading to a photo section—called either "Photos from the Road" or "Photo Gallery"—from their home pages. Each contained numerous photos from various campaign events, showing the candidates speaking, posing with supporters, or talking with small groups of supporters in a conversation-style setting; both candidates were shown with diverse demographic groups in their photos.

Even with such sections becoming increasingly popular on campaign Web sites, a viewer might not be interested in looking through a section devoted solely to photos of the candidate during the campaign. Therefore, the photos—and thus the images of the candidates—that were shown in the other sections become perhaps more important. An analysis focusing on those photos revealed an interesting difference: Bowles' site completely lacked photos on its main pages, except for four on his "Women for Bowles" page. Although he did use thumbnail photos as graphics to draw attention to specific links on his home page, the photos were clearly too small to constitute anything more than a graphic.

Dole, however, actively used photos in her Web site design. On every page of every section of her site Dole had three state-related photos to the right of her logo, reinforcing that her U.S. Senate campaign was about the people and state of North Carolina. On her home page, Dole also had a series of different photos that would move on and then off the screen, just to the right of a head-and-shoulders shot of a smiling Dole. On her "The Dole Plan" page, she featured a collage of ten photos that included a senior citizen couple, a teacher and student, a farmer, a tractor, construction workers, a nurse and patient, military personnel, and a grandmother, mother, and daughter. Dole also incorporated photos in her issues section. Beside "tax relief" was a photo of Dole at a podium draped in an American flag with a crowd of supporters looking on; beside "jobs and the economy" was a photo of Dole working alongside a worker making furniture; beside "strengthening national defense" was a photo of Dole speaking at a podium with a group of formally dressed men and the American flag behind her; and beside "education—local control" was a photo of Dole standing with a group of students outside a school.

In Dole's photos, she was predominantly dressed in formal attire; in the photos available on Bowles' site, he was predominantly dressed casually, a finding consistent with the earlier discussions on VideoStyle in chapter 3.

Dole and Bowles were shown looking at the camera, and thus the viewer, only sometimes, and they were predominantly smiling in the photos. Bowles was more open with his posture, a traditionally masculine nonverbal communication style, whereas Dole was featured in a more closed posture, a traditionally feminine nonverbal style. Photos of both candidates were more likely to feature an indoor setting.

With regard to graphics on the candidate's sites, Dole used more graphics, particularly on her home page. Bowles, on the other hand, focused on using design elements to organize and separate textual material to direct attention instead of graphics to capture attention. Not only did Dole use moving photos and a waving flag on her home page, but she also used graphics to illustrate main sections of her site. On her home page, two thumbnail photos served as graphics on which viewers could click to visit either the Spanish version of her Web site or the section containing online versions of her advertising.

Bowles' use of graphics was minimal throughout his site. Although his logo traveled on almost every page of his site, the primary design of his site followed a very businesslike tone. The different portions of his home page were divided by what resembled the tab of a folder in either orange or blue, and this folder-style design outlined most of his text throughout his Web site. Very little of the typical patriot colors of red and blue were used, and they were seen most consistently on the American flag displayed within his logo. Dole, on the other hand, used red and blue as her consistent color scheme, which encouraged a patriotic tone and a more visually interesting journey throughout her site.

Interactive Content

Interactive Content, Montana 2000. The candidates in the 2000 Montana gubernatorial race made attempts, if tentative ones, to utilize the interactive features that a Web site can offer. This analysis of the interactive content follows that outlined by the WebStyle framework, focusing on the various links throughout the site, electronic feedback and communication options, use of forms for submitting information, and availability of campaign messages originally presented in other formats (speeches, debates, advertisements).

In the Montana governor's race, Martz' home page was structured nontraditionally and left the viewer wondering exactly which page was her home page. The campaign Web site address directed the viewer to a page that included the campaign's logo, a photo of the governor and lieutenant governor candidates, three separate links to each of her issue plans, a list of supporters and endorsements, and the opportunity to sign up for an e-mail newsletter. A link titled "For News, Information and More, Please Visit Martz/Ohs—Victory 2000" also was featured on this page. If a viewer chose to click on this link, he or she was directed to a home page with a more traditional format, with links to such sections as biography, campaign news, and campaign contact information. However, where the viewer was given the option of returning to the home page, the viewer was directed back to the original page.

O'Keefe hosted a more traditional home page, including the logo, a photo of the candidates, an opportunity to sign up for e-mail updates and to read about recent endorsements, and links to such sections as accomplishments, bios, get involved, contributions, and kids' pages. When comparing the links and types of links available from the home pages, O'Keefe had seven section links, whereas Martz included a total of only four links, three of which were to pages that included information about each of her issue plans.

Neither candidate seemed interested in receiving spontaneous feedback, as both Martz and O'Keefe made their e-mail addresses available in only a few locations. Martz' site had a section titled "Contact the Campaign" in which the e-mail address was posted, and they also posted that address on the Martz/Ohs Victory 2000 page. O'Keefe posted his e-mail address at the bottom of his home page underneath the campaign contact information and again on his get-involved page. O'Keefe was the only candidate who encouraged the viewer to use e-mail for contacting the campaign, however, as on his get-involved page he stated, "Tell Mark and Carol if you have an idea to make Government work better. E-mail your ideas to Campaign HQ."

When it came to the provision of additional information to support the candidate's positions on issues, there were no links to legislation sponsored by the candidates, supporting documentation from experts, or press coverage about the issues. Although both candidates did suggest hosting a fund-raiser or coffee hour as a way in which the viewer could help the campaign, Martz did not indicate that she would be present or encourage the viewer to invite her to any special appearance; O'Keefe did suggest in his get-involved section that the viewer could "[h]ost a coffee with Mark or Carol in your home. If you are interested, check 'host a coffee' on our electronic volunteer form." O'Keefe also provided contact information for each of his campaign offices in the state, whereas Martz did not even indicate whether there were any campaign offices outside of her Helena office; neither candidate provided any information about local campaign coordinators across the state.

That O'Keefe had a more sophisticated site design became evident once again when analyzing the interactive content of the sites. First, O'Keefe's form allowed for the viewer to click his or her preferences in the options for getting involved, although, as has already been mentioned, there was no option to include a message. Also on this page was a link to download wallpaper for the viewer's desktop and also to send an electronic postcard to a friend. Although some of the links included within this section were to other sections, such as the contribution section, or to e-mail the campaign, the layout suggested there were many options for making involvement convenient. In addition, the site did include the capability for contributing through a secure online connection.

Martz' get-involved section did have a convenient form for viewers to submit information and send a message, but the preferences for how a viewer could help the campaign did require that they be typed into the message. Martz did not link the viewer to any other section in her Web site beyond the "Martz/Ohs—Victory 2000" page. Further, Martz did not include any special section for contributing nor a form for contributing anywhere on her site. As has been discussed, she did mention that as an option for helping the campaign, but her Web site was not conducive to online fund-raising or even encouragement of contributing apparently due to the associated costs (Johnson 2000a). Like her opponent, she did not provide any campaign messages designed for original distribution on other channels (direct mail pieces, advertisements, videos of debates). Both candidates did provide links to press coverage about the campaign.

Interactive Content, North Carolina 2002. Both candidates in the 2002 North Carolina Senate race utilized what had become standard interactive features of Web sites. Numerous links from the home page to various standard sections on the Web site—a contribution section, biographies, a get-involved/volunteer section, contacts, campaign photos, and campaign news—were included. Both candidates also had search engine capabilities for their sites, and, like the logo and main section links, this option traveled throughout the site for a viewer to use at any time.

Neither candidate in this race seemed to welcome spontaneous feedback or much general feedback at all, as the e-mail address was not listed for either candidate at any point in their campaign Web site. Granted, a viewer could send Dole a message asking to be an E-Leader, a role in which volunteers agreed to help distribute information and provide e-mail addresses of friends and neighbors so that the campaign could send them information. Further, a viewer could send the campaign comments through the "Contact" section, but only by completing a form in which a first name, last name, and return e-mail address were required before the e-mail could be sent. In addition, the e-mail would then be sent not through the user's e-mail program but through this form, making retrieval of a previously sent message not possible.

Bowles' site was even less encouraging about contact; the form through which viewers could contact his campaign appeared in his get-involved section and seemed to be intended for those who wanted to join the campaign. The form required visitors to fill out their first and last names, address, city, zip code, home phone, and e-mail address. Viewers could then click options to identify "how [they] want to help." Notably, there was a comments section, consisting of a box only one line deep; any information entered longer than the line of the box would just continue to scroll horizontally. Of course this would not allow any author to review his or her message at a glance, and it strongly suggested that long-winded comments or messages were not welcome. Again, as with Dole's site, the e-mail would not be sent through the user's e-mail program and therefore could not be retrieved.

Dole's site was more advanced than Bowles' in the type of content that could be downloaded—such as material for making buttons and desktop wallpaper—and the manner in which one could promote the campaign to others. Dole's site allowed viewers to send e-postcards to their friends promoting the campaign and encouraged viewers to send letters to the editor and make calls to talk-radio stations. The Web site did not provide a template or material to be used in the letters to the editor but did provide names of what they called "major metro newspapers" and the mailing address, fax number, and e-mail address of each. The site also listed a number of talk-radio stations and their phone numbers. Both candidates provided means by which viewers could make contributions online and a form that a viewer could print and mail in to the campaign. Both candidates also had links to news articles that had been printed as well as news releases created by the campaign.

Conclusions

Studies such as this help illustrate that although candidates may include similar information on their sites, the presentation of that information—rhetorically and visually—may in fact indicate key differences in campaign strategies. In 2000, both Montana candidates sought to create an informative tool through which viewers could access issue stands, press releases, and contact information, as well as submit information for volunteering. The structures that the candidates presented to facilitate these actions were quite different in design, with O'Keefe's appearing more sophisticated and Martz' appearing more simplistic. However, both candidates did make use of one important element Web sites offer—ample room for lengthy information dissemination, particularly with issue discussion. The differences discussed in the analysis of this race appear far less gendered and more directly related to resources. O'Keefe clearly enjoyed greater monetary advantages in his campaign, and his Web site featured a design that was perhaps more elaborate than Martz could afford. However, the analysis also reflects how a candidate can utilize a minimalist site design and still incorporate the information we generally deem important: issue discussion, identification with the viewer, encouragement to join the cause, and an opportunity to get to know the background and qualifications of the person for whom we are considering voting.

The North Carolina race further illustrates what a larger war chest can provide in terms of Web site design. Both candidates offered online contribution options and many more links to a greater variety of pages and sections. However, neither candidate provided much issue discussion; instead, they used the site as a tool for making other types of information available such as news articles, press releases, speeches, and advertising. Dole also provided downloadable promotional campaign materials. As in the Montana race, however, the differences that emerged in this race cannot be attributed to gender alone. More distinctly, Dole assumed an incumbent role on her Web site, and Bowles clearly assumed a challenger role. Dole did integrate feminine style strategies more effectively in her site, and Bowles' site remained mostly masculine in style, although as our VideoStyle research indicates, male candidates do actively employ feminine strategies in televised messages. Perhaps a Web site will soon need to be viewed by candidates as a channel that, not unlike television, requires more attention to personalness, identification with the viewer, and encouragement of action on the campaign's behalf. This approach, which was more actively utilized by both female candidates in this case study, clearly suggests there are benefits to be gained.

9
Voter Reactions to Candidate WebStyle

As the last two chapters have demonstrated, candidates of both genders have found the World Wide Web to be a new vehicle for projecting themselves to voters. A candidate's WebStyle provides almost limitless information about issues, endorsements, political statements, and manifestos, and it permits the presentation of all kinds of sound, graphic, and visual representations.

As our research on WebStyle shows, female candidates may face a more level playing field when it comes to Web sites as a form of self-presentation. With the content and styles of Web sites containing similar information, allowing women a better opportunity to overcome the advantages of male incumbency and better financing, it is important to understand whether voter reactions to the information in this format and channel are also similar. Or does the gender of the voter make a difference in how the information is received, evaluated, or processed? To date, there is only limited research on these questions.

Research on the effects of voter use of and exposure to Web sites has been primarily descriptive, but a few studies have discovered that viewing Web sites has a positive effect on evaluations of candidates (Hansen 2000; Hansen and Benoit 2002). Although Johnson, Braima, and Sothirajah (1999) found that exposure to political Web sites in the 1996 campaign had very limited effect on levels of candidate image or issue knowledge, Tedesco and Kaid (2000) concluded that respondents who interacted with a 2000 presidential candidate Web site were less cynical after the activity than before, regardless of whether they were attuned to informational or entertainment content. One reason for this positive effect of Web site exposure may be that those who use online sources of information ascribe higher credibility to online information than to information in traditional media (Flanigan and Metzger 2000; Johnson and Kaye 1998).

Research also has shown that the level of interactivity on a candidate's Web site may affect the perception of the candidate. Candidates with high levels of interaction on their sites were perceived as more sensitive, responsive, and trustworthy (Sundar, Hesser, Kalyanaraman, and Brown 1998). Such research may suggest that female candidates might have an edge because they are more likely to take advantage of interactive aspects on their Web sites (Puopolo 2001).

Differences in Gender Exposure to Candidate Web Sites

Early research on exposure to information on the World Wide Web suggested that women were less likely to use the Internet for political information (Bimber 1998). However, the Pew Research Center for the People and the Press (2003) reported after the 2002 election that although overall Internet use for political information was down, as expected in an off-year election, the gap between male and female users was lessening. Overall, this national survey found that 13 percent of adults polled went online for election information in 2002 (16 percent of men and 11 percent of women). Thus, men constituted 57 percent of online election news seekers in 2002, but women increased their percentage from only 39 percent of political news users in 1998 to 43 percent in 2002.

Measuring Gender Differences in Reactions to Candidate Web Communication

As we did in our analysis of gendered reactions to candidate VideoStyle, we examined the differences in how male and female voters respond to information presented on the Web. These data come from studies of responses to the 2000 presidential campaigns, in which we considered the responses of voters who were shown political information for both Al Gore and George W. Bush. In a series of experiments, 224 respondents (55 percent female, 45 percent male) were exposed to various types of information about these candidates in a laboratory setting.[1] Each respondent was seated at a personal computer and provided with Internet access that provided candidate ads, debate excerpts, or news segments from the campaign. Each respondent was also provided with other typical political information that they might find on the Internet, including access to candidate Web sites, additional information from media sources about the campaign, polls, and so on.

To measure differences in how male and female voters reacted to the candidate Web information, they filled out a pretest questionnaire that asked for demographic information, ratings of both presidential candidates on the feeling thermometer (0–100) described in chapter 6, and a vote preference question. After exposure to the Web information, each respondent was then given a posttest questionnaire that repeated the feeling thermometer rating and also asked them to indicate how likely they were to engage in a list of political and information-seeking behaviors.

In another, similar experiment on the 2000 presidential candidate Web sites, respondents were exposed to material from George W. Bush's Web site and asked to evaluate the material for its informational content and for its entertainment content.[2] The respondents were 35 percent male and 65 percent female. This experiment also contained measures of images of and feelings about the candidate and questions about willingness to engage in other political and information-seeking behaviors.

Effects of Political Web Information on Male and Female Voters

Exposure to the political information on the Web for Bush and Gore, as explained in the first experiment discussed above, made a difference by gender in how the voters rated both candidates and in their vote choices. Table 9.1 shows that going into the Internet sessions, there were no significant differences by gender in the feeling thermometer (0–100) for Bush or Gore. However, in the posttest ratings, after viewing the Internet materials, the ratings show that women rated Gore significantly higher than did men. Conversely, men rated Bush higher than women by a significant margin. These results from the feeling thermometer were reinforced by the vote choice differences, also shown in Table 9.1. Although there was no significant difference between men and women in vote preferences before

TABLE 9.1 Ratings of 2000 Presidential Candidates after Web Exposure

	Females (n = 123)	Males (n = 101)
Al Gore		
Pretest Rating	46.15	40.47
Posttest Rating	49.17	41.11*
Pretest Vote	41%	30%
Posttest Vote	46%	31%**
George W. Bush		
Pretest Rating	57.22	62.36
Posttest Rating	58.32	65.06*
Pretest Vote	59%	70%
Posttest Vote	54%	69%**

Ratings based on feeling thermometer ranging from 0–100.
* T-test indicates difference between male and female voters is significant at $p \leq .05$.
** Chi square for difference in posttest vote for male and female voters is significant at $p \leq .05$.

TABLE 9.2 Gender Differences in Response to Political Information on the Web: Political Behavior and Information Seeking

	Experiment 1		Experiment 2	
	Females (n = 123)	Males (n = 101)	Females (n = 42)	Males (n = 23)
See more ads	4.33	4.46	4.60	4.17
Watch news for more information	4.85	4.92	4.81	4.52
Volunteer for campaign	2.27	2.32	1.57	1.74
Participate in online chat	2.37	2.72	1.67	1.83
Talk with friends	5.19	5.23	5.10	4.91
Read newspapers	5.10	5.08	5.02	4.91
Contact candidate	2.75	3.04	2.14	2.22
Use Internet for general campaign information	3.85	3.95	4.17	4.26
Vote in next election	6.42	6.41	5.93	5.65
Contribute money to candidate	1.98	2.51*	1.48	1.83
Use Internet for more info on issues	4.24	4.31	4.26	4.30
Go to candidate's Web site	4.02	3.91	4.40	4.17

* T-test indicates difference between Internet and traditional exposure is significant at $p \leq .05$.

exposure to the Web information, after viewing the Web material for both candidates, women were significantly more likely to vote for Gore and men for Bush.

However, there are very few differences in male and female reactions to the Internet information in terms of general political behaviors or information seeking. Table 9.2 indicates that there is no difference between men and women voters in their likelihood or desire to see more ads about the candidates, to watch news programs to obtain more information, to volunteer for campaigns, or to use the Internet for a variety of other informational and participatory functions. Particularly important is the finding that there was no difference at all for male or female voters in the likelihood of voting in the next election. Only one difference in gender surfaced: men were significantly more likely than women to want to contribute money to the candidate after exposure to the Internet information.

The results of exposure to Bush's Web site in the second experiment produced similar results. After exposure to the Web site, there were no differences by gender in the ratings of George Bush or Al Gore on the feeling thermometer (0–100) or on any of the individual semantic differential scales (qualifications, honesty, success, sincerity, friendliness, etc.). As Table 9.2 shows, there was also no difference in the way men and women reacted to the Web site on the same political and information activities used in the first experiment.

TABLE 9.3 Reasons for Using the Web for Male and Female Voters

	Females (n=42)	Males (n=23)
To do research	8.93	7.91*
It relaxes me	4.74	6.39*
It helps me unwind	3.98	5.48*
To communicate with family/friends	9.26	8.43*
To look for information	9.19	8.43*

* T-test indicates difference between Internet and traditional exposure is significant at $p \leq .05$.

In this second experiment, we also asked the respondents to tell us something about their reasons for surfing the Web. These Internet-related motives were assessed using a 10-point Likert scale (1 = strongly disagree, 10 = strongly agree) of forty-two statements adapted from Rubin (1981) and Papacharissi and Rubin (2000). These items ranged from relaxation and entertainment motivations ("it relaxes me," "it amuses me," "it entertains me," etc.) to social interactions ("to communicate with family and friends," "to meet new people," "so I won't feel alone") and information seeking ("to do research," "to get information"). On these forty-two different reasons, male and female voters responded very similarly. In Table 9.3, we list the only five reasons that represented a significant difference between males and females. Females were significantly more likely to use the Web for doing research, to communicate with family and friends, and to look for information. Male surfers, on the other hand, were more likely to use the Web for personal recreation or relaxation, citing reasons such as "it relaxes me" and "it helps me unwind" more often than females.

Conclusion

Overall, the data presented in this chapter on male and female voter responses to information on the Internet are striking for the lack of substantial differences. Taken together, these data suggest that males and females react very similarly to information about political candidates on the Internet. Unlike research reported on VideoStyle, where women seem to react differently than men to the same video messages, the Internet's presentation of information seems to level the field.

These findings seem particularly significant in light of our findings about the WebStyle of men and women candidates. In looking at WebStyles, our research indicates that the differences between men and women candidates are less striking and present women with fewer disadvantages than traditional video and news presentations of their messages. The findings in this chapter that male and female voters also react similarly to these WebStyle messages provide real hope for female candidates to compete with male candidates on the World Wide Web.

Part IV
Media Coverage of Candidates: *Gendered Messages, Gendered Reactions*

10
NewsStyle: *Media Coverage of Candidate Presentation*

As noted in chapter 2, extensive studies by Kim Fridkin Kahn (1991, 1992, 1994a, 1994b, 1996; Kahn and Goldenberg 1991) examining the newspaper coverage of women candidates running for election in the 1980s found that this medium stereotypes female candidates not only by emphasizing "feminine traits" and "feminine issues," but also by questioning their viability as candidates. Studies conducted since Kahn's work (Banwart, Bystrom, and Robertson 2003; Bystrom, Robertson, and Banwart 2001; Devitt 1999; Robertson et al. 2002; Smith 1997), however, have given some hope that media coverage of women candidates might be improving in the late 1990s and early twenty-first century (see chapter 2).

Based on media coverage studies of female and male candidates by Robertson, Banwart, and Bystrom (2002, 2001), this chapter lays out the construct of NewsStyle—that is, how the media respond to female and male political candidates in the coverage of their campaign presentations to potential voters.

Candidate Gender, Media Coverage, and Effects on Voters

The role of the mass media in creating and communicating the NewsStyle of candidate presentations is an important element in understanding the interaction of gender and political campaigns. Researchers have illustrated that the influence of the mass media in predicting political outcomes is strong and complex (Hayes and Makkai 1996; Iyengar and Kinder 1987; Kahn and Goldenberg 1991). Furthermore, the agenda-setting function of the media—telling readers not what to think, but what to think about—has been well documented (Ansolabehere, Behr, and Iyengar 1993;

McCombs and Shaw 1972). The media have been shown to "set the table" for voters by covering the most extant, serious, and salient issues of concern to the nation (Iyengar 1979; McCombs and Shaw 1972). Agenda setting is, however, only one aspect of media influence upon voting behavior. A number of factors involving the media may inhibit women's elected representation within the American political landscape.

Chang and Hitchon (1997) argue that the role of mass media in shaping the public's expectations about politicians—and the political participation of women, in particular—is indeed immense. Using gender schema theory as a framework, the authors suggest that voters have more positive attitudes toward candidates who are portrayed through the media in a gender-appropriate manner. Kraus (1974) suggests that women are restricted by engendered structural factors far more than men. Media coverage tends to abet "structural factors by helping to shape and reinforce voter's schemas" (Chang and Hitchon 1997: 42).

Investigation of the research, however, reveals that straightforward gender bias by the media or voters is difficult to uncover (Darcy, Welch, and Clark 1994). It is clear that a candidate's gender is politically relevant (Jamieson 1995; Kahn 1996). However, gender is not necessarily a predictor of electoral success or defeat. More significant, as Huddy and Terkildsen (1993) illustrate, is how voters' expectations of male and female competency on traditionally gender-related issues may affect campaign outcomes. They found when candidates exhibited "masculine" traits, voters perceived them as more competent. The inverse is also true. "Feminine" traits tend to limit perceived competence on a wide variety of issues. How this plays out in the electoral process is of significant interest to political communication scholars.

Our focus on candidate gender and media coverage is important to understanding how female and male candidates are presented to voters during a campaign through the construct that we call NewsStyle. This chapter will provide the foundation for understanding this construct by analyzing longitudinally the media's depiction of female and male candidates over the last three elections (1998, 2000, 2002).

Candidate NewsStyle: U.S. Senate and Gubernatorial Races 1998–2002

The universe of 1998, 2000, and 2002 mixed-gender U.S. Senate and gubernatorial political races was included in this study. The newspapers with the largest circulation, as identified by the Audit Bureau of Circulation, from each respective state, were used in the study (see Appendices A, B, and C). The newspaper articles were initially researched through an online computer search, with the names of each candidate used to conduct the search.

Newspaper articles are a significant source of information for the electorate. Studies have found that at the presidential level, the patterns of coverage for candidates from television and newspapers are similar (Graber 1987; Joslyn 1980). Additionally, Goldenburg and Traugott (1987) posit that newspaper coverage influences voters' view of candidates. Kahn (1996) argues that since newspaper coverage is influential, it should be studied to see how campaigns are covered in the press. Finally, Lichter and Noyes (1996) suggest that voter knowledge does not increase with exposure to television but will show a modest increase when voters read a newspaper daily.

The universe of articles from the front section mentioning either the female or male candidate was analyzed from September 1 until Election Day during each year, except in the case of Jean Carnahan's 2000 U.S. Senate race in Missouri. This race was unique, as Carnahan replaced her husband in the race after his death in an airplane crash while campaigning. Newspaper articles were gathered for that race from October 15 until Election Day.

Written instruments were developed to code the newspaper articles. The coding instruments explain in detail the procedures utilized. Recording of the data required techniques ranging from frequency distribution to identifying stereotypes or slants of coverage. The categories for the coding of differences in presenting male and female candidates evolved from a review of previous research investigating political communication (Davis 1978; Kahn 1993; Kahn and Goldenberg 1991; Miller 1996).

Categories were employed to describe the candidate and publication (i.e., name, sex, publication date, and page number). Next, categories were established to measure the number of paragraphs in which the candidate's name was mentioned. In addition, a category was established that enabled coders to depict the focus of the article (i.e., predominantly focused on the male or the female candidate).

The next set of categories was designed to identify characteristics and representation of each candidate. These categories included character (scandals linked to the candidate or questions about trustworthiness) and credibility references (depiction of the candidate as truthful), mentions of traits associated with sex, and candidate viability (for example, labeling one candidate or the other as a "front-runner"). Next, categories for mentions of the candidate's sex, children, and marital status were developed.

In addition, categories associated with the slant of the coverage were included. These categories were evaluative and asked coders to judge the overall slant of the coverage. Evaluations were made on the article in its entirety and asked coders, for example, if one candidate was treated more favorably in the article than the other. Finally, a category was created that listed issues associated with candidates, including the economy, reproductive choice, the environment, poverty, gun control, health care, government ethics, education, crime, youth violence, and defense. The issue categories were adopted from Bystrom's (1995) research on political candidates.

Coders from communication and political science classes were recruited to evaluate the newspaper content of articles. After training,

176 • Gender and Candidate Communication

10 percent of the articles were coded by all coders in order to calculate intercoder reliability. Intercoder reliability on the news articles, calculated using the formula suggested in North, Holsti, Zaniovich, and Zinnes (1963), averaged 0.88 across all categories, with a range of 0.78 (on candidate strategy mentioned in news articles) to 1.00 (on the demographic data, issue identification, and mention of marital status).

Quantity of News Coverage

One way in which media bias can be manifested in mixed-gender campaigns is through the amount of coverage. Coverage can be assessed in terms of total coverage, i.e., the number of articles that mention the candidate, as well as dominant focus, i.e., the number of articles that predominantly feature one candidate, though both may be mentioned. As has been noted in earlier research (Kahn 1992, 1993, 1994a, 1994b, 1996), when women candidates receive less coverage than their male counterparts, the media are influencing the public awareness of a given candidate. If the media do not cover or provides less coverage for a candidate, that candidate is less likely to be supported by the electorate (Kahn 1996). Our research indicates that women candidates are quickly gaining ground and might even, at times, surpass men in the amount of coverage they receive as well as the predominant focus of that coverage (see Table 10.1).

According to our research, the 1998 campaign mirrored the results of earlier research by Kahn (1992, 1993, 1994a, 1994b, 1996), which found that male candidates receive more total coverage than female candidates and were the dominant focus in most of the coverage (in 39 percent of the articles compared to 26 percent that focused predominantly on women). By 2000 this had changed.

In the 2000 elections, women were significantly more likely to be the dominant focus in articles (in 43 percent compared to 14 percent of the articles that focused on men). In the 2000 election coverage, journalists did not reveal an inherent bias toward women by giving men more coverage. U.S. Senate candidate and former First Lady Hillary Rodham Clinton (D-NY) played a large role in the turnaround between the 1998 and 2000 campaigns. She was the dominant focus in many more articles than her opponent, Rick Lazio (R-NY), which most likely skewed the results in the 2000 study. However, even when the Clinton/Lazio race is removed from the data, female candidates were still the dominant focus in more newspaper

TABLE 10.1 Predominant Focus of Candidates in Newspaper Articles

Year	Male	Female	Equal	Total
1998	233 (39%)	153 (26%)	207 (35%)	593
2000	79 (14%)	247 (43%)	250 (43%)	578
2002	232 (35%)	227 (34%)	211 (31%)	670

TABLE 10.2 Number of Paragraphs That Mention the Candidate

Year	Male	Female	Equal	Total
1998	1,832 (34%)	1,720 (32%)	1,855 (34%)	5,407
2000	1,423 (28%)	1,765 (35%)	1,918 (37%)	5,106
2002	2,014 (31%)	1,989 (30%)	2,536 (39%)	6,539

articles than their male counterparts. Female candidates were dominant in 28 percent of the coverage; male candidates were dominant in 12 percent.

The 2002 election revealed more parity between the candidates in mixed-gender races in terms of the quantity of their coverage, with 35 percent of the articles covering men and 34 percent covering women.

Further, when examining the number of paragraphs that mention each candidate from all three election cycles, a remarkable similarity is revealed in the quantity of coverage afforded women and men candidates (see Table 10.2).

Quality of News Coverage

Another way to measure the influence of sex stereotypes on the media coverage of the political campaigns of female and male candidates is to look at the quality of the coverage, including slant; mentions of viability, appearance, and marital status; and issue and image coverage.

Negative or Positive Slant. In 1998, there were no significant differences in the slant with which male and female candidates were covered in the newspaper articles (see Table 10.3). For the most part, both candidates were treated in a neutral manner in the articles. Male candidates were treated positively in 20 percent of the articles, and female candidates

TABLE 10.3 Slant of Candidate Treatment in Articles

Candidate Year	Male	Female
1998 Candidates	n = 593	
Positive	117 (20%)	87 (15%)
Negative	32 (5%)	39 (6%)
Neutral/cannot determine	318 (54%)	
2000 Candidates	n = 578	
Positive	67 (12%)	121 (21%)*
Negative	65 (11%)	42 (7%)*
Neutral/cannot determine	283 (49%)	
2002 Candidates	n = 670	
Positive	156 (23%)	161 (24%)
Negative	52 (8%)	59 (9%)
Neutral/cannot determine	242 (36%)	

* Significant at $p \leq .05$.

were presented favorably in 15 percent of the articles. In addition, male candidates were treated negatively in 5 percent of the articles, and female candidates were presented negatively in 6 percent of the articles.

The 2000 election featured a much different story. It found that women candidates were treated significantly more favorably in articles than men candidates. Women candidates received positive treatment in 21 percent of the articles, and men candidates received positive treatment in 12 percent of the articles. Men also received more negative coverage (11 percent to 7 percent) than women. For example, the *Concord Monitor* included a report of a Jeanne Shaheen (D) supporter attacking Gordon Humphrey (R) in the 2000 gubernatorial election in New Hampshire. "Gordon Humphrey does not have a plan," she said. "He has a recipe for two more years of costly litigation and stalemate" (Filosa 2000).

However, in 2002, the coverage reverted once again to being nearly identical, with positive coverage in 23 percent of the articles on men candidates and 24 percent of the articles on women candidates, and negative coverage in 8 percent of the articles on men candidates and 9 percent of the articles on women candidates (see Table 10.3).

Viability. In terms of the quality of coverage, the viability category in the study revealed no significant differences between male and female candidates in any of the election years studied, suggesting that journalists now present female candidates to be at least as viable as men. For example, the *Detroit Free Press* treated Debbie Stabenow (D-MI) as a viable candidate in every article printed concerning her 2000 race for the U.S. Senate. This is notable since she was running against an entrenched incumbent, Spencer Abraham (R-MI). As past research (Kahn 1996) indicates that females were not treated as viable candidates in the 1980s, these results suggest that newspaper journalists are recognizing that women's campaigns are just as strong as those of their male opponents and that gender is not as important in determining the newsworthiness of a campaign.

Candidate Appearance, Gender, and Marital Status. In our analysis, women candidates continued to be treated in a biased manner by the media in terms of their appearance, gender, and marital status (see Table 10.4). Chang and Hitchon (1997) postulate that gender bias in the public is likely due to the bias of reporters and the media and their insistence on perpetuating electoral stereotypes. Kahn (1992, 1996) and Kahn and Goldenberg (1991) also argue that media coverage negatively affects the electability of female candidates through stereotypical references to women in terms of their appearance, gender, and marital status. The data from all three election years tend to reinforce these previous research findings.

For example, when newspaper stories mentioned the candidate's appearance, they were much more likely to comment on the female candidate rather than on the male candidate (see Table 10.4). In these stories,

TABLE 10.4 Cross Tabulation Results of References to Candidate Appearance, Sex, and Marital Status in Newspaper Articles

	Gender	
Reference to Candidates	Female	Male
Appearance 1998 (n = 593)	29 (5%)*	10 (2%)
Appearance 2000 (n = 578)	33 (6%)*	2 (1%)
Appearance 2002 (n = 670)	41 (6%)*	3 (1%)
Candidate sex 1998 (n = 593)	50 (8%)*	7 (1%)
Candidate sex 2000 (n = 578)	38 (7%)*	1 (1%)
Candidate sex 2002 (n = 670)	64 (10%)*	9 (1%)
Marital status 1998 (n = 593)	53 (9%)*	16 (3%)
Marital status 2000 (n = 578)	62 (11%)*	4 (1%)
Marital status 2002 (n = 670)	52 (8%)*	8 (1%)

Note: "Not applicable" and "not present" categories are not included in this table.
* Significant at $p \leq .05$.

women candidates were often depicted in newspaper articles as wearing a certain outfit or sporting a new hairstyle. Hillary Rodham Clinton's (D-NY) suits became a major area of comment for the *New York Times* in her 2000 race for the U.S. Senate.

The female candidates' gender also is more apt to be mentioned in articles. And female candidates are significantly more likely to have their marital status mentioned in articles (see Table 10.4). These references may reinforce gender stereotypes held by voters concerning the appropriate role of women in society.

Issue Coverage. Previous research (Kahn 1996) has shown that the media are more likely to cover "male issues" rather than "female issues" in their coverage of political campaigns as well as to link some issues more often with male candidates than female candidates. Specifically, Kahn posits that "women are viewed as more competent in certain policy areas—education, health, environment, maintaining honesty in government, helping disabled and aged—while the expertise of male candidates resides in alternative domains—e.g., military, farm policy, foreign policy, and the economy" (1996: 9). This is of concern, as differences in the issue coverage of female and male candidates may determine the quality of information available to the electorate in making their voting decisions. For example, Wright and Berkman (1986) argue that media appraisal of a candidate's position concerning issues influences voter perception of the candidate.

Our findings, consistent with previous research conducted by Kahn (1994b, 1996) and Miller (1996), indicate that the media link some issues to male candidates more often than to female candidates (see Table 10.5),

180 • Gender and Candidate Communication

TABLE 10.5 Cross Tabulation Results of Issues Linked with Male and Female Candidates in Newspaper Articles Covering Mixed-Gender Campaigns

Issue/Year	1998 n = 593, 2000 n = 578, 2002 n = 670	
	Present/Male	Present/Female
Taxes 1998	73 (12%)*	44 (7%)
Taxes 2000	34 (6%)	45 (8%)
Taxes 2002	81 (12%)*	38 (6%)
Budget 1998	10 (2%)	11 (2%)
Budget 2000	2 (1%)	1 (1%)
Budget 2002	4 (1%)	7 (1%)
Unemployment 1998	27 (4%)	22 (4%)
Unemployment 2000	4 (1%)	3 (1%)
Unemployment 2002	12 (2%)	15 (2%)
Cost of living 1998	13 (2%)	5 (1%)
Cost of living 2000	1 (1%)	1 (1%)
Cost of living 2002	7 (1%)	9 (1%)
Recession 1998	3 (1%)	5 (1%)
Recession 2000	0 (0%)	0 (0%)
Recession 2002	14 (2%)	21 (3%)
Immigration 1998	8 (1%)	0 (0%)
Immigration 2000	3 (1%)	4 (1%)
Immigration 2002	9 (1%)	5 (1%)
Economy 1998	28 (5%)	18 (3%)
Economy 2000	32 (6%)	36 (6%)
Economy 2002	48 (7%)	37 (7%)
Education 1998	62 (10%)	83 (14%)
Education 2000	25 (4%)	26 (4%)
Education 2002	58 (8%)	89 (13%)
Crime 1998	37 (6%)*	10 (1%)
Crime 2000	2 (1%)	2 (1%)
Crime 2002	13 (1%)	9 (1%)
Health care 1998	25 (4%)	38 (6%)
Health care 2000	12 (2%)	41 (7%)*
Health care 2002	23 (3%)	45 (6%)
Senior citizens 1998	13 (2%)	28 (5%)
Senior citizens 2000	2 (1%)	18 (3%)*
Senior citizens 2002	17 (3%)	22 (3%)
Poverty 1998	7 (1%)	12 (2%)
Poverty 2000	2 (1%)	0 (0%)
Poverty 2002	3 (1%)	6 (1%)
Welfare 1998	12 (2%)	6 (1%)
Welfare 2000	4 (1%)	4 (1%)
Welfare 2002	3 (1%)	7 (1%)
Environment 1998	20 (3%)	31 (4%)

TABLE 10.5 (continued) Cross Tabulation Results of Issues Linked with Male and Female Candidates in Newspaper Articles Covering Mixed-Gender Campaigns

Issue/Year	1998 n = 593, 2000 n = 578, 2002 n = 670	
	Present/Male	Present/Female
Environment 2000	2 (1%)	12 (2%)
Environment 2002	14 (2%)	24 (3%)
Drugs 1998	10 (2%)	9 (1%)
Drugs 2000	2 (1%)	7 (1%)
Drugs 2002	1 (1%)	3 (1%)
Dissatisfaction with government 1998	24 (5%)*	9 (2%)
Dissatisfaction with government 2000	6 (1%)	3 (1%)
Dissatisfaction with government 2002	11 (2%)	5 (1%)
Ethics 1998	9 (2%)	3 (1%)
Ethics 2000	2 (1%)	5 (2%)
Ethics 2002	3 (1%)	11 (2%)
Women's issues 1998	11 (2%)	42 (7%)*
Women's issues 2000	3 (1%)	33 (6%)*
Women's issues 2002	6 (1%)	48 (7%)*
Defense 1998	15 (3%)	5 (1%)*
Defense 2000	2 (1%)	9 (2%)
Defense 2002	21 (2%)	19 (2%)
International issues 1998	6 (1%)	9 (1%)
International issues 2000	4 (1%)	32 (5%)*
International issues 2002	20 (3%)	19 (3%)
Youth violence 1998	2 (1%)	4 (1%)
Youth violence 2000	2 (1%)	5 (1%)
Youth violence 2002	0 (0%)	3 (1%)

* Significant at $p \leq .05$.

particularly with issues that resonate with voters. The content analysis of the sample news articles revealed that the masculine issues of taxes, crime, dissatisfaction with government, and defense were significantly tied to male candidates more often than to female candidates in at least one of the elections, but primarily in the 1998 campaign. Male candidates were not linked significantly more often to these issues than female candidates were in the 2000 campaign, and in 2002 men were linked significantly more often only with taxes.

In keeping with the results of previous research (Kahn 1996), women were linked significantly more often with the feminine issues of health care and senior citizens' issues in 2000 (see Table 10.5). However, unlike the results of previous research (Kahn 1996; Riggle et al. 1997), the masculine issue of international affairs was linked significantly with women candidates in 2000, most likely because of the salience of Palestinian-Israeli relations to New York City Jewish voters and its effect on Hillary Rodham Clinton's (D-NY) U.S. Senate campaign that year.

In addition, women candidates were significantly linked with "women's issues" in all three election years, but sometimes in a negative manner. For example, the following is the lead-in to a newspaper story concerning Ellen Sauerbrey's (R-MD, 1998 gubernatorial candidate) previous run for governor:

> The Fells Point Festival was in full swing, smiles all around, politicians thrusting their right hands out, trying to shake loose a few votes. It was 1994 and Ellen R. Sauerbrey, the Republican nominee for governor, was all smiles as well. When a young woman approached her, Sauerbrey presented her hand. The woman ignored it.
>
> "I could never vote for you," she told Sauerbrey. "I know you're a pro-lifer. And what really gets me sick is you could never understand what you're doing—you don't even have kids."
>
> Sauerbrey's face fell. She mumbled something. She had no good answer. Friends were embarrassed for her.
>
> Later, Sauerbrey—the hard-nosed, tax-slashing, old war-horse who upset the liberal status quo of Maryland politics—thought about her day. She was angry.
>
> She wanted to cry.
>
> She had no good answer to the woman's comment. (Richissin 1998: A1)

Although the article is somewhat more complimentary later, the writer of the piece mentions a stereotypical women's issue, reproductive choice, but to the detriment of the candidate, particularly when paired with references to Sauerbrey as having no children, referring to her as an "old war-horse," and then adding that she wanted to cry.

Image Coverage. Trait or image coverage in newspapers is also an important factor that may influence the electorate's choice for office. As Kahn has noted, "voters use personality traits as a basis for evaluations of candidates in both national and statewide elections" (1996: 53).

Our study found some significant differences in the ways in which candidate image was portrayed by the media (see Table 10.6). For example, the media paid significantly more attention to the female candidates' backgrounds and to the male candidates' competency in each election year.

TABLE 10.6 Cross Tabulation Results of Candidate Image Characteristics Linked with Male and Female Candidates in Newspaper Articles Covering Mixed-Gender Campaigns

1998 n = 593, 2000 n = 578, 2002 n = 670

Image Characteristic	Male	Female
Candidate background 1998	36 (6%)	76 (13%)*
Candidate background 2000	49 (8%)	108 (19%)*
Candidate background 2002	43 (6%)	122 (18%)*
Candidate personality 1998	30 (5%)	34 (6%)
Candidate personality 2000	27 (5%)	31 (5%)
Candidate personality 2002	31 (5%)	27 (4%)
Candidate party 1998	71 (12%)	58 (9%)
Candidate party 2000	68 (12%)	60 (10%)
Candidate party 2002	87 (12%)	71 (11%)
Candidate experience 1998	84 (14%)*	43 (7%)
Candidate experience 2000	42 (7%)	37 (7%)
Candidate experience 2002	54 (8%)	47 (8%)
Candidate honesty 1998	51 (9%)	42 (7%)
Candidate honesty 2000	15 (2%)	34 (6%)*
Candidate honesty 2002	33 (5%)	44 (7%)
Candidate toughness 1998	57 (10%)	37 (6%)
Candidate toughness 2000	61 (11%)	57 (10%)
Candidate toughness 2002	56 (9%)	42 (6%)
Candidate warmth 1998	11 (2%)	12 (2%)
Candidate warmth 2000	18 (3%)	36 (6%)*
Candidate warmth 2002	13 (2%)	11 (2%)
Candidate competence 1998	62 (10%)*	21 (4%)
Candidate competence 2000	51 (9%)*	27 (5%)
Candidate competence 2002	44 (7%)*	14 (2%)
Candidate aggression 1998	55 (9%)*	26 (4%)
Candidate aggression 2000	40 (7%)	37 (6%)
Candidate aggression 2002	51 (8%)	61 (9%)

* Significant at $p \leq .05$.

Although covering the backgrounds of women candidates, particularly challengers, could be seen as positive, many of these stories discussed the woman's family life, husband, and children, a slant that tends to work against the female candidate by perpetuating voter stereotypes concerning women's ability to perform in office.

The following excerpt from the *Denver Post* covering the Colorado 1998 gubernatorial race between Gail Schoettler (D) and Bill Owens (R) illustrates the use of gender stereotypes in the background coverage of female and male candidates:

> Gail Schoettler, born Gail Sinton, grew up on a rolling cattle ranch just outside the tiny rural town of Shandon, Calif.
>
> Owens, now 48, went to St. Andrew's Elementary School, where nuns doled out both education and punishment with an even hand.
>
> Schoettler, now 55, attended Shandon Elementary School. Her class—the kids of ranch hands, rodeo riders, and landowners—fluctuated from a dozen to a grand total of 17 students from kindergarten to graduation.
>
> Owens became a Republican at an early age, arguing his theory of conservative government during the unrest of the '60s with his older brother Mike. By the age of 13, he was president of the Young Republicans in his high school.
>
> Schoettler, according to her classmates, never seemed very political. She was a "quiet leader," at one point organizing a class project to send relief to refugees. (Johnston 1998: A-1)

The article paints very different pictures of Owens and Schoettler. Owens is portrayed as the consummate political professional, active and aggressive in his beliefs. Schoettler, on the other hand, is depicted as a "quiet leader" and nurturing (in her relief efforts).

Although we found no significant differences in mentions of candidate personality in the coverage of female and male candidates (see Table 10.6), the following example from the *Chicago Tribune* concerning Carol Moseley-Braun's (D-IL) 1998 reelection campaign for the U.S. Senate also illustrates how gendered stereotypes in media coverage can emphasize the woman's personality and appearance over their issue stances:

> Though she boasts that her legislative record is one of the best in the Senate, it is not her votes that make many of her supporters go weak in the knees. It is her personality, featuring a signature smile that she flips on like a light switch, leaving her admirers aglow.
>
> That same smile and charisma propelled her to a historic victory in 1992. The question is whether it is still enough to win again. (Dorning 1998: B-1)

This study also found that female candidates were significantly more likely to be discussed in terms of their warmth and honesty in the 2000 election, whereas male candidates were significantly more likely to be discussed in terms of their experience and aggression in 1998.

Conclusion

Although newspaper stereotyping toward female candidates still exists, this research illustrates that in the 2000 and 2002 elections, women received at least as much coverage as well as more evenly balanced coverage than in previous elections in the 1980s and 1990s.

Rather than depending upon gender-based schemas (Kahn 1992; Riggle et al. 1997) to make choices about candidates, voters in the 2000 election had quantifiably more, as well as more favorable, information about female candidates before making their choices in the voting booth.

Still troubling, however, is the media's penchant to stereotype women with regard to mentioning their sex and marital status more often than they do for men. Such portrayals of women may nourish stereotypical images of them as wives and mothers that may not be favorable to their election to political office. Further, newspapers' continuing obsession with female candidates' appearance is apparent in this study as well as in previous work (Kahn 1996). By focusing on the appearance of women political candidates, the media treat them less seriously than men candidates and distract attention from their issue positions.

Overall, in terms of issue and image coverage, the findings of this study reveal some significant differences in the portrayal of male and female candidates. But most of these differences were in the 1998 campaign and had disappeared by 2000 and 2002. For example, the media linked male candidates more often with issues of taxes, crime, dissatisfaction with government, and defense and the images of competence, aggression, and experience in the 1998 campaign, but with only taxes in 2002. The media linked female candidates more often with women's issues in all three election years and with the feminine issues of health care and senior citizens and the images of honesty and warmth in 2000. The media also covered the backgrounds of women candidates more often, including mentions of their marital status and families.

As we approach subsequent elections in the twenty-first century, we find the NewsStyle of female and male candidates running against each other in mixed-gender U.S. Senate and gubernatorial campaigns to be mostly equitable in the quantity of media coverage as well as in the quality of coverage in terms of assessment of their viability and positive versus negative slant. However, our construct of NewsStyle also finds notable differences in the newspaper presentation of female and male candidates, with men candidates more often associated with the masculine issue of taxes and masculine image of competence and women candidates most often associated with the feminine issues of health care and senior citizens and the feminine images of honesty and warmth. As part of their News-Style, women candidates also continue to receive less equitable coverage in mentions of their appearance, sex, and marital status.

Although differences in coverage—especially in the quantity of coverage—seem to be changing, the differences that remain may interact with gender biases within the electorate to create an untenable position for female candidates. For instance, although Fox (1997) and Miller (1996) to some extent argue that there may be a certain amount of pro-woman bias in the electorate, there is also a strong anti-woman bias. Salient in this argument is the fact that there is no formidable anti-man bias—for example, there has been no public opinion research that illustrates that there is a group of voters who believe men should not be elected due to their sex.

Ultimately, the findings of our research imply that the media still support some of the traditional stereotypes held by the public about men and women and their roles in society. This portrayal may have an impact on the outcome of elections and thus upon how the nation is governed.

Appendix A
1998 Election—Candidates and Newspapers

Female Candidate	Opponent	Newspaper
Blanche Lincoln	Fay Boozman	*Arkansas Gazette*
Barbara Boxer	Matthew Fong	*Los Angeles Times*
Dottie Lamm	Ben Campbell	*Denver Post*
Crystal Young	Daniel Inouye	*Honolulu Star Bulletin*
Carol Moseley-Braun	Mike Fitzgerald	*Chicago Tribune*
Barbara Mikulski	John Pierpont	*Baltimore Sun*
Mary Boyle	George Voinovich	*Cincinnati Post*
Jane Hull	Paul Johnson	*Arizona Republic*
Gail Schoettler	Bill Owens	*Denver Post*
Barbara Kennelly	John Rowland	*Hartford Courant*
Linda Lingle	Ben Cayetano	*Honolulu Star Bulletin*
Ellen Sauerbrey	Parris Glendening	*Baltimore Sun*
Jeanne Shaheen	Jay Lucas	*Concord Monitor*
Jan Laverty Jones	Kenny Guinn	*Las Vegas Sun*
Laura Boyd	Frank Keating	*Daily Oklahoman*
Myrth York	Lincoln Almond	*Providence Journal*
Ruth Dwyer	Howard Dean	*Burlington Free Press*

Appendix B
2000 Election—Candidates and Newspapers

Female Candidate	Opponent	Newspaper
Hillary Rodham Clinton	Rick Lazio	*New York Times*
Dianne Feinstein	Tom Campbell	*Los Angeles Times*
Olympia Snowe	Mark Lawrence	*Bangor Daily News*
Debbie Stabenow	Spencer Abraham	*Detroit Free Press*
Kay Bailey Hutchison	Gene Kelly	*Houston Post*
Maria Cantwell	Slade Gordon	*Seattle Times*
Jean Carnahan	John Ashcroft	*St. Louis Post Dispatch*
Judy Martz	Mark O'Keefe	*Independent Record*
Heidi Heitkamp	John Hoeven	*Bismarck Tribune*
Jeanne Shaheen	Gordon Humphrey	*Concord Monitor*
Ruth Dwyer	Howard Dean	*Rutland Herald*
Ruth Ann Minner	John Burris	*Delaware News Journal*

Appendix C
2002 Election—Candidates and Newspapers

Female Candidate	Opponent	Newspaper
Fran Ulmer	Frank Murkowski	*Anchorage Daily News*
Jimmie Lou Fisher	Mike Huckabee	*Arkansas Democratic Gazette*
Janet Napolitano	Matt Salmon	*Arizona Republic*
Mazie Hirono	Linda Lingle	*Honolulu Star Bulletin*
Kathleen Sebelius	Tim Shallenburger	*Wichita Eagle*
Shannon O'Brien	Mitt Romney	*Boston Globe*
Kathleen Kennedy Townsend	Robert Ehrlich	*Baltimore Sun*
Jennifer Granholm	Dick Posthumus	*Detroit Free Press*
Myrth York	Don Cercieri	*Providence Journal*
Susan Parker	Jeff Sessions	*Birmingham News*
Lois Weinberg	Mitch McConnell	*Louisville Courier-Journal*
Mary Landrieu	Susan Terrell	*New Orleans Times-Picayune*
Chellie Pingree	Susan Collins	*Bangor Daily News*
Jean Carnahan	Jim Talent	*St. Louis Post Dispatch*
Jeanne Shaheen	John Sununu	*Concord Monitor*
Gloria Tristani	Pete Domenici	*Albuquerque Journal*
Joyce Corcoran	Mike Enzi	*Casper Star-Tribune*
Elizabeth Dole	Erskine Bowles	*Winston-Salem Journal*

11
NewsStyles in the 2000 New York U.S. Senate Campaign: *A Case Study*

> You know the rules are basically as follows: If you don't get married you are abnormal. If you get married but don't have children, you're a selfish yuppie. If you get married and have children but then go outside the home to work you're a bad mother. If you get married and have children but stay at home, you've wasted your education. And if you don't get married but have children and work outside the home as a fictional newscaster you get in trouble with the vice president. (Clinton 1994)

In the preceding excerpt, Hillary Rodham Clinton expressed to the graduating class at Wellesley College the conflicting role expectations all women face, but especially the "double bind" (Jamieson 1995) women face as they run for political office. This case study investigates one such election, the 2000 U.S. Senate campaign in New York between Democrat Hillary Rodham Clinton and Republican Rick Lazio, applying the construct of NewsStyle, as outlined in chapter 10. The case study begins with a short biography and political history of Rodham Clinton as well as a history of the 2000 New York U.S. Senate election. Next, a rhetorical analysis of the political advertising used in the campaign is provided to establish a foundation for our examination of media coverage of candidate messages. The study then explores the race from the construct of NewsStyle by examining, through content analysis, the media coverage of the Rodham Clinton/Lazio race. Finally, a few thoughts about why Rodham Clinton won the election are offered.

Biography of Hillary Rodham Clinton

In *Living History* (2003), Rodham Clinton describes her middle-class, mid-America upbringing. Her book begins, "I wasn't born a first lady or a senator. I wasn't born a Democrat. I wasn't born a lawyer or an advocate for women's rights and human rights. I wasn't born a wife or a mother." Her life began in Chicago, where she was born and nurtured by a conservative family who held deeply rooted middle-class values. At the beginning, she was active as a Republican in student politics. Indeed, in high school, she says she was "an active Young Republican and, later, a Goldwater girl, right down to my cowgirl outfit and straw cowboy hat emblazoned with the slogan AuH$_2$0" (Clinton 2003:21). At Wellesley College, she was elected president of the College Young Republicans during her freshman year. However, due to the Vietnam War and influence by her college friends, she dropped out of Republican politics, and by the time she was a junior, she was working for the campaign of antiwar activist Eugene McCarthy. She entered Yale Law School in 1969, and it was there, in the spring of 1970, she met Bill Clinton.

Bill Clinton and Hillary Rodham moved to Austin to work for the McGovern presidential campaign in 1972. After President Nixon's reelection in 1974, Rodham moved to back to Washington, where she worked for the House Judiciary Committee's special counsel, John Doar, on the impeachment of President Nixon. In October 1975, she returned to Arkansas and married Bill Clinton. He was elected attorney general of Arkansas in 1976, and she worked on Jimmy Carter's presidential campaign. Afterward, she joined the Rose Law Firm in Little Rock and, in 1977, was appointed part-time chair of the Legal Services Corporation.

Bill Clinton ran for and won the gubernatorial seat in Arkansas in 1978. It was during 1978 that Rodham Clinton made a small (approximately $1,000) investment in commodities futures on a tip given to her by an attorney at Tyson Foods. That investment later yielded more than $100,000 and has been the target of much legal investigation.

Rodham Clinton continued practicing law, served on the boards of Wal-Mart and TCBY, and chaired the Arkansas Education Standards Committee from 1980 to 1990. She and Clinton also invested heavily in the Whitewater real estate project during the decade. The project's funding source and bank, Morgan Guaranty Savings, failed and eventually cost taxpayers nearly $73 million. This, too, came under investigation, and eventually an independent counsel was selected to scrutinize the matter.

Clinton won the presidency in 1992, and one of his first acts was to appoint Rodham Clinton as leader of a task force on health care reform. This panel, surrounded by controversy, produced a plan that never left committee in either the U.S. House or the Senate and was abandoned by the time of the midterm elections. Rodham Clinton began to take lesser roles in the Clinton presidency. She began work that included legislation for breast cancer research funding and child defense statutes. By 1998, her husband, already involved in scandal, was accused of having an affair with White House intern Monica Lewinsky. The Starr Report revealed the truth of the affair and led to subsequent impeachment proceedings. By midyear, the country was engulfed in the scandal. Rodham Clinton, however, continued to convey constant public support for her husband (Alvarez 2004).

A History of the 2000 New York U.S. Senate Campaign

New York Senator Patrick Moynihan, the retiring seventy-three-year-old Democrat, was arguably among the U.S. Senate's strongest intellects. He had held his Senate seat for twenty-five years, after previously serving in the cabinets of Presidents Kennedy, Johnson, Nixon, and Ford. The campaign to fill the seat became one of the most fiercely fought contests in the 2000 elections.

The campaign began as a challenge between New York City mayor Rudolph Giuliani and Hillary Rodham Clinton. When Giuliani dropped out of the race for health reasons in late spring, Rick Lazio, a four-term U.S. Congressman from Long Island, took his place. Lazio quickly narrowed the focus of the race to character issues, with President Clinton at the epicenter of the attacks. Polls illustrated that the race was deeply divisive—one in three New Yorkers had an unfavorable opinion of Rodham Clinton (e.g., see the Marist Institute for Public Opinion, 2000).

However, Rodham Clinton's largest problem was the "carpetbagger" label. Lazio argued extensively, both in campaign speeches and in ads, that she was not a "real" New Yorker, often reminding voters that she had established residency in New York only in the last year, when she decided to run for the Senate. He portrayed himself as the "moderate, homegrown" alternative to the liberal carpetbagger.

Rodham Clinton conceded that if the race were based on "who has lived in New York the longest," she would lose. She attempted (largely successfully) to promote the issues in the campaign and portray Lazio as a rabid right-winger with ties to former Speaker of the U.S. House of Representatives Newt Gingrich (Lazio served as deputy whip under Gingrich).

Lazio, to his detriment, directed voters' attention to the issue of "soft money." During the first debate, Lazio walked across the stage, confronting Rodham Clinton and making a demand that she sign a pledge eliminating soft money from her campaign. After a terse exchange, Rodham Clinton declined. However, polls revealed that many New Yorkers, especially women, disapproved of Lazio's aggressive tactics and found him unlikable (Nagourney and Connelly 2000).

Both candidates agreed to stop accepting soft money in late September 1999. However, the issue reemerged in the second Rodham Clinton–Lazio debate when Rodham Clinton charged that Lazio violated the agreement by accepting $1.8 million in ad money from the Republican National Committee. Lazio responded by stating, "Please, no lectures from Motel 1600 on campaign finance reform" (CNN.com 2000).

With less than a month remaining before Election Day, polls showed Rodham Clinton leading by about 3 percentage points, a margin that narrowed even further in the last weeks of the campaign (Hirschkorn 2000). Despite early problems in the campaign and the accusations of carpetbagging and corruption, Rodham Clinton was able to prevail in what is generally seen to be an extraordinary campaign. Spending more than $41 million, she beat popular Republican Lazio by a surprisingly wide margin—55 percent to 43 percent.

NewsStyle: The Media Coverage of the Campaign

Because of the interest in the Rodham Clinton/Lazio race, media coverage was extensive—international and national as well as local. Both Rodham Clinton and Lazio made strong attempts to play not only to the more obvious news sources, but also to more minor media in the news market (especially in upstate New York).

We chose the following three newspapers to investigate the NewsStyle of the Rodham Clinton/Lazio campaign: the *New York Daily News*, *Buffalo Times*, and *Albany Union-Trade*. Although television is the primary source of news for a majority of the country, studies illustrate that newspapers provide appropriate information concerning elections (Goldenberg and Traugott 1987). Newspaper articles are a significant source of information for the electorate. Voters' discernment of political candidates is affected by what they read. As explained in chapter 10, newspapers shape the NewsStyle of candidates by how they cover campaigns. Hence, their content is worthy of investigation

These three newspapers were chosen for substantive and practical reasons. First, these newspapers cover both upstate New York and New York City and boast large readerships. We did not use the *New York Times* in this case study due to its reputation as a "national newspaper." Second, articles from these newspapers were easily obtained off microfiche and through archives on the Internet. The universe of articles mentioning either candidate from September 1, 2000, to November 7, 2000, Election Day, was selected for analysis. A total of four hundred articles were identified that contained the names of Hillary Rodham Clinton and/or Rick Lazio.

Written instruments were developed to code the newspaper articles. Recording of the data required techniques ranging from frequency distribution to identifying stereotypes or slants of coverage. The categories for coding media content evolved from previous research investigating political communication (Davis 1978; Hofstetter 1976; Kahn 1993; Kahn and Goldenberg 1991; Miller 1996) as well as sex stereotyping (Campbell 1989; Jansen 1993; Kramarae 1995; Miller 1996; Trent and Sabourin 1993). Categories were employed to describe the demographic data of the candidate and newspaper as well as the number of paragraphs mentioning each candidate's name. The next category asked coders to evaluate issues as they were linked with certain candidates. The issue categories were developed from Miller's (1996) newspaper article code book and Bystrom's (1995) political advertising code book. Another set of categories was designed to identify characteristics and representation of each candidate. These categories included character and credibility references, mentions of traits associated with sex, and candidate viability.

A set of categories also was included to investigate discussion of political ads from the campaign in these newspapers. In addition, categories associated with the slant of the coverage were included. These categories were evaluative and asked coders to judge the overall slant—positive, negative, or neutral—of the coverage. Evaluations were made on the article in its entirety and included statements concerning the use of any gender stereotypes in the article.

Three coders—one female political science major and two male communication majors—were recruited from a graduate political communication class to code the newspaper content of the articles identified. During a training session, the coders read the coding instrument and coded five articles of like content. After additional coding and training, 10 percent of the total number of articles was then utilized in the intercoder reliability test. Intercoder reliability was 0.85 across all categories, with a range of 0.72 to 1.00.

Analysis of the NewsStyle of the Rodham Clinton/Lazio Campaign

The study used descriptive statistics to record frequencies and presence or absence of defined categories. Frequencies were calculated for the articles concerning each candidate. The chi square statistic was used to test for significant difference in the coverage of Rodham Clinton and Lazio in the respective categories. Analysis of the four hundred newspaper articles revealed important, significant, and interesting results with regard to issue and image coverage of these candidates.

Issue Coverage

Significant differences were revealed in the issues linked to each candidate by the newspapers studied (see Table 11.1). Discussion concerning taxes was linked to Lazio significantly more often than to Rodham Clinton. However, references to the budget and economy in general were more often linked to Rodham Clinton. In addition, issues related to national defense were linked strongly to Rodham Clinton. All of these issues are considered "masculine," according to previous research.

Social, "feminine" issues were linked to Rodham Clinton more often than to her Republican counterpart. Education and health care, for example, were linked to Rodham Clinton significantly more often (see Table 11.1). Rodham Clinton also was linked to environmental issues significantly more often than Lazio. Finally, in the category labeled women's

TABLE 11.1 Issues Linked to Candidates

Issue	Clinton	Lazio
Taxes	26 (6%)	45 (11%)*
Budget	27 (7%)*	11 (3%)
Economy	25 (6%)*	10 (2%)
Defense	15 (4%)*	2 (1%)
Education	57 (14%)*	22 (6%)
Health care	28 (7%)*	9 (2%)
Environment	13 (3%)*	1 (1%)
Women's issues	29 (8%)*	10 (2%)

* Significant at $p \leq .05$.

TABLE 11.2 Images Linked to Candidates

Image Characteristic	Clinton	Lazio
Candidate appearance	24 (6%)*	7 (2%)
Marital status	68 (17%)*	10 (2%)
Aggressive	13 (3%)	55 (13%) *
Sex of candidate mentioned	63 (15%)*	4 (1%)

* Significant at $p \leq .05$.

issues (representing such issues as reproductive choice, sexual harassment, etc.), Rodham Clinton also proved to be significantly referenced.

Image Coverage

Significant differences in the portrayal of candidate image characteristics also emerged in our analysis of the newspaper coverage of Rodham Clinton and Lazio (see Table 11.2). For example, Rodham Clinton's appearance was mentioned significantly more often than that of her male opponent. References to Rodham Clinton's marriage also were significantly more frequent than references to Lazio's marriage. And Rodham Clinton's sex was mentioned significantly more often than Lazio's. Rodham Clinton was referred to as the "female candidate" in sixty-three articles (15 percent), whereas Lazio was coined the "male candidate" in only four of the articles (1 percent). References to candidate appearance, marital status, and sex can be considered sex stereotyping by the media. Also stereotypically, Lazio was presented as much more aggressive than Rodham Clinton.

However, there were no significant differences in how the media presented the favorability or viability of these candidates.

Discussion

The results of our case study show that Hillary Rodham Clinton and Rick Lazio received mostly equitable coverage by the newspapers studied. There were no significant differences in the slant of the stories about their campaigns or in how these newspapers presented their viability as candidates to voters. There were, however, differences in their issue and image coverage, which worked to both advantage and disadvantage Rodham Clinton.

These results imply that the media's discussion of issues in their coverage of the Rodham Clinton/Lazio campaign may be at the heart of Rodham Clinton's success. Wright and Berkman (1986) argue that media appraisal of a candidate's position concerning issues influence voter perception of the candidate. This study determined that journalists spent more time focusing on many of Rodham Clinton's issues. Furthermore, these newspapers were more likely to link many salient masculine and feminine issues with Rodham Clinton. In particular, linking Rodham Clinton with the most salient issue of most political campaigns—the economy—most likely helped her, especially in upstate New York. She also was linked more often than Lazio with the politically salient issues of national defense, education, and health care. Beyond the obvious benefit of being linked with issues that resonate with voters, Rodham Clinton also enjoyed being linked to a greater number of issues than Lazio.

However, Rodham Clinton's image coverage could have disadvantaged her campaign with voters, as her appearance, marital status, and sex were mentioned much more often than Lazio's appearance, marital status, and sex. The mention of such factors can disadvantage female candidates by underscoring sex stereotypes held by voters.

Rodham Clinton did receive much more coverage of her appearance than her opponent, and this probably did not help her campaign. Her blue dresses and hairstyle received much more attention than Lazio's suit color or receding hairline. However, Rodham Clinton's strong issue coverage may have offset the tendency of these newspapers to cover her image in stereotypical ways. In addition, Lazio's aggressive debate behavior may have damaged him. Many newspapers reported on his aggressive behavior at the Buffalo debate, where he crossed the stage waving a no-soft-money contract at Rodham Clinton. Most of the newspaper reports about Lazio's behavior were not complimentary, and polls (e.g., CNN 2000) revealed that the action did not appeal to moderate voters, especially women.

It is also important to note that one factor—marital status—that usually disadvantages female candidates (Kahn 1996) may have helped Rodham Clinton in this campaign. Bill Clinton, the candidate's husband, was mentioned far more often than Rick Lazio's spouse, Pat. However, since President Clinton had an extraordinarily high approval rating at the time of the New York U.S. Senate campaign, Rodham Clinton may have benefited from being linked to her husband.

Political Advertising in the Campaign

To better understand the media dynamics, this case study also explores the influence of candidate advertising. Rodham Clinton's first ads were, for the most part, positive, and were created while she was running against Giuliani. Her ad campaign began with a spot titled "First." The thirty-second ad highlighted Rodham Clinton before her tenure as first lady in the White House. In the ad, a male announcer discussed her work as a lawyer and leader in the Children's Defense Fund charity. She did not, however, make mention of her work in the Rose Law Firm. The strategy behind "First" was to attempt to educate voters about Rodham Clinton's pre–White House life and her thirty years of work on child and family issues. This ad was an attempt to inoculate voters against Giuliani's constant reference to Rodham Clinton as "the First Lady." The ad uses wordplay, redefining Rodham Clinton not as a First Lady, but as a woman with many other "firsts."

Rodham Clinton's other campaign ad, also released while Giuliani was a candidate but at a time when there was doubt about whether he would remain in the race, was a positive thirty-second ad featuring Dr. Betty Lowe, an Arkansas pediatrician who served as Chelsea Clinton's physician, and, much like the first ad, reflected Rodham Clinton's commitment to children and families.

Giuliani's first Senate ad was a sixty-second spot titled "Integrity." In it, U.S. Senator John McCain and Giuliani were portrayed riding together on McCain's 2000 presidential campaign bus. The ad clearly attempted to draw from McCain's strong support in New York state. Giuliani ran a total of seven ads during his time in the race. The last ad aired by his campaign was a sixty-second spot titled "A New York Senator" that portrayed Giuliani as a "true New Yorker." Though the ad did not mention Rodham Clinton directly, it quite clearly attempted to place her in the unenviable position of a carpetbagger. The ad provided details concerning Giuliani's native status as well as his straightforward style.

Rodham Clinton's Political Advertising Campaign versus Lazio

Two days after Lazio entered the campaign, Rodham Clinton launched her third ad, titled "Mission," which featured her speaking about health care, education, targeted tax cuts for families, and creating new jobs. "Mission" discussed popular centrist issues and attempted to portray Rodham Clinton as a positive, above-the-trenches candidate in contrast to Lazio, who went on the attack in his candidacy speech by stating that Rodham Clinton was "carpetbagging" by running for the Senate in a state in which she did not live (PBS.org 2000).

Her fourth ad, titled "Plan," featured Rodham Clinton presenting a plan to improve the state's economy. It was obvious that at this point, early in the campaign, Rodham Clinton's camp wanted a race based on issues and not character, personalities, or images. In her next set of ads, however, she went on the attack. Two ads, titled "I Love New York" and "Trust Me," featured former New York City mayor Ed Koch attacking Lazio on behalf of

Rodham Clinton. The issues raised in the ads included Lazio's perceived right-wing stance on gun control and abortion rights. Koch also linked Lazio with conservative former presidential candidate Pat Buchanan (Lazio, according to Koch, had once considered joining Buchanan in the Independence Party). Rodham Clinton's approach in these negative ads was to link Lazio to the far right wing of the Republican Party. Further, by utilizing Koch, Rodham Clinton attempted to deflect the carpetbagger criticism. Once started, Rodham Clinton continued to attack Lazio for being too far to the right. The Rodham Clinton camp's next set of ads included attacks on Lazio for his vote on the Patients' Bill of Rights (he voted against it), his alleged flip-flop on hate crimes legislation, and his supposed propensity to miss important votes in Congress. With the skipped-vote ads, Rodham Clinton's campaign used a tactic employed by former Republican senator Alfonse D'Amato of New York, who accused his opponent, Charles Schumer, of the same offense in their previous campaign. Further, the ad gave Rodham Clinton a "safe" attack, since she had not previously held office and, therefore, there was no question of her having missed votes.

Rodham Clinton released a series of five attack ads in late September 2000 aimed at her opponent, with the most potent being an ad titled "News Update: Heating Oil." In the ad, an anonymous announcer criticized Lazio for missing a House vote (the measure lost by two votes) on legislation to create a home heating oil reserve for the Northeast. The ad mimicked a news broadcast and was particularly timely. Escalating gas prices were an issue in the 2000 presidential campaign, and Rodham Clinton's ad helped turn it into a local issue. Further, the ad targeted upstate New Yorkers and was especially relevant to the area's low-income and blue-collar voters. Another thirty-second ad, titled "Won't See," attacked Lazio's voting record on an array of issues. The ad accused him of cuts to education and Medicare and being against adding new teachers in schools, raising nursing home standards, and improving prescription drug benefits for senior citizens. It also linked Lazio to former Speaker Gingrich. "Won't See" also was a response to a Lazio ad titled "Effective," which was released two weeks earlier. In it, Lazio was portrayed as a particularly effective congressman.

Two other ads released in the series included "Important" and "Ostrich." Both of these ads, once again, posited a link between Lazio, former Speaker Gingrich, and the Republican far right. A final negative ad, titled "Stand," also attempted to link Lazio to Gingrich. In it, Lazio and Gingrich were pictured together; the ad also featured people expressing shock at the fact that Lazio supported Gingrich. Moreover, the ad used the line "Who knew?" at the end, implying that Lazio had attempted to conceal his right-wing positions.

After the series of attack ads in late September and early October 2000, the Rodham Clinton camp changed tactics and once again began to release positive ads. One of the ads, titled "Economy," aired only in upstate New York and portrayed the surprising strength that Rodham Clinton seemed to hold in the normally conservative upstate area. Another of the ads attempted to change a negative into a positive by portraying Rodham Clinton's long-standing commitment to health care. The ad, titled "Cause," even mentioned Rodham Clinton's failed 1994 health care reform bill. The spot was directed toward women, as it discussed mammograms and child health insurance. A third positive ad, titled "Six R's," highlighted the traditional trio of reading, writing, and arithmetic along with an additional three, "responsibility, respect, and results." This ad used the rhetorical strategy of stating a message (values and discipline) that spoke to traditionally Republican voters in upstate New York as well in the suburbs. By doing so, Rodham Clinton separated herself from the idea that Democrats shy away from issues concerning character and values in the classroom.

During the final weeks of the campaign, the Rodham Clinton team released new television ads attacking Lazio. One of those ads, titled "Affordable," discussed Rodham Clinton's tax plan and contrasted it to Lazio's tax plan. The ad claimed Lazio's tax cut plans would "squander the whole surplus" and were "just like Rick Lazio." Ultimately this ad also was a response to the Lazio commercial that claimed Rodham Clinton supported fifteen tax increases.

Analysis of Rodham Clinton's Political Advertising Strategy

Rodham Clinton's advertising campaign was based upon positive and negative emotive appeals (Kaid, Leland, and Whitney 1992). Lang (1991) notes that this rhetoric may focus the attention of the viewer on the commercial as well as leading the viewer to more fully engage with certain aspects within the commercial. Indeed, Kaid et al. (1992) conclude that voters may or may not be influenced by the intellectual questioning of a candidate's platform, but may instead be moved by emotive appeals. Rodham Clinton began her campaign by portraying herself as a positive candidate upon whom the electorate could depend to achieve goals. Rodham Clinton's early ads played upon the appeals of security (jobs), love of family (health care and education issues), and children's defense as well as honored female baby boomers' work ethic (by portraying Rodham Clinton as a type of "supermom"). However, the negative appeals associated with the Rodham Clinton advertising campaign were perhaps even more powerful. Fear appeals (Kaid et al. 1992; Kern 1989) attack voters' security concerning a candidate and provide a sense of disconcertment toward issues an opposing candidate might support.

Rodham Clinton's ads did this in a number of ways. First, by linking Lazio to a candidate with many negatives (Gingrich), she was able to cause voters to question Lazio's appropriateness for the position. Next, Rodham Clinton attempted (somewhat successfully) to portray Lazio as incompetent and uncaring concerning the heating oil issue. This ad, in particular, played to the insecurities of the lower-middle-class, older, mostly conservative voters in upstate New York. Lazio had difficulty answering the charge and attempted to deflect the issue with a generic "Clinton gasoline tax" charge. Research indicates that to be effective, fear appeals must be accompanied by a method of avoiding what is feared (Leventhal, Meyers, and Nerenz 1980). In this particular instance, Rodham Clinton continually followed her spurts of negative campaigning with extremely positive "security" commercials, many not even mentioning Lazio's name. Overall, Rodham Clinton was able to portray Lazio as an incompetent villain, to be feared just as Gingrich was to be feared. Further, the Rodham Clinton camp used transfer appeals to impute Gingrich's negative qualities to Lazio. Conversely, Rodham Clinton portrayed herself as a heroic leader who embodied the basic fundamental themes and values of New York's culture. Further, she was able to lessen the impact of the "carpetbagger" label by providing evidence that she, not Lazio, had the best interests of the New York voter at heart.

Lazio's Political Advertising Campaign versus Rodham Clinton

Lazio began his political advertising campaign by running a positive "getting to know me" ad featuring Republican governor Rick Pataki praising Lazio as a trusted congressman. The ad portrayed Lazio as a moderate with a strong commitment to the environment and tax cuts for working people. But Lazio quickly began what became essentially a negative, defensive political ad campaign. Although the Lazio camp accused the Rodham Clinton campaign of running the first negative ad (which was true), this did not change the fact that she ran several different positive ads during the Giuliani and early Lazio periods of the campaign. Because of her early involvement in the race, Rodham Clinton was able to remain positive for a much longer time than Lazio.

Lazio's first negative ad foreshadowed much of the rest of his ad strategy. This early negative commercial, titled "Guess What," attempted to serve two purposes: to attack Rodham Clinton and to defend himself from one of her attacks. The ad states:

> I've been in the Senate campaign for about a month now, and guess what? Hillary Clinton has already started running attack ads designed to fool you about me. Her ads are simply untrue. I voted for a Patients' Bill of Rights and I oppose hate crimes. So why is she doing this? Because it's a lot easier for Mrs. Clinton to attack me than to name a single thing she has ever done for New York. So Mrs. Clinton, you can run the negative campaign about tearing people down. I'm going to run a campaign about building New York up.

In this ad, Lazio tried to thwart Rodham Clinton's attempt to define him before he could define his own candidacy. Further, he attempted to occupy the moral high ground by claiming he was a victim of a personal character attack. Lazio's next ad also was a response to the Rodham Clinton camp's assertion that the congressman was bowing to big drug companies and voted against the Patients' Bill of Rights legislation. The ad, titled "Know," was unique in featuring Lazio's spouse, Pat, a registered nurse, as the major character in the commercial. The commercial included a character attack on Rodham Clinton, with Pat Lazio making the claim that "Mrs. Clinton isn't telling it straight."

The Lazio camp's next set of ads also was negative. The first, a fifteen-second spot titled "Taxes," accused Rodham Clinton of supporting fifteen tax hikes and stated that people could not trust her on taxes. In the next, a fifteen-second ad titled "Ringer," Lazio defended himself against charges that he supported Gingrich on health care. It was a response ad to the Rodham Clinton camp's attack ad, "Stand." Lazio claimed that one of the people interviewed in the "Stand" ad was a Democratic Party employee. Again, Lazio charged that voters could not trust Rodham Clinton. Lazio's next strategy was to borrow an idea from the Giuliani campaign and use Senator McCain in an ad. However, unlike Giuliani's earlier ad, which was positive, this ad also attacked Rodham Clinton. As the principal character in the ad, titled "Believe," Senator McCain expressed disappointment that Rodham Clinton had backed off her pledge to refuse soft money. The ad also declared that Lazio was the only candidate the voters could trust.

Lazio's next ad, "Positive," responded to the Rodham Clinton ad "Won't See." With "Positive," Lazio attempted to both defend himself against the Rodham Clinton ad and attack her character. The ad claimed, again, that Rodham Clinton could not be trusted, and brought back the carpetbagger issue by claiming that Rodham Clinton had never done anything for New York. The Lazio campaign's next ad was more positive. "Effective" emphasized Lazio's credentials as a successful legislator. The ad never mentioned Rodham Clinton by name, but it implicitly contrasted Lazio's congressional record to Rodham Clinton's lack of one.

Analysis of Lazio's Political Advertising Strategy

Lazio's advertising campaign differed from Rodham Clinton's in many ways. First, Lazio did not have the luxury of introducing himself the way Rodham Clinton did, because of the timing of his entry into the race. Giuliani and Rodham Clinton spent weeks airing positive "get to know the candidate" ads. They were able to portray a likeable persona early, which tended to deflect some of the backlash from the negative ads that would be run as the campaign progressed. Lazio could not do this.

Second, Lazio spent much of his political ad campaign on the defensive, responding to ads created by the Rodham Clinton camp. The negative association with Gingrich, the redefinition of Lazio as a far right wing candidate by the Rodham Clinton camp, and his congressional record were continually mentioned in both the Rodham Clinton ads and the Lazio response. Further, just as the Lazio campaign had attempted to make "liberal" a demonic epithet in his 1988 campaign for the U.S. House, the Rodham Clinton campaign used the term "far right" as a demon phrase to influence moderate voters in the 2000 U.S. Senate race. Third, Lazio attempted to utilize reassurance appeals (Kern 1989) in his ads. This type of ad often uses symbols that focus on a local heritage in order to establish a common ground with the electorate. Pat Lazio's soft-spoken voice in the commercial "Know" would seem to appeal to one of Rodham Clinton's natural constituencies—moderate suburban women.

Ultimately, Lazio's political ad campaign may have failed due to a variety of reasons. The first is timing and how that affected the lack of positive ads at the beginning of his campaign. Second, Lazio may have overestimated the impact of the "carpetbagger" label. History teaches that Robert Kennedy also was successful as a carpetbagger candidate running in the state of New York. Finally, however, Lazio's defensiveness may have been his undoing. Unlike Rodham Clinton, who tended to present either positive ads or negative ads with little mention of Lazio's attacks upon her, the Lazio camp presented several ads that, in the process of defending his positions or character, restated Clinton's attacks, a tactic that in fact may have merely reinforced them.

Conclusion

In the aftermath of the November 7, 2000, election, many journalists claimed that Hillary Rodham Clinton won against all odds to become New York's U.S. senator-elect. According to Margaret Carlson of *Time* magazine, "only in hindsight does Hillary's run look plausible" (2000: 59).

However, the NewsStyle presentation of Rodham Clinton and Lazio by the media provides several salient reasons for her victory. Rodham Clinton was covered similarly to Lazio in terms of favorability and viability, and she received stronger issue coverage than Lazio on several concerns salient to voters—the economy, national defense, health care, and education. The media's stereotypical portrayal of her appearance, marital status, and sex may have been offset by her strong issue coverage as well as the fact that she was married to a popular president.

In addition, Lazio's defensive posture in his advertising campaign may have worked to Rodham Clinton's advantage by leading the media to cover him as more aggressive. Mike Murphy, Lazio's political consultant, used a pit bull approach in designing the campaign against Rodham Clinton, attempting to drive her negatives as high as possible. This strategy may have failed because Rodham Clinton had been in the public eye for many years as First Lady, whereas Lazio was not as well known, especially in upstate New York. When Lazio presented himself as extremely aggressive, especially in the Buffalo debate—and this aggressiveness was emphasized in his newspaper coverage—voters may have been turned off.

Beyond the results reported in this case study, there were other reasons for Rodham Clinton's victory. For example, she was able to utilize the positive aspects of Bill Clinton's presidency—for instance, economic vitality as well as his high approval ratings in New York. According to a CNN poll (2000), about two-thirds of the voters in New York State approved of the job President Clinton had been doing, and three-quarters of them voted for Rodham Clinton in the U.S. Senate election.

Also, Lazio made no attempt to garner the black vote. At one point late in the campaign, a Marist College public opinion poll (2000) had Rodham Clinton winning 95 percent of the black vote, with 0 percent for Lazio and 5 percent undecided. Ultimately, time also played a role in the race. Rodham Clinton kicked off a listening tour in upstate New York in July 1999. Her marathon, sixteen-month campaign was just too much for Lazio to overcome.

12
Gendered Reactions to Media Coverage

As women have become more important forces in the political system, political observers have considered the significance of gender as a filter for media coverage of politics. In the last two chapters, we have examined how the media cover male and female candidates when they run for political office. As with political advertising (VideoStyle) and Internet presentations (WebStyle), we compare and contrast in this chapter the reactions of male and female voters to news media coverage of political figures (NewsStyle).

Gender and Political Knowledge Levels

Some political observers suggest that differences in how men and women voters process news and information can be seen in their different levels of political knowledge. The often-discussed "gender gap" in voting also has been extended to encompass a "knowledge gap" between male and female citizens. For decades, voting and policy issue research has documented that women tend to be less informed about and less interested in political issues than men (Bennett and Bennett 1989; Delli Carpini and Keeter 1991, 1996, 2000; Kenski and Jamieson 2001; Verba, Burns, and Schlozman 1997). In a study of perceptions about political knowledge in the 2000 election, Banwart and Bystrom (2001) also found that male citizens are more confident about their level of information and knowledge than are female citizens.

Researchers have considered that differences in education and socialization might account for these differences in political knowledge levels (Delli Carpini and Keeter 1996, 2000) and for the fact that women seem more knowledgeable about and more involved in local politics than men (Delli Carpini and Keeter 2000; Verba, Burns, and Schlozman 1997). However, there is also some evidence that knowledge level differences may be related to media use.

Delli Carpini and Keeter found that attention to the media did have "at least modest correlations" with political knowledge at the end of the 1980s, although not as strong as factors such as gender and education (1996: 182).

One reason for suspecting that there may be differences in how men and women react to the political messages they receive in campaigns comes from findings that there are gender differences in the channels and formats of information reliance. For example, men are more likely than women to gather political information from newspapers, newsmagazines, political television talk shows, political radio talk shows, and the Internet (Kenski and Jamieson 2001; Verba, Burns, and Schlozman 1997). Women are more likely than men to obtain political information from local television news, morning television shows, and talking with others (Banwart and Bystrom 2001; Kenski and Jamieson 2001).

Banwart and Bystrom (2001) extended the findings of previous research by looking at the relationship between perceived political knowledge and interest and media use by women and men. Interestingly, women who perceived themselves as "highly informed" or "highly interested" relied on most of the same sources of political information (morning talk shows and local television news) as women who perceived themselves as uninformed and disinterested. In contrast, "highly informed" and "highly interested" men relied on more traditional media sources (newspapers and magazines), which researchers also have found to be most correlated with political knowledge (Delli Carpini and Keeter 1996).

Media Use and Reactions to Political Candidates

A few studies have looked at audience reactions to the media coverage of political women, including the First Lady. For example, Brown used focus groups to look at middle-class attitudes toward First Lady Hillary Rodham Clinton's image as constructed by television news coverage. She found that "despite the endless remakes of her image, apparently to make her seem more domestic, Hillary Clinton was consistently seen as powerful" by members of the focus groups (1997: 266).

Other researchers have examined the relationship between newspaper and television coverage and the perceived viability of male and female candidates. Using American National Election Studies (ANES) data from 1988, 1990, and 1992, Knopf and Boiney (2001) found that increased exposure to media coverage on radio and television increased the perception of viability of male candidates more than of female candidates.

The findings that male and female voters traditionally have relied on different sources of news and information about political candidates suggest that the NewsStyle presentations of male and female candidates may be received differently, depending upon the gender of the receiver. Although we do not have data to test the specific reactions of voters to all of the candidates in our analysis of NewsStyle in the preceding chapters, we do have data that compare more generally how male and female voters receive their information and how that may have affected their reactions to presidential candidates in the last two presidential elections (1996 and 2000) and to Senate candidates in the 1996 and 2002 election cycles.

Measuring Media Use Differences of Male and Female Voters

One of the continuing concerns about gender differences in reactions to political candidates involves the extent to which male and female voters have different information-seeking patterns. Some of the research mentioned above certainly points to such a conclusion, and our own research confirms this. For instance, in the 2000 presidential campaign, we gathered data on media use from more than two thousand voters who were gathered to watch presidential campaign materials in the form of television ads and debates. We asked these voters, who were a mixture of students from universities around the country and citizens from the communities in which these universities were located, about their media usage.[1]

In Table 12.1, we show a breakdown of these respondents' media use patterns. In almost every category of media use, there are significant differences between men and women. Men read the newspaper an average of 3.7 days per week, almost a full day more per week than women, who only read a newspaper 2.8 days per week. Men also watch national television news more frequently than women, watching an average of 2.8 days per week, compared with only 2.2 days per week for women. On the other hand, women watch local television news more than men (2.9 days per week versus 2.6 days per week).

TABLE 12.1 Gender Differences in News Exposure to Political Information in 2000

	Males (n = 849)	Females (n = 1,219)
Mean days of newspaper*	3.7	2.8
Mean days national TV news*	2.8	2.2
Mean days local TV news*	2.6	2.9
Amount of use (5 = a lot, 0 = never)		
Television talk shows*	2.2	1.9
Late-night talk shows*	2.3	2.1
Morning talk shows*	1.2	1.9
Newspapers*	3.2	3.0
Newsmagazines*	2.4	2.2
Political talk radio*	1.4	1.2

* T-test for differences in males and females is significant at $p \leq .05$.

Other differences in media use are apparent as well. For instance, men are more likely than women to watch television talk shows, but men more often watch late-night talk shows, whereas women tend to watch morning talk shows. Although the difference is less strong, men also rely on newsmagazines more often than women.

Measuring Reactions to NewsStyle in the 2000 Presidential Campaign

How do these substantial differences in media usage between male and female voters relate to perceptions of the candidates? Table 12.2 gives some idea of how these differences may affect ratings of the presidential candidates in 2000. Using the same data discussed above, we correlated the feeling thermometer ratings of Bush and Gore with media usage by male and female voters. Some of these differences are not very strong, but they do indicate that there may be some relationship between NewsStyle and voter responses by gender.

As the data indicate, the use by males of national television news, which men use more than women, relates significantly in a positive way ($r = .07$) to the ratings of Gore by male voters, but not for female voters. However, exposure to local television news is more helpful to Bush's image among male voters, but not among females, who watch more local news.

The greatest effect on the candidate images for both genders is apparent in regard to political talk radio shows. Whereas men rely on political talk

TABLE 12.2 Correlations by Gender of News Use and Political Candidate Perceptions

	Gore Rating	Bush Rating
Males (n = 849)		
National TV news	.07*	.05
Local TV news	.03	.13*
Radio news	−.06	.11*
Political talk radio shows	−.14*	.16*
News magazines	.01	−.02
Newspapers	.05	−.05
Morning TV talk shows	.05	.02
Females (n = 1,219)		
National TV news	.04	.08
Local TV news	.03	−.01
Radio news	.00	−.00
Political talk radio shows	−.12*	.11*
News magazines	.06*	−.03
Newspapers	.09*	−.02
Morning TV talk shows	.07*	.03

* Pearson correlation is significant at $p \leq .05$.

radio more than women, both groups are similarly affected by it in regard to candidate ratings. For both genders, listening to political talk radio has a negative correlation with Gore's ratings ($r = -.14$ for men and $r = .12$ for women) and a positive effect on Bush's evaluations ($r = .16$ for men and $r = .11$ for women). All of these are strong, significant correlations.

Further examination of these findings suggests that particular character traits of the candidates may be related to gender differences in media usage. Perceptions of Gore by male voters were particularly affected by use of national television news, which was correlated with Gore being perceived as qualified, sophisticated, successful, and active. Men who saw Gore on television talk shows or read articles in the newspapers about him also were likely to see him as qualified and successful. On the other hand, male voters who used the newspapers for campaign information had more negative views of how qualified Bush was for the presidency. Men who relied on local television news, however, found Bush to be qualified, honest, successful, sincere, and active. National network television also helped his image as a successful man.

Women who relied on newspapers for information had similar reactions to Gore, finding him qualified, honest, friendly, sincere, and strong. However, where men's perceptions of Gore's were particularly affected by national network news, local news shaped perceptions of his traits for female voters, who found him friendly, sincere, and strong when viewed on that medium. Like male voters, women who relied on newspapers for information thought Bush was not particularly well qualified. Like their perceptions of Gore, female perceptions of Bush were more positive in terms of his qualifications, sincerity, sophistication, successfulness, and friendliness as a result of reliance on local television news. Another difference for female voters was the relationship between reliance on talk show formats and viewing Bush as honest and active.

Reactions to Specific Television News Segments

To further explore possible gender differences in reactions to news portrayals of candidates, we also examined data from experiments that exposed respondents to specific news segments about the 2000 presidential campaign. These experiments were part of the same research reported in chapter 9 on reactions to WebStyle in the 2000 campaign. These data come from studies of responses to the 2000 presidential campaigns in which we considered the responses of voters who were shown political information for both Al Gore and George W. Bush in a news format. These news segments were edited and adapted from real news segments shown on the national television networks during the campaign. In a series of experiments, 139 respondents (43 percent male, 57 percent female) were exposed to the news segments in a laboratory setting.[2] Respondents filled out questionnaires before and after viewing the television news segments.

TABLE 12.3 Gender Differences in Reactions to News about 2000 Presidential Candidates

	Males (n = 58)	Females (n = 81)
Ratings of Bush		
Pretest	64.0	62.0
Posttest	65.2	61.5
Ratings of Gore		
Pretest	40.2	44.8
Posttest	39.2	47.1
Information seeking		
See more ads	3.5	4.3*
View more TV news	4.4	5.0*
Read newspapers	4.5	5.1*
Go to candidates' Web site	3.6	3.7

* T-test for differences in males and females is significant at $p \leq .05$.

Comparisons of male and female voter reactions to the television news segments in these experiments showed that male and female voters reacted similarly to the presidential candidates after viewing. Table 12.3 shows that when subjects rated Bush and Gore on a feeling thermometer (0–100), there were no substantial differences related to gender in either the pretest or posttest measures. Thus, exposure to the news segments did not affect respondents, regardless of gender.

Table 12.3 also shows the results of comparisons by gender of respondents' reports of their likelihood of seeking additional information about the political candidates after viewing the news segments. Respondents were asked to respond on a scale of 1 (not very likely) to 7 (very likely) if they would like to "watch more ads about the candidates," "view more television news about the candidates," "read more newspaper information," or "seek more information on the candidates' Web sites" after viewing the news segments. These data suggest that female voters were stimulated to seek more information than were male voters. This was true for every type of information seeking except Web site material, suggesting that women voters may question what they see in the news more than men, and that they find themselves actively thinking about pursuing more information in such situations.

Gender Reactions to NewsStyle of Male and Female Candidates

Since our work on the presidential campaign did not allow us to examine differences in male and female voters to candidates of different genders, we turned to the ANES surveys for additional information. We used the pre- and posttest data from the 1996 and 2002 data sets for this purpose, and

TABLE 12.4 Media Use of Male and Female Voters in 1996 and 2002: Mixed-Gender Senate Races

	1996 Male (n = 128)	1996 Female (n = 155)	2002 Male (n = 73)	2002 Female (n = 88)
Mean days newspaper	3.3	2.7*	3.4	3.2
Mean days national news	2.9	3.4*	3.8	4.0
Mean days local news	3.5	4.6*	3.9	4.6*

Note: Source is 1996 and 2002 American National Election Studies.
* T-test for differences in males and females is significant at $p \leq .05$.

we selected from these data only the states in which a male and female candidate were running for the U.S. Senate against each other. This provided some data that related to our VideoStyle analyses for these two election years (1996 and 2002). In 1996, this provided data for the states of Michigan, Texas, Louisiana, Wyoming, Kansas, and West Virginia; respondents from these states totaled 283. In 2002, there were 175 voters in the ANES survey who voted in states with a mixed-gender Senate race (North Carolina, Louisiana, Alabama, New Hampshire, Kentucky, Missouri, and Maine).

Table 12.4 shows that these respondents exhibited some of the same media use differences uncovered in the studies we reported for presidential candidates in 2000. For instance, in 1996, men read the newspaper significantly more often than women, and women watched local news on television significantly more often than men. However, in this 1996 subset of the ANES data, women also watched national television news more frequently than men. The differences are similar in the 2002 data set, but with the smaller sample sizes, only the difference between male and female voters is significant when examining local news viewing, where, as expected, women watched more often than did men.

More interesting, however, is that these data allowed us the chance to examine whether there were differences in how men and women voters voted for men and women candidates based on media usage. Table 12.5 provides the simple answer. None of the media use differences between men and women voters can be directly related to their choice of a male or female candidate for the U.S. Senate in either 1996 or 2002. In other words, men who voted for male Senate candidates exhibited media use patterns similar to those of men who voted for female Senate candidates. The same was true for female voters. The source of their news media information did not relate to their selection of a male or female Senate candidate in either 1996 or 2002.

These interesting findings, although based on small sample sizes and using very simple measurement techniques, provide some additional reassurance for those who continue to be concerned about the differences in coverage given to male and female candidates. Although our research suggests

TABLE 12.5 Relationship of Media Use to Voting for Male or Female Senate Candidates, 1996 and 2002

	Voted for Senate Candidate			
	1996		2002	
Male Voters	Male (n = 41)	Female (n = 38)	Male (n = 24)	Female (n = 20)
Media usage				
Mean days newspaper	3.7	4.2	3.8	3.1
Mean days national TV news	3.4	3.6	3.8	3.1
Mean days local TV news	3.7	3.84	3.6	3.7

	Voted for Senate Candidate			
	1996		2002	
Female Voters	Male (n = 52)	Female (n = 45)	Male (n = 22)	Female (n = 27)
Media usage				
Mean days newspaper	2.7	3.0	3.6	3.1
Mean days national TV news	3.5	4.1	4.2	4.0
Mean days local TV news	5.2	4.3	4.7	4.2

Note: Source is 1996 and 2002 American National Election Studies.

that male and female voters may react differently to news about presidential candidates in differing media and different formats, these differences disappear when considering mixed-gender U.S. Senate races.

Part V
Gender and Political Communication in Future Campaigns

13
Gendered Political Campaign Communication: *Implications for the Future*

After looking at how female and male candidates are presented in political advertising, Web sites, and campaign news coverage, and how potential voters react to these presentations, our conclusions sometimes raise more questions than answers. Nonetheless, there are several recurring trends that help to guide our expectations for the future role of gendered political communication.

Candidate-Controlled Styles

The first two concepts used for our comparisons of gendered communication in electoral contests are analyses of message types controlled primarily by the candidates themselves: political television advertising and Web sites. Political television advertising is still the dominant form of candidate communication for most major-level races in which female candidates must compete with male opponents. This has made the comparison of VideoStyle particularly important to our analysis of gendered communication. Our research on matched-gender races, encompassing the last decade of the twentieth century and the first two major elections (2000 and 2002) of the twenty-first century, suggests that female candidates in major-level races are establishing successfully their own competitive style of political advertising.

Our analysis of VideoStyle has shown that female candidates have overcome the stereotypical admonishment that women must avoid negative ads; female candidates running against male candidates are sometimes able to use even higher percentages of attack spots than their male opponents. They have been able to adopt some incumbent strategies, even when challengers, to give themselves authority. Winning female candidates also seem to be successful at achieving a VideoStyle that (1) is overall positive, (2) emphasizes personal traits of toughness and strength, (3) capitalizes on the importance of "feminine" issues such as education and health care, and (4) balances feminine campaign issues with "masculine" issues such as the economy, defense, and homeland security. What other pragmatic advice do our findings suggest for a female candidate in her spots? Winning female candidates also top their male opponents by keeping their attire formal (business/professional dress) and their smiles bright.

When it comes to self-presentation in the newest campaign medium, the Internet, our research shows fewer differences between male and female candidates. Both men and women candidates' WebStyles are marked by significant amounts of issue information; unlike the balance between feminine and masculine issues observed in VideoStyle presentations, Web sites for both genders seem to focus on masculine issues. Traits emphasized on the Web also center on past accomplishments for both genders. Perhaps the newness of this medium has not provided sufficient development of a differing style for female and male candidates, but currently neither gender has taken full advantage of the Web's ability to provide message segmentation for different types of groups. Both genders have made only limited use of the Web to showcase the candidate's performance in other venues by providing streaming video of live appearances, speeches, debates, ads, or other messages. Although the 2002 campaign Web sites of both genders provided some additional use of linking technology on their sites and more attempts to solicit contributions and volunteers, both genders are still lagging behind commercial development trends in providing interactivity and personalization in their WebStyles.

What advice does our research provide the female candidate for developing a successful WebStyle in the future? Several points are clear. The Web may be the best venue for female candidates wanting an equal competition with male candidates, especially in situations where resources are limited. A female candidate can do much more for much less on the Web than through television advertising. Female candidates should develop sophisticated WebStyles that allow them to (1) provide more specialized messages to specific groups (either through expansion of their main Web sites or through development of specialized Web sites than can be linked to the main site), (2) be a leader in innovative types of interactivity on their Web sites, and (3) use the Web to generate a more personalized presence for the candidate with voters (through audiovisual presentations by the candidate on the Web site and by providing opportunities for citizens to "tune in" for personal chats and question and answer sessions with the candidate or campaign representatives).

Elizabeth Dole's 2002 U.S. Senate campaign in North Carolina provides a good baseline for this type of Web use. Although there is still room for many adaptations and increased technological sophistication, our case study example demonstrated the superiority of Dole's WebStyle in many of these categories.

NewsStyle: Out of the Candidate's Control?

Candidates can control their VideoStyles and their WebStyles, but they do not have complete control of how the news media decide to cover their campaigns. In the past, female candidates have suffered in this particular genre of campaign information. However, our research provides very encouraging news about NewsStyle.

It appears that the stereotypical news coverage trends of the last century are no longer dominant. In the 2000 and 2002 campaign cycles, female candidates had achieved sufficient status as candidates to be given equal and sometimes greater coverage in newspapers than their male opponents. In fact, in 2000 (due largely to the Hillary Rodham Clinton candidacy for U.S. Senate in New York) female U.S. Senate candidates received more total coverage than males. Since 1998, women candidates have also been getting their share of positive coverage, and there are no longer great differences in the viability or electability quotient accorded to female candidates.

There is one area where news coverage remains troublesome for female candidates. The tendency to emphasize candidate gender, appearance, marital status, and masculine issues in news coverage still haunts the female candidate. Candidate gender is still mentioned more frequently for women, reporters still comment more often on a female candidate's dress or appearance, and reports still refer to a female candidate's marital status more frequently. Issue discussions by the media also have continued to emphasize topics traditionally considered masculine, such as taxes, crime, and defense.

Rodham Clinton's 2000 U.S. Senate race in New York was a prime example of this stereotypical news coverage. Our case study on NewsStyle showed that whereas Rodham Clinton did get more total coverage than her male opponent, she was subjected to frequent commentary on her personal appearance and dress as well as her marital relationship with former president Bill Clinton. She overcame the problem of masculine issue discussion by focusing her own campaign strongly on economic issues.

Rodham Clinton's campaign also demonstrated some of the advice that a female candidate should heed in order to influence her own NewsStyle. Whereas neither male nor female candidates can directly control news coverage, they can have considerable influence on it. By focusing on a mixture of masculine and feminine issues, a female candidate can achieve a balance that helps to ensure the media will not leave her out of a discussion of masculine issues.

Female candidates also should remember that they can influence NewsStyle in another way. They can use their controlled communication, their VideoStyle and their WebStyle, to impact NewsStyle. For the past three decades, particularly since the 1988 presidential campaign, the news media have increased their coverage of candidate television advertising. Although they came late to the realization, reporters finally recognized that television advertising was the dominant form of candidate-voter communication in major races. Consequently, reporters began to cover political advertising as a part of the campaign dialogue and even designated themselves as watchdogs for the public in "policing" political ads (Broder 1989). Since that time, the "ad watch" has become a common feature of news coverage of political campaigns (Kaid, Gobetz, Garner, Leland, and Scott 1993; Kaid, Tedesco, and McKinnon 1996). Research on the 1996 campaign indicated that female candidates have not had their ads subjected to as much scrutiny as have male candidates (Kaid, McKinney, Tedesco, and Gaddie 1999). However, with research showing that female candidates are receiving equal or greater coverage of their campaigns than male candidates in the twenty-first century, it is likely that more ad watch coverage will follow. This provides female candidates with opportunities to influence their news coverage through the production of high-quality ads that will attract media attention. In addition, the fact that ad watches focus more often on negative ads (Kaid et al. 1999; Kaid, Tedesco, and McKinnon 1996), coupled with the increased freedom of female candidates to escape stereotypes and use negative ads, may open the door for more ad watch coverage of their campaigns.

It is also likely that as Web campaigning becomes more popular and more developed, news media will expand their coverage of candidates' Web sites as part of the campaign dialogue. Thus, a candidate's WebStyle may become a topic for increased news coverage, and voters may see emergence of regular "Web watches."

Gender Reactions: Implications for the Female Candidate

If female candidates can control their VideoStyles and their WebStyles and influence their NewsStyles, then what can they expect from male and female voters in the years to come? Our research suggests that there are very few differences in how male and female voters react to candidates of either gender. This is true across all of the media styles we have discussed in this volume. Our research on the 1996 and 2000 presidential campaigns, for instance, showed that male and female candidates reacted differently to different candidates (women were more positive to Clinton and to Gore, respectively). However, there was nothing to indicate that these reactions were due to the video presentations of either candidate in a way that related to gender.

Overall, the advice for women candidates seems in line with our findings about the impact of winning candidate VideoStyle: go positive. Winning female candidates have demonstrated that their VideoStyles are characterized by substantial positive messages, and our research on audience reactions indicates that women voters are more often supportive of women candidates who use positive messages. This does not suggest a moratorium on negative advertising, but merely that a female candidate should seek a balance of negative and positive messages that points to an overall positive campaign message.

Similar balance should prevail in the selection of masculine and feminine issue and image traits. Women are very strongly influenced by the issues and qualities characteristic of feminine style. When women preferred a male candidate in our studies, it was usually because the male candidate co-opted the feminine qualities by appearing honest, caring, personal, and positive. Female candidates must walk a careful road here. They must discuss masculine issues that are on the minds of voters (such as the economy, defense, and crime) without abandoning their own strength in feminine issues (education, health care). The same is true for personal qualities: women candidates must show they are strong, aggressive, and experienced, but also caring and compassionate.

The successful use of WebStyle to influence male and female voters requires more complex strategies. On one hand, men use the Web much more for political information than do women, although overall women use the Web more for information and research generally, whereas men use the Web more for recreation and relaxation. On the other hand, our research shows that when they are exposed to Web information, men and women react similarly in terms of political and information-seeking behaviors. However, our research showed that, as with VideoStyle, there may be differences between men and women in candidate preferences after Web exposure, but there is no certainty that this is due to the WebStyle presentations of the candidates.

Overall, our findings about WebStyle, both in terms of the content of the candidates' sites and the potential reactions of voters to this new form of communication, lead to the conclusion that the Web may offer female candidates a productive new force for achieving equality in electoral battles. The female candidate's WebStyle can be achieved and maintained with fewer financial resources and with unlimited opportunities for balancing masculine and feminine issues and traits in self-presentation. These advantages seem particularly strong in the context of the findings about similar reactions of male and female voters to WebStyle presentations. It is premature to suggest that the Web will be the communication tool that gives female candidates presentational and financial parity with their male counterparts. However, as more and more citizens become "wired" and turn to the Web for political information, the potential for that equality may be inherent in the Web.

This potential of the Web to equalize female and male candidate self-presentation to voters also may be related to the evolving deemphasis of traditional news media on political coverage. Over the last few election cycles, the traditional news media, particularly television network news, have devoted less and less coverage to campaigns (Center for Media and Public Affairs 2000; Lichter, Noyes, and Kaid 1999). And citizens are turning less and less to traditional network news for their information; this is especially true for young voters (Pew Research Center 2004).

Complicating the future news environment, of course, is the gender differences in the use of traditional and new media—men tend to read newspapers, watch national network news, and tune in to late-night television talk shows more frequently than do women. Women watch local television news and watch morning talk shows more often. Our studies show some relationship between male voter exposure to television news and attitudes toward Bush and Gore in 2000. However, there were very few differences between male and female voters in terms of political and information-seeking behaviors stimulated by exposure to television news about the 2000 campaign. This finding was very much the same as our research on gender reactions to VideoStyle and WebStyle. The only substantial gender difference in reactions to NewsStyle in our studies was the finding that women voters express a desire to seek out more information after viewing news, suggesting that female voters may be more involved and engaged by the news material than their male counterparts.

Finally, our examination of National Election Studies data from 1996 and 2002 also substantiated that there are no significant differences between female and male voter media use that can be related to the choices of female and male candidates in 1996 or 2000. In other words, the type of traditional media to which voters are exposed, even though it may differ by gender, does not result in any influence on candidate choice.

Conclusions

Women are becoming a much greater force in the political landscape. Their success at the polls in the last decade of the twentieth century and the first two election cycles of the twenty-first century have demonstrated that female candidates can be successful in challenging for political status and power at most levels of government. Only at the presidential level do women remain barred by stereotypical perceptions that devalue their legitimacy and question their mettle.

As female candidates compete for office at all levels, there is a greater need than ever for scholars, political consultants, and the media to understand the elements that make up female and male VideoStyles, WebStyles, and NewsStyles. The research we have presented in this volume offers some descriptions and measures some effects that have led us to recommend some ways female candidates might improve their success through

VideoStyle and WebStyle, two message styles under their direct control, and through attempts to influence how the media present their candidacies in NewsStyle.

However, there can be no doubt that such research is in its infancy. We need far more comprehensive studies of gendered communication and gendered reactions. It is especially important that work on WebStyle be advanced because of its potential for creating a level playing field for female candidates. Even more important is the need for more experimental and survey research that can test directly the conclusions and indications provided by the descriptive work that has already been done on VideoStyle, WebStyle, and NewsStyle.

The next few election cycles may be particularly challenging for female candidates as the United States faces the threats of terrorism and increased involvement in military conflicts. One reason female candidates may have been so successful in the 1990s is that it was an era dominated by domestic concerns. Female candidates were often fighting an issue battle that focused on their own natural turf; issues such as education and health care allowed them to play to their strengths and often forced male candidates to turn their own campaigns to feminine issues. In the aftermath of the collapse of communism, and devoid of a clear external threat, the United States found little reason to be focused on foreign affairs or military matters. After the tragic terrorist attacks of September 11, 2001, the political landscape changed in many ways. An increased concern with military and defense matters would seem to put female candidates at a disadvantage, particularly in races with national import. Despite the concentration on defense, the 2002 election was a midterm election that seemed to turn more on the president's ability to rally the nation than on specific issues of domestic or foreign significance. However, the 2004 and following elections may test the ability of female candidates to sustain their advances and demonstrate their credibility on issues of economic strength and military engagement. This will particularly affect female candidates contesting for seats in the U.S. Senate and Congress.

Despite these challenges, we believe that female candidates have the tools under their own control to be successful. They can be successful in applying the VideoStyles and WebStyles that set them on a winning path. Candidates who can apply the lessons of VideoStyle and WebStyle successfully also may be able to capitalize on these controlled messages to influence NewsStyle for a synergistic communication effort.

Notes

Chapter 3[1] The campaign spot was the unit of analysis in each study. Coders were primarily graduate and undergraduate students who were trained in the use of the coding instrument. Using Holsti's formula, intercoder reliability was calculated for a randomly selected subsample of the spots in each year. Individual category reliabilities ranged from 0.80 to 1.00 in each year, and the average intercoder reliability across all categories and years was 0.87.

Chapter 5[1] Three coders—two female and one male undergraduate student—were recruited and trained to code the sample in this study. The students were political science or communication studies majors interested in political campaigns. The training of coders included one two-and-a-half-hour session that familiarized the coders with the coding instrument, code book, and procedures for coding. The coders coded a political spot ad from a separate sample to discuss and clarify any areas in question. The coders then participated in three additional training sessions in which they coded twenty-three practice ads from a separate sample. At the conclusion of the training sessions, the coders were then assigned four spot ads from the sample (24 percent of the total sample) to be coded and analyzed for intercoder reliability. To test for intercoder reliability on the political spot ads and appropriateness of the training session and coding instrument, Holsti's formula (North et al. 1963) was used. Intercoder reliability across all categories was calculated at 0.96. Following the calculation of intercoder reliability in each set of the sample, the coders were then assigned random sets of the political spot ads to code.

Chapter 6[1] The nineteen universities were located in the following regions: East and Southeast (Maryland, Pennsylvania, Florida, Alabama, South Carolina), Midwest (Illinois [two locations], Indiana, Ohio, Minnesota, Arkansas, Iowa, Missouri), Southwest (Oklahoma [two locations], Texas), and West (California [two locations], Oregon). Because of differing subject availability, not all subjects were chosen in the same way (i.e., in some locations, subjects were chosen randomly from student subject pools, and in others, students were used as part of intact general communication, mass communication, and political science classes).

[2] The spots were: (1) a Dole spot called "Truth on Spending" that attacks Clinton's support for big-money projects, such as $48 million for alpine slides and midnight basketball; (2) a Clinton negative ad with split screens of Bob Dole saying he was fighting against Medicare and the creation of the Department of Education; (3) a positive Dole ad called "From the Heart" in which Elizabeth Dole talks about her husband keeping his commitment to a 15 percent tax cut; (4) a Clinton positive spot titled "Second" in which Jim Brady endorses Clinton as a man of strong character for supporting gun control legislation; (5) a Clinton negative ad, "Wrong in the Past," attacking Dole for his Washington insider status by showing Dole's actions in the 1960s, 1970s, and 1980s against such legislation as the creation of Medicare, the Brady bill, the Family and Medical Leave Act, the creation of the Department of Education, and the establishment of the office of the drug czar; (6) a negative Dole ad called "Riady," which plays on Clinton's creation of a large government bureaucratic health care system and his tax increase and uses clippings to emphasize his ethical uncertainties; (7) a Dole spot called "Nicole," which describes an editorial from the *New York Times* about a teenage girl named Nicole who thinks it's okay to smoke marijuana because President Clinton did it; and (8) a Clinton spot titled "Look" that emphasizes how risky the Dole tax scheme is and accuses Dole of voting for legislation that would total $900 million in higher taxes.

[3] The spots used in the 2000 experimental sessions, in the order of their appearance, were: (1) a positive Bush spot titled "Trust" in which Bush talks about trusting America and renewing America's purpose; (2) a positive Gore ad, "College," in which Gore's college tuition tax deduction for middle-class families is featured; (3) a negative Bush ad, "Gore-Gantuan," which attacks Gore's spending plan and says it will wipe out the surplus and increase governmental spending; (4) a Gore ad titled "Down" that uses a graphic of a dissolving dollar bill to attack Bush's tax cut plan, ending with the message that Gore will pay down the debt, protect Social Security, and give a tax deduction for college tuition; (5) a Bush ad titled "Education Recession" that suggests there is a Clinton/Gore education recession, states Bush has raised education standards in Texas, and tells the viewer how to obtain the "Bush blueprint for education" that features accountability, high standards, and local control; (6) a Gore ad titled "Apron" that attacks Bush on the minimum wage in Texas and promotes the "Al Gore plan" of increasing the minimum wage and investing in education, middle-class tax cuts, and a secure retirement; (7) a Bush ad called

"Big Relief vs. Big Spending" that compares Bush's tax cut plan with Gore's spending plan, stating that Gore's spending plan threatens America's prosperity; (8) a negative Gore ad called "Needle" that opens with a foggy Houston skyline, attacks Bush on his environmental policies in Texas, and ends with a foggy Seattle skyline, asking the viewer to "imagine Bush's Texas-style environmental regulations" in Seattle.

[4] These universities were located in the following states: Arkansas, California, Colorado, Florida, Idaho, Illinois, Indiana, Iowa, Kansas, Massachusetts, Missouri, Ohio, Oklahoma, Pennsylvania, Texas, Virginia, and South Carolina. Because of differing subject availability, not all subjects were chosen in the same way (i.e., in some locations, subjects were chosen randomly from student subject pools, and in others, students were used as part of intact general communication, mass communication, and political science classes).

[5] The twelve bipolar adjective pairs used were: qualified/unqualified, sophisticated/unsophisticated, honest/dishonest, believable/unbelievable, successful/unsuccessful, attractive/unattractive, friendly/unfriendly, sincere/insincere, calm/excitable, aggressive/unaggressive, strong/weak, and active/inactive.

[6] The specific items used in the cynicism scale were: (1) "Whether I vote or not has no influence on what politicians do"; (2) "One never really knows what politicians think"; (3) "People like me don't have any say about what the government does"; (4) "Sometimes politics and government seem so complicated that a person like me can't really understand what's going on"; (5) "One can be confident that politicians will always do the right thing" (reversed in coding); (6) "Politicians often quickly forget their election promises after a political campaign is over"; (7) "Politicians are more interested in power than in what the people think"; and (8) "One cannot always trust what politicians say."

[7] The ten bipolar adjective pairs used were: unassertive/assertive, incompetent/competent, inexperienced/experienced, dishonest/honest, uncaring/caring, unfair/fair, passive/aggressive, weak leadership/strong leadership, negative/positive, and impersonal/personal. Cronbach's alpha reliability for this scale was 0.85.

[8] The thirteen bipolar adjective pairs used were: unqualified/qualified, dishonest/honest, unbelievable/believable, unattractive/attractive, uncaring/caring, insincere/sincere, incompetent/competent, passive/aggressive, inexperienced/experienced, inactive/active, weak leader/strong leader, impersonal/personal, and negative/positive.

Chapter 7[1] The application of a computer program designed to download Web sites was used to collect the sites. Programming complications prohibited the gathering of all identified Web sites. In addition, in 2000, three candidates did not have an identified Web site, and in 2002, three candidates did not have an identified Web site. The typically fluid nature of the Internet and, thus, of Web sites poses a potential difficulty for content analysis procedures (McMillan 2000). In order to control for the content in the Web site, all Web sites were downloaded during each election cycle and stored for coding purposes. Because the study was interested in candidate WebStyle and not changes in candidate WebStyle over time, the Web sites were collected at a time when the candidates would have finalized their desired presentations. With this in mind, the Web sites for each year were collected during the week prior to the election. Intercoder reliability for the 2000 election cycle was assessed on a sample of 22 percent of the sites collected and averaged 0.89 across all categories. Intercoder reliability for the 2002 election cycle was assessed on a sample of 20 percent of the sites collected and averaged 0.86 across all categories. The formula used to calculate intercoder reliability and appropriateness of the training sessions and coding instrument is that given in North et al. 1963: $R = 2(C_{1,2})/C_1 + C_2$, where $C_{1,2}$ = number of category assignments both coders agree on, and $C_1 + C_2$ = total category assignments made by both coders

Chapter 8[1] The link to "more images" was not available for viewing.

Chapter 9[1] These experiments took place in the fall of 2000 and were part of a larger study that compared exposure to the same information on television and on the Internet. Only the results from the Internet exposures are reported here. The respondents were a mixture of students at the University of Oklahoma and adult residents recruited from the Norman/Oklahoma City communities. Although the conclusions are their own, the authors would like to thank the Carnegie Corporation of New York for supplying partial funding for these experiments.

[2] The second experiments took place at Virginia Tech University; respondents were sixty-five students randomly assigned to two groups. Candidate image was assessed in both the pretest and the posttest using the same twelve-item semantic differential scale discussed in chapter 6. The scales produced high reliability when assessed using Cronbach's alpha: 0.80 for Gore pretest, 0.82 for Bush pretest, 0.84 for Gore posttest, 0.83 for Bush posttest. Other measures of Internet use motives and political cynicism were employed. Since control of stimulus material was an essential characteristic of this experimental design, a twenty-two-minute video of a surveillance of George Bush's official presidential Web site was produced using the MultiPro 2000, a PC-to-TV scan converter. In order to show subjects a variety of information that constituted the site, audio, video, audiovisual, and text-only frames were shown. In an effort to assess motivation effects on learning about candidate issue and image, participants were instructed to evaluate the Web site content either for its informative value or for its entertainment value. More details on this study are

reported in Tedesco and Kaid 2002. The authors thank John Tedesco for the use of these data.

Chapter 12 [1] These data were gathered in a number of sessions between Labor Day and Election Day in 2000. The university communities were in several different states, representing geographic diversity throughout the United States: Alabama, Arkansas, California, Colorado, Florida, Idaho, Illinois, Indiana, Iowa, Kansas, Massachusetts, Missouri, Ohio, Oklahoma, Pennsylvania, Texas, Virginia, and South Carolina. The total number of participants was 2,081. Of these, 41 percent were male and 59 percent were female. Political party identification was distributed, with 40 percent Democrats, 38 percent Republicans, and 22 percent independents/others.

[2] These experiments took place in the fall of 2000 and were part of a larger study that compared exposure to the same information on television and on the Internet. Only the results from the news exposures are reported here. The respondents were a mixture of students at the University of Oklahoma and adult residents recruited from the Norman/Oklahoma City community. In total, 139 respondents participated. They had a mean age of twenty-eight years, they were 43 percent male and 57 percent female, and their partisan affiliation was distributed, with 31 percent Democratic, 54 percent Republican, and 15 percent independent/other. Although the conclusions are their own, the authors would like to thank the Carnegie Corporation of New York for supplying partial funding for these experiments.

References

Aday, S., & Devitt, J. (2001). *Style over substance. Newspaper coverage of female candidates: Spotlight on Elizabeth Dole.* Washington, DC: The Women's Leadership Fund.
Alexander, D., & Andersen, K. (1993). Gender as a factor in the attribution of leadership traits. *Political Research Quarterly, 46,* 503–525.
Alliance for Better Campaigns (2001, February 5). *Alliance criticizes TV station for airing little candidate discourse, while profiting from a windfall of political spending in 2000.* Available at: www.bettercampaigns.org/press/release.
Alvarez, A. (2004). Hillary Clinton—A quick biography and career dossier. Available at: www.politics-now.com/news/hillaryclintonbiography.htm.
Anez, B. (2000a, February 5). O'Keefe accuses foes of digging for political dirt. *Helena Independent Record* [available: www.helenair.com].
Anez, B. (2000b, September 29). Martz, O'Keefe debate turns ugly. *Helena Independent Record* [available: www.helenair.com].
Anez, B. (2000c, November 5). Term limits assure turnover on Tuesday. *Helena Independent Record* [available: www.helenair.com].
Ansolabehere, S., Behr, R., & Iyengar, S. (1993). *The media game: American politics in the television age.* New York: Macmillan Publishing Company.
Ansolabehere, S., & Iyengar, S. (1995). *Going negative: How political advertisements shrink and polarize the electorate.* New York: The Free Press.
Ansolabehere, S., Iyengar, S., & Simon, A. (1999). Replicating experiments using aggregate and survey data: The case of negative advertising and turnout. *American Political Science Review, 93*(4), 901–909.
Ansolabehere, S., Iyengar, S., Simon, A., & Valentino, N. (1994). Does attack advertising demobilize the electorate? *American Political Science Review, 88,* 829–838.
Ashmore, R. D., Del Boca, F. K, & Wohlers, A. J. (1986). Gender stereotypes. In R. D. Ashmore & F. K. Del Boca (Eds.), *The social psychology of female-male relations: A critical analysis of central concepts* (pp. 69–119). Orlando, FL: Academic Press.
The Associated Press (2000, November 8). Key findings from voter survey: Updates throughout. *The Associated Press State & Local Wire* [available: www.lexis-nexis.com].
Banwart, M. C. (2002). *Videostyle and webstyle in 2000: Comparing the gender differences of candidate presentations in political advertising and on the Internet.* Unpublished doctoral dissertation, University of Oklahoma, Norman.
Banwart, M. C., & Bystrom, D. G. (2001, November). *Gender influences on gathering political information: Examining perceptions of and sources for obtaining political knowledge in elections.* Presented at the annual meeting of the National Communication Association, Atlanta, GA.

Banwart, M. C., Bystrom, D. G., & Robertson, T. (2003). From the primary to the general election: A comparative analysis of media coverage of candidates in mixed-gender races for governor and U.S. Senate in 2000. *American Behavioral Scientist, 46*(5), 658–676.

Banwart, M. C., Bystrom, D. G., Robertson, T., & Miller, J. (2003). Issue agendas in candidate messages vs. media coverage: Are women and men on the same page? In L. L. Kaid, J. C. Tedesco, D.G. Bystrom, & M. S. McKinney (Eds.), *The millennium election: Communication in the 2000 campaign.* Boulder, CO: Rowman & Littlefield Publishers Inc.

Banwart, M. C., & Carlin, D. B. (2001, November). *The effects of negative political advertising on gendered image perception and voter intent: A longitudinal study.* Paper presented at the meeting of the National Communication Association, Atlanta, GA.

Banwart, M. C., & Kaid, L. L. (2003). Behind their skirts: Clinton's appeal to women voters. In R. E. Denton & R. L. Holloway (Eds.), *Images, scandal, and communication strategies of the Clinton presidency* (pp. 91–112). Westport, CT: Praeger/Greenwood.

Bem, S. L. (1993). *The lenses of gender: Transforming the debate on sexual inequality.* New Haven, CT: Yale University Press.

Bennett, L. M., & Bennett, S. E. (1989). Enduring gender differences in political interest: The impact of socialization and political dispositions. *American Politics Quarterly, 17*(1), 105–122.

Benze, J. G., & Declercq, E. R. (1985). Content of television political spot ads for female candidates. *Journalism Quarterly, 82,* 278–283, 288.

Bimber, B. (1998, June/July). The gender gap in electronic democracy. *The National Voter, 47*(4), 8–9.

Braden, M. (1996). *Women politicians and the media.* Lexington, KY: The University of Kentucky Press.

Broder, D. A. (1989, 19 January). Should news media police accuracy of ads? *Washington Post,* p. A22.

Broder, D. S. (2002). N.C. race narrows for Dole, Bowles: GOP hopeful still in lead for senate. *Washington Post,* A06.

Brown, M. E. (1997). Feminism and cultural politics: Television audiences and Hillary Rodham Clinton. *Political Communication, 14,* 255–270.

Bystrom, D. G. (1994, November). *Gender differences and similarities in the presentation of self: The videostyles of female vs. male U.S. Senate candidates in 1992.* Paper presented at the meeting of the Speech Communication Association, New Orleans, LA.

Bystrom, D. G. (1995). *Candidate gender and the presentation of self: The videostyles of men and women in U.S. Senate campaigns.* Unpublished doctoral dissertation, University of Oklahoma, Norman.

Bystrom, D. G. (1999, November). *Why not a woman? Reactions to the presidential candidacy of Elizabeth Dole.* Paper presented at the National Communication Association convention, Chicago, IL.

Bystrom, D. G. (2003, November). *Winning strategies: Viewer reactions to female and male videostyles.* Paper presented at the annual meeting of the National Communication Association, Miami, FL.

Bystrom, D. G. (in press). Media content and candidate viability: The case of Elizabeth Dole. In M. S. McKinney, D. G. Bystrom, L. L. Kaid, & D. B. Carlin (Eds.), *Communicating politics: Engaging the public in democratic life.* New York: Peter Lang Publishing.

Bystrom, D. G., & Kaid, L.L. (1996, November). *Videostyle and technology in political advertising: An update on women candidates in the 1994 election.* Paper presented at the meeting of the Speech Communication Association, San Diego, CA.

Bystrom, D. G., & Kaid, L. L. (2002). Are women candidates transforming campaign communication? A comparison of advertising videostyles in the 1990s. In C. R. Rosenthal (Ed.), *Women transforming Congress.* Norman, OK: University of Oklahoma Press.

Bystrom, D. G., & Miller, J. L. (1999). Gendered communication styles and strategies in campaign 1996: The videostyles of women and men candidates. In L. L. Kaid & D. G. Bystrom (Eds.), *The electronic election* (pp. 303–318). Mahwah, NJ: Lawrence Erlbaum Associates, Inc.

Bystrom, D. G, & Miller, J. L. (1999). Gendered communication styles and strategies in campaign 1996: The videostyles of women and men candidates. In L. L. Kaid & D. G. Bystrom (Eds.), *The electronic election: Perspectives on the 1996 campaign communication* (pp. 293–302). Mahwah, NJ: Lawrence Erlbaum Associates, Inc.

Bystrom, D. G., Robertson, T., & Banwart, M. C. (2001). Framing the fight: An analysis of media coverage of female and male candidates in primary races for governor and U.S. Senate in 2000. *American Behavioral Scientist, 44*(12), 1999–2013.

Campbell, K. K. (1989). *Man cannot speak for her: A critical study of early feminist rhetoric.* New York: Greenwood Press.

Campbell, K. K., & Jerry, E. C. (1988). Woman and speaker: A conflict in roles. In S. S. Brehon (Ed.), *Seeing female: Social roles and personal lives* (pp. 123–133). New York: Greenwood Press.

Carlson, M. (2000, November 20). Capitol Hill: If time doesn't heal all wounds, a Senate seat just might; after a dogged campaign, the First Lady gets a chance to work on a legacy all her own. *Time, 156,* 58–59.

CBS News Poll. (2004, January 18). *04 election could be 2000 redux.* Available at: www.cbsnews.com/stories/2004/01/17/opinion/polls/main593848.

Center for American Women and Politics (1997). *Gender gap: Voting, party identification and presidential ratings.* Rutgers University, Eagleton Institute of Politics. Available at: www.rci.rutgers.edu/~cawp/facts/ggap.pdf.

Center for American Women and Politics. (2002). *Summary of women candidates for selected offices: 1970–2002 (major party nominees).* Rutgers University, Eagleton Institute of Politics. Available at: www.rci.rutgers.edu/~cawp/ facts/canhistory/can_histsum.pdf.

Center for American Women and Politics. (2004). *National information bank on women in public office.* Rutgers University, Eagleton Institute of Politics. Available at: www.rci.rutgers.edu/~cawp/facts1.html.

Center for Media and Public Affairs (2000). Campaign 2000 final: How TV news covered the general election campaign. *Media Monitor, XVI*(6), 1–9.

Chang, C., & Hitchon, J. (1997). Mass media impact on voter response to women candidates: Theoretical development. *Communication Theory, 7,* 29–52.

Clinton, H. R. (2003). *Living history.* New York: Simon & Schuster Adult Publishing Group.

Clinton, H. R. (1992). Remarks to Wellesley College class of 1992. Available at: www.wellesley.edu/publicaffairs/commensement/1992/speecheshrc.html.

CNN.com. (2000, October 10). Lazio denies Hillary Clinton's 'soft money' charges. Available at: www.cnn.com/2000/ALLPOLITICS/stories/10/10/lazio.king/ index.html.

Curtis, A., Shuler, S., & Grieve, P. (1994, November). *Feminine and masculine style in political communication: A content analysis.* Paper presented at the meeting of the Speech Communication Association, New Orleans, LA.

Damico, D., & Rice, D. (2002, September 11). Bowles, Dole are nominees in high-profile senate race. *Winston-Salem Journal Online Edition* [available: www.lexis-nexis.com].

Darcy, R., Welch, S., & Clark, J. (1994). *Women, elections, & representation.* Lincoln: University of Nebraska Press.

Daughton, S. M. (1995). Women's issues, women's place: Gender-related problems in presidential campaigns. In K. E. Kendall (Ed.), *Presidential campaign discourse* (pp. 221–239). Albany, NY: SUNY Press.

Davis, L. (1978). Camera eye-contact by the candidates in the presidential debates of 1976. *Journalism Quarterly, 55,* 431–437.

Davis, R. (1999). *The web of politics: The Internet's impact on the American political system.* New York: Oxford University Press.

Delli Carpini, M. X., & Keeter, S. (1991). Stability and change in the U.S. public's knowledge of politics. *Public Opinion Quarterly, 55,* 583–612.

Delli Carpini, M. X., & Keeter, S. (1996). *What Americans know about politics and why it matters.* London: Yale University Press.

Delli Carpini, M. X., & Keeter, S. (2000). Gender and political knowledge. In S. Tolleson-Rinehart & J. J. Josephson (Eds.), *Gender and American politics: Women, men, and the political process* (pp. 21–54). Armonk, NY: M. E. Sharpe.

Deloitte & Touche, LLP. (2000, January 13). *Women in elected office survey identifies obstacles for women as political leaders* [On-line], 1–5. Available: www.us.deloitte.com.

DeRosa, K. L. (1996, March). *The voice of women in American political discourse.* Paper presented at the meeting of the South Central Women's Studies Association, Norman, OK.

DeRosa, K. L., & Bystrom, D. (1999). The voice of and for women in the 1996 presidential campaign: Style and substance of convention speeches. In L. L. Kaid & D. G. Bystrom (Eds.), *The electronic election: Perspectives on the 1996 campaign communication* (pp. 97–111). Mahwah, NJ: Lawrence Erlbaum Associates, Inc.

Devitt, J. (1999). *Framing gender on the campaign trail: Women's executive leadership and the press.* Washington, DC: The Women's Leadership Fund.

Dolan, K. (1997). Gender differences in support for women candidates: Is there a glass ceiling in American politics? *Women & Politics, 17,* 27–41.

Dorning, M. (1998, October 22). Carol Moseley-Braun for senator, image is asset and curse: Though she stresses here record, the democrat finds her personality and a series of missteps in the spotlight. *The Chicago Tribune,* A1.

Dow, B. J., & Boor Tonn, M. (1993). Feminine style and political judgment in the rhetoric of Ann Richards. *Quarterly Journal of Speech, 79,* 286–332.

Dulio, D. A., Goff, D. L., & Thurber, J. A. (1999). Untangled web: Internet use during the 1998 election. *P.S. Politics: Political Science & Politics, 32*(1), pp. 53–59.

Dyer, E. (2002a, June 17). Senate race grows more partisan: Democrat Erskine Bowles goes after Republican Elizabeth Dole. *News & Record,* B1.

Dyer, E. (2002b, July 16). Cash in senate race exceeds $1.2 million: The two front-runners collected about $3.7 million between April and June, recent finance reports show. *News & Record,* B3.

Filosa, G. (2000, October 1). Shaheen and Humphrey neck and neck. *The Concord Monitor,* pp. A1, A3.

Finkel, S. E., & Geer, J. G. (1998). A spot check: Casting doubt on the demobilizing attack advertising. *American Journal of Political Science, 42,* 573–595.

Flanagin, A. J., & Metzger, M. J. (2000). Perceptions of Internet information credibility. *Journalism & Mass Communication Quarterly, 77*(3), 515–540.

Fox, R. L. (1997). *Gender dynamics in congressional elections.* Thousand Oaks, CA: Sage.

Freedman, P., & Goldstein, K. (1999). Measuring media exposure and the effects of negative campaign ads. *American Journal of Political Science, 43*(4), 1189–1208.

Frey, L. R., Botan, C. H., Friedman, P. G., & Kreps, G. L. (1991). *Investigating communication: An introduction to research methods.* Englewood Cliffs, NJ: Prentice Hall.

Garramone, G. M. (1984). Voter responses to negative political ads. *Journalism Quarterly, 61,* 250–259.

Garramone, G. M., Atkin, C. K., Pinkleton, B. E., & Cole, R. T. (1990). Effects of negative political advertising on the political process. *Journal of Broadcasting & Electronic Media, 34,* 299–311.

Geiger, S. F., & Reeves, B. (1991). The effects of visual structure and content emphasis on the evaluation and memory of political candidates. In F. Biocca (Ed.), *Television and political advertising: Vol. 1. Psychological processes* (pp. 125–143). Hillsdale, NJ: Lawrence Erlbaum Associates, Inc.

Glass, A. J. (1998, October 8). 1998 elections will test Web's political boundaries. *The Atlanta Constitution,* A14.

Goffman, E. (1973). *The presentation of self in everyday life.* Woodstock, NY: The Overlook Press.

Goldenberg, E. N., & Traugott, M. W. (1987). Mass media effects in recognizing and rating candidates in U.S. Senate elections. In J. Vermeer (Ed.), *Campaigns in the news: Mass media and congressional elections.* New York: Greenwood Press.

Graber, D. A. (1987). Framing election news broadcasts: News context and its impact on the 1984 presidential election. *Social Science Quarterly, 68,* 552–568.

Greer, J., & LaPointe, M. (2001). *Cyber-campaigning grows up: A comparative content analysis of senatorial and gubernatorial candidates' Web sites, 1998–2000.* Presented at the Annual Meeting of the American Political Science Association, San Francisco, September 2001.

Hanna, J. (2002, November 6). Analysis: Sebelius followed "a winning formula." *Topeka Capital Journal.* [On-line]. Available: www.c-jonline.com.

Hansen, G. J. (2000, November). *Internet presidential campaigning: The influences of candidate Internet sites on the 2000 election.* Paper presented at the National Communication Association Convention, Seattle.

Hansen, G. J., & Benoit, W. L. (2001). The role of significant policy issues in the 2000 presidential primaries. *American Behavioral Scientist, 44*(12), 2082–2100.

Hansen, G. J., & Benoit, W. L. (2002, November). *Presidential campaigning on the* Web: The influence of candidate World Wide Web sites in the 2000 general *election*. Paper presented at the National Communication Association Convention, New Orleans.

Hayes, B. C., & Makkai, T. (1996). Politics and the mass media: The differential impact of gender. *Women & Politics, 16*, 45–74.

Hayes, B. C., & McAllister, I. (1997). Gender, party leaders, and election outcomes in Australia, Britain, and the United States. *Comparative Political Studies, 30*, 3–26.

Heldman, C., Carroll, S. J., & Olson, S. (2000, August). *Gender differences in print media coverage of presidential candidates: Elizabeth Dole's bid for the Republican nomination*. Paper presented at the meeting of the American Political Science Association, Washington, DC.

Hirschkorn, P. (2000, October 31). Poll indicates Clinton-Lazio race tight entering final week. Available at: www.cnn.com/2000/ALLPOLITICS/stories/10/31/newyork. senate/.

Hitchon, J. C., & Chang, C. (1995). Effects of gender schematic processing on the reception of political commercials for men and women candidates. *Communication Research, 22*, 430–458.

Hitchon, J. C., Chang, C., & Harris, R. (1997). Should women emote? Perceptual bias and opinion change in response to political ads for candidates of different genders. *Political Communication, 14*, 49–69.

Hofstetter, C. R. (1976). *Bias in the news: Network television coverage of the 1972 election campaign*. Columbus: Ohio State University Press.

Huddy, L., & Terkildsen, N. S. (1993). *The consequences of gender stereotype for influence the conduct and consequences of political campaigns*. New York: Columbia University Press.

Iyengar, S. (1979). Television news and issue salience. *American Politics Quarterly, 7*, 395–416.

Iyengar, S., & Kinder, D. R. (1987). *News that matters: Television and American opinion*. Chicago: The University of Chicago Press.

Iyengar, S., Valentino, N. A., Ansolabehere, S., & Simon, A. F. (1997). Running as a woman: Gender stereotyping in political campaigns. In P. Norris (Ed.), *Women, Media, and Politics* (pp. 77–98). New York: Oxford University Press.

Jalonick, M. C. (2000). Greatest hits: GOP campaign Web sites. *Campaigns & Elections, 21*(15), 56, 87.

Jamieson, K.H. (1988). *Eloquence in an electronic age: The transformation of political speechmaking*. New York: Oxford University Press.

Jamieson, K. H. (1995). *Beyond the double bind: Women and leadership*. New York: Oxford University Press.

Jamieson, K.H., Falk, E., & Sherr, S. (1999, March). The enthymeme gap in the 1996 presidential campaign. *PS: Political Science & Politics, 32*, 12–17.

Jansen, J. (1993). Sex role stereotypes and clinical judgement. *Journal of Substance Abuse, 10*, 383–289.

Jesdanun, A. (2002, October 31). Candidates turn to Net to mobilize supporters. *The Associated Press State & Local Wire* [available: www.lexis-nexis.com].

Johnson, C. S. (2000a, January 30). Montana politicians on the "dot.com" campaign trail. *Helena Independent Record* [available: www.helenair.com].

Johnson, C. S. (2000b, May 11). Gubernatorial candidates take-on economy. *Helena Independent Record* [available: www.helenair.com].

Johnson, C. S. (2000c, September 3). Martz, O'Keefe ready to step up campaigning efforts. *Helena Independent Record* [available: www.helenair.com].

Johnson, C. S. (2000d, September 22). GOP buys TV ads for Martz. *Helena Independent Record* [available: www.helenair.com].

Johnson, C. S. (2000e, November 3). O'Keefe edge at $2.1 million. *Helena Independent Record* [available: www.helenair.com].

Johnson, C. S. (2000f, November 8). GOP sweeps state. *Helena Independent Record* [available: www.helenair.com].

Johnson, T. J., Braima, M. A., & Sothirajah, J. (1999). Doing the traditional media sidestep: Comparing the effects of the Internet and other nontraditional media with traditional media in the 1996 presidential campaign. *Journalism & Mass Communication Quarterly, 76*, 99–123.

Johnson, T. J., & Kaye, B. K. (1998). Cruising is believing?: Comparing Internet and traditional sources on media credibility measures. *Journalism & Mass Communication Quarterly, 75*(2), 325–340.

Johnston, A., & White, A. B. (1994). Communication styles and female candidates: A study of political advertisements of men and women candidates for U.S. Senate. *Political Research Quarterly, 46*, 481–501.

Johnston, M. (1998, October, 25). Owens, Schoettler spring from different states, stock. *The Denver Post*, p. A20.
Joslyn, R. A. (1980). The content of political spot ads. *Journalism Quarterly, 57,* 92–98.
Kahn, K. F., &. Kenney, P. J. (1999). Do negative campaigns mobilize or suppress turnout? Clarifying the relationship between negativity and participation. *American Political Science Review, 93,* 877–889.
Kahn, K. F. (1991). Senate elections in the news: Examining campaign coverage. *Legislative Studies Quarterly, 16,* 349–374.
Kahn, K. F. (1992) Does being male help? An investigation of gender and media effects in the U.S. Senate races. *Journal of Politics, 54,* 497–517.
Kahn, K. F. (1993). Gender differences in campaign messages: The political advertisements of men and women candidates for US Senate. *Political Research Quarterly, 46*(3), 481–502.
Kahn, K. F. (1994a). The distorted mirror: Press coverage of women candidates for statewide office. *Journal of Politics, 54,* 154–173.
Kahn, K. F. (1994b). Does gender make a difference? An experimental examination of sex stereotypes and press patterns in statewide campaigns. *American Journal of Political Science, 38*(1), 162–195.
Kahn, K. F. (1996). *The political consequences of being a woman: How stereotypes influence the conduct and consequences of political campaigns.* New York: Columbia University Press.
Kahn, K. F., & Geer, J. G. (1994). Creating impressions: An experimental investigation of political advertising on television. *Political Behavior, 16,* 93–116.
Kahn, K. F., & Goldenberg, E. N. (1991). Women candidates in the news: An examination of gender differences in U.S. Senate campaign coverage. *Public Opinion Quarterly, 55*(2), 180–199.
Kaid, L. L. (1994). Political advertising in the 1992 campaign. In, R. E. Denton (Ed.), *The 1992 presidential campaign: A communication perspective* (pp. 111–127). Westport, CT: Praeger.
Kaid, L. L. (1995). Measuring candidate images with semantic differentials. In K. Hacker (Ed.), *Candidate images in presidential election campaigns* (pp. 131–134). New York: Praeger.
Kaid, L.L. (1997, October). *Political television advertising: A comparative perspective on styles and effects.* Paper presented at the International Conference on Images of Politics, Amsterdam.
Kaid, L. L. (1998). Videostyle and the effects of the 1996 presidential campaign advertising. In R. E. Denton, Jr. (Ed.), *The 1996 presidential campaign: A communication perspective* (pp. 143–159). Westport, CT: Praeger.
Kaid, L.L. (1999). Political advertising: A summary of research findings. In B. Newman (Ed.), *The handbook of political marketing* (pp. 423–438). Thousand Oaks, CA: Sage Publications.
Kaid, L. L. (2002). Political advertising and information seeking: Comparing the exposure via traditional and Internet media channels. *Journal of Advertising, XXXI,* 27–35.
Kaid, L. L., & Davidson, D. K. (1986). Elements of videostyle: Candidate presentation through television advertising. In L. L. Kaid, D. Nimmo, & K. R. Sanders (Eds.), *New perspectives on political advertising* (pp. 184–209). Carbondale, IL: Southern Illinois University Press.
Kaid, L. L., Gobetz, R. H., Garner, J., Leland, C. M., & Scott, D. K. (1993). Television news and presidential campaigns: The legitimization of televised political advertising. *Social Science Quarterly, 74*(2), 274–285.
Kaid, L. L., Haynes, K. J. M., & Rand, C. E. (1996). The Political Communication Center: A Catalog and Guide to the Archival Collections. Norman, OK: Political Communication Center.
Kaid, L. L., & Holtz-Bacha, C. (2000). Gender differences in response to televised political broadcasts: A multicountry comparison. *Harvard Journal of International Press/Politics, 5*(2), 17–29.
Kaid, L. L., & Johnston, A. (1991). Negative versus positive television advertising in US presidential campaigns, 1960–1988. *Journal of Communication, 41,* 53–64.
Kaid, L. L., & Johnston, A. (2001). *Videostyle in presidential campaigns: Style and content of televised political advertising.* Westport, CT: Praeger/Greenwood.
Kaid, L. L., Leland, C. M., & Whitney, S. (1992). The impact of televised political ads: Evoking viewer responses in the 1988 presidential campaign. *The Southern Speech Communication Journal, 57*(4), 285–295.
Kaid, L. L., McKinney, M. S., & Tedesco, J. C. (2000). *Civic dialogue in the 1999 presidential campaign: Candidate, media, and public voices.* Cresskill, NJ: Hampton Press.

Kaid, L. L., McKinney, M., Tedesco, J. C., & Gaddie, K. (1999). Journalistic responsibility and political advertising: A content analysis of coverage by state and local media. *Communication Studies, 50*(4), 279–293.

Kaid, L. L., Myers, S. L., Pipps, V. & Hunter, J. (1984). Sex role perceptions and televised political advertising: Comparing male and female candidates. *Women & Politics, 4*(4), 41–53.

Kaid, L. L., & Tedesco, J. (1999). Presidential candidate presentation: Videostyle in the 1996 presidential spots. In L. L. Kaid & D. G. Bystrom (Eds.), *The electronic election* (pp. 209–222). Mahwah, NJ: Lawrence Erlbaum Associates, Inc.

Kaid, L. L, Tedesco, J. C., & McKinnon, L. M. (1996). Presidential ads as nightly news: A content analysis of 1988 and 1992 televised adwatches. *Journal of Broadcasting and Electronic Media, 40*, 297–308.

Kaid, L. L., & Wadsworth, A. J. (1989). Political television commercials: An experimental study of type and length. *Communication Research, 5*, 55–70.

Kansas Secretary of State. (1996). *1996 general election official vote totals.* Available at: www.kssos.org/elections.

Kansas Secretary of State. (2002a). *2002 general election official vote totals.* Available at: www.kssos.org/elections.

Kansas Secretary of State. (2002b). *Voter Registration and Party Affiliation.* Available at: www.kssos.org/elections/02elec/voterreg102102.html.

Kansas Secretary of State. (2000). *2000 Kansas general election results (president).* Available at: www.kssos.org/elections/elections_statistics.html.

Kenski, K., & Jamieson, K. H. (2001, August). *The 2000 presidential campaign and differential growths in knowledge: Does the "knowledge gap" hypothesis apply to gender as well as education?* Paper presented at the meeting of the American Political Science Association, San Francisco, CA.

Kern, M. (1989). *30-Second politics: Political advertising in the 1980s.* New York: Praeger.

Kern, M., & Just, M. (1997). A gender gap among viewers? In P. Norris (Ed.), *Women, media, and politics.* New York: Oxford University Press.

Klotz, R. (1997). Positive spin: Senate campaigning on the web. *P.S.: Political Science & Politics, 30*, 482–486.

Knopf, M. E., & Boiney, J. A. (2001) The electoral glass ceiling? Gender, viability, and the news in U.S. Senate campaigns. In K. O'Connor (Ed.), *Women and Congress: Running, winning, and ruling* (pp. 79–101). New York: The Haworth Press Inc.

Koch, J. W. (1999). Candidate gender and assessments of Senate candidates. *Social Science Quarterly, 80*, 84–96.

Kondracke, M. M. (2002, December 9). The new Elizabeth Dole is anything but "uptight." *Roll Call* [available: www.nationaljournal.com].

Kramarae, C. (1995). A backstage critique of virtual reality. In S. Jones (Ed.), *Cybersociety* (pp. 36–56). London: Sage Publications.

Kraus, W. (1974). Political implication of gender roles. *American Political Science Review, 68*, 176–1723.

Krippendorf, K. (1980). *Content analysis: An introduction to its methodology.* Beverly Hills, CA: Sage Publications.

Laceky, T. (1999, July 19). Martz says she's running for governor. *Associated Press State & Local Wire* [available: www.lexis-nexis.com].

Lang, A. (1991). Emotion, formal features, and memory for televised political advertisements. In F. Biocca (Ed.), *Television and political advertising, Vol. 1* (pp. 221–243). Hillsdale, NJ: Lawrence Erlbaum Associates, Inc.

League of Women Voters. (1996). *Women see responsive role for government.* Available at: www.lwv.org/elibrary/pub/ladieshj.

Leeper, M. S. (1991). The impact of prejudice on female candidates: An experimental look at voter inference. *American Politics Quarterly, 19*(2), 248–261.

Lemert, J. B., Wanta, W., & Lee, T. (1999). Party identification and negative advertising in a U.S. Senate election. *Journal of Communication, 49*, 123–134.

Leventhal, H., Meyer, D., & Nerenz, D. (1980). The common sense representation of illness danger. In S. Rachman (Ed.), *Medical psychology* (Vol. 2, pp. 7–30). New York: Pergamon.

Lichter, S. R., & Noyes, R. E. (1996) *Good intentions make bad news: Why Americans hate campaign journalism* (2nd ed.). Lanham, MD: Roman & Littlefield.

Lichter, S.R., Noyes, R. E., & Kaid, L. L. (1999). No news or negative news: how the networks nixed the '96 campaign. In L. L. Kaid & D. G. Bystrom (Eds.), *The electronic election: Perspectives on the 1996 campaign communication* (pp. 3–13). Mahwah, NJ: Lawrence Erlbaum Associates, Inc.

Lutey, T. (2000, September 14). Martz goes on attack. *Bozeman Daily Chronicle* [available: www.gomontana.com].

Marist Institute for Public Opinion. (2000, September 21). Clinton vs. Lazio: After the scuffle off in Buffalo. Available at: www.maristpoll.marist.edu/nyspolls/ 000921hc.htm.

Martinez, M. D., & Delegal, T. (1990). The irrelevance of negative campaigns to political trust: Experimental and survey results. *Political Communication and Persuasion, 7*(1), 25–40.

McCombs, M. E., & Shaw, D. (1972). The agenda-setting function of the mass media. *Public Opinion Quarterly, 36,* 176–187.

McLean, J. & Grenz, C. (2002, November 5). Sebelius wins: Governor-elect: it's 'time for a change'. *The Topeka Capital–Journal.* Available at: www.cjonline.com.

McMillan, S. J. (2000). The microscope and the moving target: The challenge of applying content analysis to the World Wide Web. *Journalism & Mass Communication Quarterly, 77,* 80–98.

Miller, G. (2001). Newspaper coverage and gender: An analysis of the 1996 Illinois state legislative house district races. *Women & Politics, 22,* 83–100.

Miller, J. L. (1996). *Dynamics of political advertisements, news coverage, and candidate gender: A content analysis of the campaign messages of the 1990 and 1994 California and Texas gubernatorial elections.* Unpublished doctoral dissertation, University of Oklahoma, Norman.

Monneyham, S. (2002, October 11). Dole raps foe over textile troubles: Bowles says ads unfairly attack wife's company. *The Commercial Appeal,* A17.

Moon, C. (2002, August, 1). Poll respondents, focus groups agree—2002 legislature did poor job. *CJOnline: The Topeka Capital-Journal* [available online: www.cjonline.com].

Nagourney, A., & Connelly, M. (2000, September 21). In poll, Mrs. Clinton makes gain among women from the suburbs. *New York Times,* A1.

Nesbit, D. D. (1988). *Videostyle in senate campaigns.* Knoxville: University of Tennessee Press.

Niven, D., & Zilber, J. (2001a). Do women and men in Congress cultivate different images? Evidence from congressional web sites. *Political Communication, 18,* 395–405.

North, R., Holsti, O., Zaniovich, M., & Zinnes, D. A. (1963) *Content analysis: A handbook with applications for the study of international crisis.* Evanston, IL: Northwestern University Press.

Papacharissi, Z., & Rubin, A. M. (2000). Predictors of Internet use. *Journal of Broadcasting & Electronic Media, 44*(2), 175–196.

Patterson, T. E., & McClure, R. D. (1976). *The unseeing eye: The myth of television power in national politics.* New York: G. P. Putnam's Sons.

PBS.org. (2000, May 30). *Online NewsHour: Racing for the Senate.* Available at: www.pbs.org/newshour/bb/politics/jan-june00/nysenate_5-30.html.

Pearson, J. C., Turner, L. H., & Todd-Mancillas, W. (1991). *Gender & communication* (2nd ed.). Dubuque, IA: Wm. C. Brown Publishers.

Pew Research Center for People & the Press (2000a, December 3). *Internet election news audience seeks convenience, familiar names.* Retrieved December 1, 2003 from http/www.people-press.org.

Pew Research Center for People & the Press (2000b, December 21). *Some final observations on voter opinions.* Retrieved December 1, 2003 from http/ www.people-press.org.

Pew Research Center for People & the Press (2002a, October 10). *Americans thinking about Iraq, but focused on the economy: Midterm election preview.* Retrieved December 1, 2003 from http/ www.people-press.org.

Pew Research Center for People & the Press (2002b, November 5). *House voting intentions knotted, national trend not apparent.* Retrieved December 1, 2003 from http/ www.people-press.org.

Pew Research Center for the People & the Press (2003, January 5). *Political sites gain, but major news sites still dominant: Modest increase in Internet use for campaign2002.* Available at: people-press.org/reports/display.php3? ReportID=169.

Pinkleton, B. E. (1998). Effects of print political comparative advertising on political decision-making and participation. *Journal of Communication, 48,* 24–36.

Pinkleton, B. E., Um, N., & Austin, E.W. (2002). An exploration of the effects of negative political advertising on political decision making. *Journal of Advertising, 31*(1), 13–25.

Procter, D. E., Schenck-Hamlin, W., & Haase, A. (1994). Exploring the role of gender in the development of negative political advertisements. *Women & Politics, 14*(2), 1–22.

Puopolo, S. T. (2001). The web and U.S. Senatorial campaigns 2000. *American Behavioral Scientist, 44*(12), 2030–2047.

Raney, R. F. (1998, July 30). Politicians woo voters on the Web. *The New York Times*, p. G1.

Rausch, J. D. Jr., Rozell, M. J., & Wilson, H. L. (1999). When women lose: A study of media coverage of two gubernatorial campaigns. *Women & Politics, 20*, 1–17.

Rice, D. (2002, September 17). Dole had double-digit lead, poll shows Bowles trailing in senate race by 14 points, poll director says. *Winston-Salem Journal*, A1.

Richissin, T. (1998, October 4). Sauerbrey substituted one dream for another portrait: Candidate discusses her life—growing up poor, her father's medical problems, and her decision to pursue politics. *The Baltimore Sun*, p. A1.

Riggle, E. D., Miller P., Shields, T., & Johnson, M. S. (1997). Gender stereotypes and decision context in the evaluation of political candidates. *Women and Politics, 17*, 69–88.

Robertson, T. (2000). *Sex and the political process: An analysis of sex stereotypes in 1998 senatorial and gubernatorial campaigns.* Unpublished doctoral dissertation, University of Oklahoma, Norman.

Robertson, T., Conley, A., Scymcznska, K., & Thompson, A. (2002). Gender and the media: An investigation of gender, media and politics in the 2000 election. *New Jersey Journal of Communication, 10*, 104–117.

Rosenstone, S. J., Kinder, D. R., Miller, W. E., and the National Election Studies (1997). *American National Election Study, 1996: Pre- and Post-Election Survey*, computer file, Ann Arbor, MI: University of Michigan, Center for Political Studies (producer), Ann Arbor, MI: Inter-university Consortium for Political and Social Research (distributor).

Rosenwasser, S. M., & Dean, N. G. (1989). Gender role and political office. *Psychology of Women Quarterly, 13*, 77–85.

Rubin, A. M. (1981). An examination of television viewing motivations. *Communication Research, 8*, 141–165.

Sapiro, V. (1981/2). If U.S. Senator Baker were a woman: An experimental study of candidate images. *Political Psychology, 3*, 61–83.

Schenck-Hamlin, W. J., Procter, D. E., & Rumsey, D. J. (2000). The influence of negative advertising frames on political and politician accountability. *Human Communication Research, 26*(1), 53–74.

Selnow, G. W. (1998). *Electronic whistle-stops: The impact of the Internet on American politics.* Westport, CT: Praeger.

Seltzer, R. A., Newman, J., & Leighton, M. V. (1997). *Sex as a political variable: Women as candidates and voters in U.S. elections.* Boulder, CO: Lynne Rienner.

Serini, S., Powers, A. & Johnston, S. (1998). Of horse race and policy issues: A study of gender in coverage of a gubernatorial election by two major metropolitan newspapers, *Journalism Quarterly 75*(1), 194–204.

Shepard, S. (2002, September 9). N.C. Senate race soon to escalate: Outcome may foreshadow fate of Bush agenda. *The Atlanta-Journal Constitution*, 6A.

Shiver, J. (1999, January 15). Web clicking with more mainstream Americans. *The Los Angeles Times* (Business Section), p. 3.

Smith, K. B. (1997). When all's fair: Signs of parity in media coverage of female candidates. *Political Communication, 14*, 71–81.

Stromer-Galley, J. (2000). On-line interaction and why candidates avoid it. *Journal of Communication, 50*, 111–132.

Sundar, S.S., Hesser, K. M., Kalyanaraman, S., & Brown, J. (1998, July). *The effect of system.* New York: Oxford University Press.

Szpiech, K. M. (1992, November). *The power of feminine style: A critical analysis of Representative Patricia Schroeder's political discourse.* Paper presented at the meeting of the Speech Communication Association, Chicago, IL.

Tedesco, J. C., & Kaid, L. L. (2000, November). *Candidate Web sites and voter effects: The Los Angeles Times* (Business Section), p. 3.

Tedesco, J. C., Miller, J. L., & Spiker, J. A. (1999). Presidential campaigning on the information superhighway: An exploration of content and form. In L. L. Kaid & D. G. Bystrom (Eds.), *The electronic election* (pp. 51–64). Mahwah, NJ: Lawrence Erlbaum Associates, Inc.

Theimer, S. (2002, November 1). FEC analysis finds North Carolina with highest-spending Senate race; West Virginia costliest for House. *Associated Press State & Local Wire* [available: www.lexis-nexis.com].

Trent, J. S., & Friedenberg, R. V. (2000). *Political campaign communication* (4th ed.). Westport, CT: Praeger.

Trent, J. S., & Sabourin, T. C. (1993). Sex still counts: Women's use of televised advertising during the decade of the 80's. *Journal of Applied Communication Research, 21*(1), 21–40.

Turnbull, A. (2002, August 22). Bowles faults Dole on Social Security. *The Morning Star,* 2B.

Vavreck. L. (2000). How does it all "turnout"? Exposure to attack advertising, campaign interest, and participation in American presidential elections. In L. M. Bartels & L. Vavreck (Eds.), *Campaign reform: Insights and evidence* (pp. 79–105). Ann Arbor: University of Michigan Press.

Verba, S., Burns, N., & Schlozman, K. L. (1997). Knowing and caring about politics: Gender and political engagement. *The Journal of Politics, 59*(4), 1051–1072; *Voter, 47*(4), 8–9.

The Virginian-Pilot (2002, October 31). Bowles gains ground on Dole in N.C. Senate race, poll shows. *Landmark Communications,* A5.

Wadsworth, A. J., Patterson, P., Kaid, L. L., Cullers, G., Malcomb, D., & Lamirand, L. (1987). "Masculine" vs. "feminine" strategies in political ads: Implications for female candidates. *Journal of Applied Communication Research, 15,* 77–94.

West, D. M. (2001). *Air wars: Television advertising in election campaigns, 1952–1992* (3rd ed.). Washington, DC: Congressional Quarterly Inc.

Witt, L., Paget, K. M., & Matthews, G. (1995). *Running as a woman: Gender and power in American politics.* New York: The Free Press.

Wright, G. C., & Berkman, M. B. (1986). Candidates and policy in U.S. Senate elections. *American Political Science Review, 80,* 569–588.

Zurakowski, M. M. (1994). From doctors and lawyers to wives and mothers: Enacting "feminine style" and changing abortion rights arguments. *Women's Studies in Communication, 17,* 45–68.

Index

A
Abraham, Spencer, 103, 107–109, 122
Agenda setting, 173–174
Ali, Muhammad, 133
Andrews, Tom, 103, 106

B
Blair, Tony, 94
Bond, Christopher "Kit," 103, 104–105
Bowles, Erskine, 135, 145–146, 149–153, 155–156, 158–159, 161–163
Boxer, Barbara, 6
Brennan, John, 6
Brownback, Sam, 103, 106
Bush, George W., 6, 96–101, 145, 167–168, 206–208, 224

C
Cantwell, Maria, 6, 103, 106–108, 123, 125
Carnahan, Jean, 122, 175
Challenger candidate
    appeal strategies, 35–36, 43, 47
    VideoStyle, 48–53, 55–57
Clinton, Bill, 6, 23, 94–100, 133, 190–191, 216
Clinton, Hillary Rodham, 6, 30, 176, 182, 189–203, 215–216
Collins, Susan, 6, 143
Cooney, Mike, 144
Cynicism, voter, 100, 102, 223

D
D'Amato, Alfonse, 193, 196
Docking, Jill, 103, 106
Dole, Bob, 6, 23, 95–100
Dole, Elizabeth, 21–22, 140, 145–146, 149–150, 152–153, 155–156, 158–159, 161–163, 214–215
Domenici, Pete, 130

E
Ehrlich, Bob, 125, 133, 136

F
Feinstein, Dianne, 6, 133
Feminine
    appeal strategies, 35
    issues, 17, 20, 179–182
    traits, 15, 17, 21, 104, 182–183
Feminine style construct, 7, 9, 12–15
Fisher, Jimmie Lou, 122
Forbes, Steve, 21

G
Gender gap, 5–7, 93
Gender schema theory, 7, 16–17, 22–23, 174
Gingrich, Newt, 196, 197, 198, 199, 200
Giuliani, Rudolf, 196–197, 199, 200
Gore, Al, 6, 96–101, 133, 145, 167–168, 206–208, 216, 244

Gorton, Slade, 103, 106–108
Graham, Robert, 103–105
Granholm, Jennifer, 110, 133–134

H
Hawkins, Paula, 103–105
Hoffa, Jimmy, 133
Holsti's formula for intercoder
    reliability, 221, 224
Humphrey, Gordon, 103, 106–108

I
Incumbent candidate
    appeal strategies, 35–36, 43, 47, 123
    VideoStyle, 48–54
Internet, 113–114

K
Koch, Ed, 196

L
Lamontagne, Ovide, 103, 106
Landrieu, Mary, 6
Lazio, Pat, 200, 201
Lazio, Rick, 176, 189, 191–203
Levin, Carl, 133

M
Maddox, Jim, 102, 104–105
Major, John, 94
Martz, Judy, 143–145, 147, 149, 151–155,
    157–159, 160, 162
Mazurek, Joe, 144
Masculine
    appeal strategies, 35
    issues, 14, 20, 179–182
    traits, 14–15, 21, 182–183
McCain, John, 196, 200
McConnell, Mitch, 122, 130–131
Media use, 204–205, 208–210
Mikulski, Barbara, 30
Minner, Ruth Ann, 6, 143
Moseley-Braun, Carol, 6, 30, 184
Moynihan, Patrick, 191

Murkowski, Frank, 130, 135
Murray, Patty, 6

N
Napolitano, Janet, 135
Natelson, Rob, 144
National Election Studies, 208, 209, 210,
    218
Newspaper coverage of candidates, 19–22
    candidate appearance, 178–179, 185,
        200
    candidate gender, 178–179, 185
    candidate marital status, 178–179,
        185
    candidate viability, 178
    image coverage, 182–185, 194
    issue coverage, 179–181, 185, 193
    quality of, 177–185
    quantity of, 176–177
    slant, 177
    stereotypes, 184–186
NewsStyle
    candidate, 174–176, 185–186, 215–216
    Clinton, Hillary Rodham, 192–196
    construct, 18–22
    Lazio, Rick, 192–196
    voter reactions to, 206–210

O
O'Brien, Shannon, 128
O'Keefe, Mark, 144, 148, 150–155,
    157–160, 162
Owens, Bill, 184

P
Pataki, Rick, 199
Pew Research Center, 113
Political advertising
    appeal strategies, 35–36, 42–43, 50,
        54–57, 59, 63–64, 67, 75–76
    appeal structure, 34–35, 49
    appeal types, 34–35
    attacks, 32–34, 40, 49–50, 53, 52–63,
        65
    Clinton, Hillary Rodham, 196–199

image emphasis, 36, 40–42, 51–52, 55, 57, 59, 64–66, 75
issue emphasis, 36, 40–42, 51–52, 55, 57, 59, 64–66, 75
Lazio, Rick, 199–201
non-verbal content, 37–38, 43, 50, 55, 57, 59, 61, 65, 69–70, 77–78
production content, 38–39, 50, 55, 57, 59, 64–65, 69–70, 77–78
spending on, 29
voter reactions to, 94–95, 97–102
Political knowledge, 203–204
Polls
campaign issues, 41, 42
Clinton, Bill, job approval rating, 202
perception of female candidates, 3
2000 New York U.S. Senate race, 191–192, 202
2000 Montana governor's race, 145
Voter News Service exit, 6–7
Presentation of self. *See* Self-presentation theory

R

Richards, Ann, 7, 13, 30, 103–105
Roberts, Barbara, 6
Romney, Mitt, 128

S

Sauerbrey, Ellen, 182
Schoettler, Gail, 184
Schroeder, Pat, 13, 21
Schumer, Charles, 196
Sebelius, Kathleen, 81–88, 140
Self-presentation theory, 9–10, 11
Sex stereotypes, 4–5, 7, 16–18, 22–23
in newspaper coverage of candidates, 17–18, 20, 30
in voter perceptions of candidates, 18, 22–23, 184–186
Shaheen, Jeanne, 6, 103, 106–108
Shallenburger, Tim, 81–83, 88–91, 135, 140
Snowe, Olympia, 103, 106, 124, 133
Stabenow, Debbie, 6, 103, 107–109
Sununu, John, 124

T

Talent, Jim, 118, 123, 128
Townsend, Kathleen Kennedy, 129, 135–136
Tristani, Gloria, 125

U

Ulmer, Fran, 125, 135

V

VideoStyle
candidate, 14, 31, 213–214, 216–217
challenger, 48–51
construct, 9–12
Democrat, 62–71
female/male, 44–45
incumbent, 48–51
losers, 71–75
open race, 49–51, 59–61
Republican, 62–71
Sebelius, Kathleen, 83–88
Shallenburger, Tim, 88–92
voter reactions to, 102–109
winners, 71–75

W

Web sites
appeal strategies, 123–125, 152–153
attacks, 125–126
candidate, 114–115
images portrayed, 120–122, 149–151
interactive content, 136–139, 159–162
issues discussed, 116–120, 147–149
non-verbal content, 131–134, 156–158
production content, 134–136, 156–158
sectional appeals, 126, 128–130, 153–156
voter reactions to, 166–167, 169–170
voter use of, 165–166, 169
WebStyle
Bowles, Erskine, 135, 149–153, 155–156, 158–159, 161–163

candidate, 16, 140–141, 214–218
construct, 7, 9, 15–16, 116, 214
Dole, Elizabeth, 149–150, 152–153, 155–156, 158–159, 161–163, 214–215
effects on voters, 167–168
Martz, Judy, 147, 149–155, 157–162
O'Keefe, Mark, 148–155, 157–162
voter reactions to, 166–167

Weinberg, Lois Combs, 132–133, 135
Williams, Carol, 155
Woods, Harriett, 103, 104–105
Women political candidates, 4–5

Y

Yeakel, Lynn, 30
York, Myrth, 130